RUNNING
for
RECOVERY

RUNNING
for
RECOVERY

Marathons of the Body, Mind, Spirit

*A Marathon Runner Runs
on the Road to Repentance*

"I shall not die, but live, and
declare the works of the Lord."
— Psalm 118:17 (KJV)

CH [LTC, RET] ARTHUR W. COFFEY, JR., D. MIN.

WestBow
P R E S S
A DIVISION OF THOMAS NELSON

WestBow Press books may be ordered through booksellers or by contacting:

WestBow Press
A Division of Thomas Nelson
1663 Liberty Drive
Bloomington, IN 47403
www.westbowpress.com
1-(866) 928-1240

Because of the dynamic nature of the Internet, any web addresses or links contained in this book may have changed since publication and may no longer be valid. The views expressed in this work are solely those of the author and do not necessarily reflect the views of the publisher, and the publisher hereby disclaims any responsibility for them.

Certain stock imagery © Thinkstock.
Any people depicted in stock imagery provided by Thinkstock are models, and such images are being used for illustrative purposes only.

ISBN: 978-1-4497-7560-5 (e)
ISBN: 978-1-4497-7559-9 (sc)
ISBN: 978-1-4497-7558-2 (hc)

Library of Congress Control Number: 2012921468

Printed in the United States of America

WestBow Press rev. date: 01/29/2013

CONTENTS

Preface   vii

Introduction   ix

CHAPTER 1   The Body Marathon   1

CHAPTER 2   The Mind Marathon   90

CHAPTER 3   The Spirit Marathon   120

CHAPTER 4   The Far Journey   218

Postscript   343

Addendum   349

Author Bio   391

PREFACE

The full draft of this book was originally submitted to three publishers. All got back with me to say they liked the honesty of it but wanted more of a "story line" to hold readers' interest, something to allow the reader to step out of the classroom and into the living room. However, as Ralph Waldo Emerson said, "'Tis a good reader that makes a good book."

I also like the words of writer Sydney Smith: "The writer does the most who gives his reader the most knowledge and takes from him the least time." Therefore, it is not my job to preach to you but to tell my story as it happened. At several points, the reader may be referred to the appendices to read training regimens; the purpose of this is to allow reflection that moves the reader deeper into the story. Here, the reader will engage a pause for an expository look at what is being said. My Bible translation of preference from childhood has been the King James Version (KJV) for its scholarship in translating the Hebrew, Greek, and Aramaic texts. I have also cited in this book the Amplified Bible for doing the same into modern language and the Living Bible to assist readers who are not familiar with the Scriptures.

To write my story has been therapeutic. "Thoughts disentangle themselves when they pass through your fingertips," said Dawson Trotman, founder of the Christian organization called the Navigators. "This shall be written for the generation to come and the people which shall be created shall praise the Lord" (Ps. 102:18 King James Version, or KJV). "And the Lord answered me, and said, Write the vision, and make it plain upon tables, that he may run that readeth it" (Hab. 2:2 KJV).

INTRODUCTION

Born out of and cradled in the crucible of a near-death accident; a broken family; the loss of job and home; a stark medical and mental prognosis; a deep, dark depression; and excessive misery, the pages of this book have ached for words that speak on a theme that is timeless. And, as I could hear the hoof beats of Pharaoh's horses and the chariots of bankruptcy drawing close behind me, how would God part my "Red Sea"?

Without being simply didactic, I want to show you how God's Word can become, as he describes it, "sent out" (Is. 55:10–11); "active and alive" (Heb. 4:12); "watched over and performed" (Jer. 1:12). The central task and goal for me is to present you with the opportunity to see how God's Word can speak to and change real-life crises as it did for me—leaving a sense of wonder and comfort about God's Word. Theologically, it would mean encountering Scripture—not just as *logos* (an idea or concept), but as *rhema* (word spoken directly, meant to be personal). How could the Scriptures become more than words on a page?

Over the years, I have been encouraged to write this book more like a soap-opera script so as to hold readers' attention. But that style would have deflected your attention from the real meat of the message: God's Word as a whole tells me that it is not necessary to recall shameful things from my past. If God's forgiveness of my sins means he has forgotten, erased, healed, and covered them, who am I to raise them up again?

You may be asking, "Is this a book about running, relationships, or repentance?" It's all three—we begin with the physical marathon, continue with the mental and spiritual ones, and then assess how they interrelate for recovery. As I looked at deadly wounds to my body, mind, spirit, family, and career, I wondered how God's Word could cause seemingly impossible changes to take place in my thinking, speaking, actions, relationships, and actual life circumstances. This "recounting" is something God said I would do (Ps. 118:17) as I knocked on death's doorway while in the hospital for three months.

Chapter One, the Body Marathon, will introduce a body-mind-spirit "transfer of training dynamic." What is that dynamic? Try asking yourself the following questions: 1) What can I learn from a physical run or challenge that will help me with a mental run or challenge, and vice versa? 2) What can I learn from a spiritual run or challenge that will help me with both a physical and a mental challenge? And 3) what can I learn from a physical and a mental run or challenge that would become a living parable, a reflection of what I'm learning on the spiritual level of my life? This same training dynamic flows through Chapter Two, the Mind Marathon, and Chapter Three, the Spirit Marathon.

In this training, I will ask you to consider a hierarchy of God's Word over the human spirit, over the mind, and over the body. If I ask the questions, "Who am I?" and "What is my identity?" God's answer will be, *I am spirit, I have a mind, and I live in a body.* God's Word will address my identity as "spirit" even when I'm knocked out on the operating table. That's why I have been led over the years to pray the healing Scriptures even for patients who were in a coma. What my spirit—that part of me that connects with the Word and will live somewhere forever—hears will, then, speak to my mind; next, my mind will help direct my body to take steps according to the original Word given. My spirit is that part of my being that can perceive God "talking" to me through his Word about specific conditions in my life. I hear him in the sense that I know that I know. When John the Baptist, still in his mother's womb, sensed the presence of Jesus, who was still in Mary's womb, he "leaped" inside his mother's womb (see Luke 1:41). He had connected with the "Word made flesh" (John 1:14). "The spirit of a man is the lamp of the Lord, searching all the inner depths of his heart" (Prov. 20:27).

The Scriptures noted in this book are central and pivotal to the "wholistic" marathon journey for the reader (trainee). I invite and pray that you will read this book and, when finished, put it down and say, "Wow, look how God's Word affected the body, mind, spirit, and life history of this runner. I want to be close to the Word; I want the Word to be close to me; I want to train on God's Word so it can speak to my 'wall.'" And, as you know, to be close with the Word is to be close with God (John 1:1–14). The Holy Spirit, my Head Coach in this hierarchy, has led the training for the words that follow; he is the one who made them stand up in the midst of my thoughts and say, "Attention to orders." Read them with the eye of a trainee hungry for a word that endures to the end.

In summary, the book could become a "wounded-healer" vehicle for those encountering similar kinds of stress or crisis. The end result is that you, the reader, will move closer to and relate with God's heart on a deeper level as you move closer to and relate more deeply with His Word (John 1:1). "Let the words of my mouth, and the meditation of my heart, be acceptable in Thy sight, O Lord, my strength, and my redeemer" (Ps. 19:14 KJV). "For physical training is of some value—useful for a little; but godliness (spiritual training) is useful and of value in everything and in every way, for it holds promise for the present life and also for the life which is to come" (1 Tim. 4:7–8 The Amplified Bible, or AMP).

As we run, I want to show you the series of trials and tragedies in my life that God's Word formed into triumphs. Run, now, with me.

CHAPTER 1

The Body Marathon

Boston, Easter Monday, 1992

Doctors said I'd never run again, but here I am at long last, amid the crowd of marathon athletes—the goal of years of training, mountain runs to build endurance and wind, attempts at many qualifying runs, and various runners' injuries. As I find my place in the start-up, I can't believe that my feet are on the same pavement as the feet of world-class athletes, using this year's Boston Marathon as their qualifying run for the Olympics. Looking about, I catch the excitement of fellow runners who are stretching, warming up, and sharing experiences. I know my new wife and "Brady Bunch" of seven eagerly anticipates cheering me on to the finish line, where they now wait—the crowning end of a long, long journey. This is real; it is about to happen.

Just as I am saying, "Thank you, Father. Thank you, Jesus. Thank you, Holy Spirit," the gun fires and we are off. As we gear up for the demanding 26.2-mile race against time and our own records, we begin to test our strides and paces as seasoned veterans in this most prestigious of all runs. I feel the brisk, fresh spring air on my face and gaze into a beautiful, cloudless blue sky. My mind drifts back seven years to another season of marathon training, to another day with such a sky. The journey flashes back, and my mind leaves the race and moves toward a trilogy of trials, tragedies, and triumphs.

The Accident

No memory of it exists, but I am told that, after conducting a funeral service, I went home on my motorcycle through the small village and country parish I served in the Shenandoahs. A car suddenly pulled across the road in front of me. My oldest son, Brooke, who was riding with me, later explained: "Daddy, you slammed on all the brakes, but it was too late." Seconds later, I crashed my motorcycle into the car and went down. Bystanders said Brooke was thrown far but sustained only minor injuries; this alone was evidence of the protective "hand of God." I'm told that eyewitnesses saw me and said, "He's dead."

I can't remember anything from the June 20, 1986, accident. After asking members of my family to proofread this account, my son, who was on that motorcycle with me, wrote beside the above paragraph: "Describe the day more before the wreck; add more detail." I would if I could. Unfortunately, I'm not able to remember the contents of the day or much of the years preceding the accident. So, I asked him to help reconstruct the day, and he did. These are his words:

> I had been at Washington and Lee's basketball camp all week. You picked me up on the motorcycle at a friend's house in Lexington, VA. You were wearing a suit and had a plastic grocery bag full of books sitting on the gas tank of the motorcycle or near there. I was wearing a cut-off T-shirt and shorts. We approached

the town of Fairfield and were making our descent down the hill. I looked over at an old man riding a moped. After glancing at him for a moment, I turned around and leaned up to ask you if we were stopping at the grocery store. I think I turned once more to look back at the man on the moped. When I turned back around, I noticed a big flash of blue. Of course, this was the side of the four-door Cadillac we collided with.

I remember the sound pretty clearly. It sounded as if someone had dropped several sheets of plate glass off of a five-story building. The next thing I know, I was getting up off of the asphalt and unstrapping my helmet. I started walking over toward the curb. I noticed an elderly woman crying hysterically, saying, "What have I done? What have I done?" I must have been in shock. Two women who were working at the beauty salon ran out to me and instructed me to sit down.

At that moment, I noticed you in the middle of the road. The motorcycle was on top of your legs, and you were curled up in a ball, motionless. The women helping me had brought a pillow out for me to lie back on, but every few seconds I would look back up to the road. Cars would pass by slowly as they eased through the crash site. Minutes later, an ambulance arrived.

The next thing I remember, we were in the back of the ambulance. There was a paramedic in the back working on you. You were strapped to a stretcher, moaning, obviously in pain. Your head was especially swollen, among other things. Your pants leg had been cut up so that they could work on your knee. You kept fighting the restraints, and the paramedic was trying to tell you to be still. I remember peering through the window to the cab of the ambulance. The speedometer indicated ninety-five miles per hour. I felt a little nauseated. The next thing I knew, I was in the hospital sitting in a wheelchair. You were flown to Memorial Hospital. That's everything I can remember about the wreck.

I do not recall the three months I subsequently spent in the hospital. I'm told that, most of the time, they thought I was going to die. One of the doctors attending me in intensive care later, in post care, remarked, "Another hand was working in there with ours." He also said that my marathon training was a helpful factor. When people have asked me through the years whether or not I had an "out-of-body experience," I have had to say, "Not to my knowledge." You will soon see why I had no revelations or visions to recall from this experience; if I had died, my home today would not be heaven. However, as with many near-death cases, I do register a change in the way I view death; now, it seems more like a graduation than an end. The Scripture that says, "Absent from the body," "present with the Lord" (2 Cor. 5:6, 8) has a familiar ring.

The doctor's remark about the other hand also rings true to me. I am convinced that God brought me through the ordeal because he had plans for healing and transformation. As I knocked on death's door, a woman in one of the local churches, I was later told by church members, was praying for me while working her garden. She had a close, trusting relationship with God. A reference, Psalm 118:17, came to her mind. Setting her tools down, she went into the house to look it up and found that it said, "For he shall not die, but live to recount the works of the Lord."

Some clinicians in after-care status wrote, "Severe long- and short-term memory deficits, poor conceptual thinking and a thirty-six point lowered IQ." Following X-ray procedures, for which they placed me inside a huge cylinder and "looked" at me from the inside out, the doctor—and I can still see him sitting behind his desk with the paperwork——said, "Left brain damage, right side of body semiparalysis (from neurological injuries), left spinal cord compressed through neck, and injuries to your knee (a bolt through it) spell an end to your running days." I loved to run and was training for a marathon when the accident happened.

As I later learned, I had crashed headlong into the car and struck the pavement. One newspaper article written several years later said that I had "ended up with his motorcycle wrapped around his mangled body. A bolt from the machine rammed through his knee. He suffered massive head injuries, and everyone from the bystanders to the rescue squad workers thought they were cutting a dead man from the twisted metal."

Family members said my face was swollen to five times its normal size, despite the fact that I was wearing a helmet. With the avalanche of evil that followed this accident, I can see in retrospect that the Devil had loaded his best shot and fired it on that fateful day. One of my sisters thought to tell me years later that when she had called my dad to tell him what had happened to me, he said, "I knew for a week that something was going to happen." Our family history records that kind of "inner knowing" on his part.

The accident triggered an avalanche of troubles that cascaded in my mind for four years—leaving a hole in my soul. These mammoth explosions within my mind formed a crucible for training in God's Word. Through a trilogy of tragedies (body, mind, and spirit), the Holy Spirit coached me continually on his Word. When I would still myself to read the Bible, I was reading *logos* and could not turn it into *rhema*, but the Holy Spirit could. And, using the Scriptures, he lived up to his description as "teacher, helper, counselor, comforter and one who convicts of truth" (John 14:26; John 16:7–15; Rom. 8:26). When a verse of Scripture struck me as *rhema*, I knew that it was time to sit up; salute; say, "Yes, sir"; and become expectant. I knew that I knew that I knew. God's miracle was a trilogy of triumphs—causing my story to appear in seven newspapers in five different states, one international magazine, and now this book. Publications and speaking engagements served as tangible proof of what God said in Psalm 118:17.

The Guilt

I was finally heading home from the hospital. The hour-and-fifteen-minute drive with my wife at the time was deafeningly silent. As she turned the car into the driveway, I saw the house and saw the children coming out the door. I welled up with tears.

During the course of the following month, my wife struggled with more than my prognosis. One day, as I was coming into the living room, she stood up, looked firmly at me, and said, "I want a separation." While she suffered through the crisis of an uncertain future and the loss of the husband she had known, the crowning crisis had occurred during my hospitalization, when she became aware of my previous adultery. It was with someone she thought was her friend. Looking back, I see that, while I was in the hospital, I must have known in my spirit that she knew. That explains the drive home, enveloped in silence. That same month, she moved out.

In a marathon, somewhere around mile twenty or twenty-one, the runner hits "the wall." This is where mind and body shake hands in agreement and say, "We wanna quit." And that's where most runners will do just that—quit. At that point, "mind over matter" no longer works. Like the walls and struggles I was encountering in my physical marathon, the simultaneous mental and spiritual "marathons" began to, like chronic depression, cause my mind and body to say, "We wanna quit!" The burning question was, How does the Holy Spirit apply the Father's healing Word through the stripes of his Son, Jesus, to our wounded bodies, minds, spirits, and relationships? How does God heal lives broken from sin, and how could I train to run on the road to repentance? In short, what would I learn from the physical marathon that would apply to the mental and spiritual marathons, and vice versa? So this burning question seared the writer's soul, rooted in the following Word:

"But he was wounded for our transgressions, he was bruised for our iniquities: the chastisement of our peace was upon him; and with his stripes we are healed" (Is. 53:5 NKJV).

Therefore, to break through the "wall" in a marathon, I need to understand the hierarchy of Word over spirit over mind over body.

The Mailbox Run

As I tried to run these respective "marathons," our Head Coach, God's Holy Spirit, came to my side and coached me with the Father's Word. He kept finding ways to remind me of one of those special, lifted up (*rhema*) words that I had read one day while waiting for the three boys to come off the school bus. I had custody of them; my wife had custody of our daughter. The Word said, "But they that wait upon the LORD shall renew their strength; they shall mount up with wings as eagles; they shall run, and not be weary; and they shall walk, and not faint" (Is. 40:31 KJV).

So one day, during a seven-month string of pity parties, God's spirit kept giving me mental "taps on the shoulder," urging me to understand that he wanted me to get out and run, to get back in shape. I raised my fist and argued with these thoughts, saying, "You heard the doctors. I'll never run again."

The next tap came: "Run out to the mailbox and back." (The mailbox was at the end of the driveway, which was about one-third of a mile long through the woods.) "Okay," I replied, pointing down to my feet, "you see me hobbling, don't you?" I was somewhat sarcastic as I deliberately placed one foot in front of the other. This run was hard! (I knew from three years of studying Hebrew and two years of studying Greek that the original words for the "Holy Spirit" mean "wind" and "power." I recalled Jesus' telling folks that the Spirit works like the wind; we don't see the effects but rather feel them. Also, the creation text speaks of the Spirit brooding or hovering over the face of the deep. Scientists tell us that the wind moved and formed a lot of the earth when it was in a state of chaos.) This was significant to me. Could the Holy Spirit take the Word—much like he did when God the Father spoke it, saying. "Let there be ..."—and speak it to me, now, in a creative way, causing it to wind through the wounds to my body, mind, spirit, and relationships? As I gave thought to the Isaiah Word, I wanted but was afraid to trust what it said about renewed strength and running. But, as I reached the mailbox and turned to head back, something unexplainable happened. My leg, stride, and balance felt different. The hobbling stopped, and I could stretch out with my toes to the pavement. So, as I ran back, I said right out loud, "Yes, Father, I feel it. What did you do?"

To my mind, he said, *On the way out, you ran in faith. On the way back, I spoke my Word to your leg.* But I had run to the mailbox with sarcasm; I saw my faith as sarcastic faith. That night I referred to my concordance and read about faith. Two of the passages I found spoke as though coming from him, personally, to me about the "faith run." One said, "So then faith cometh by hearing, and hearing by the word of God" (Rom. 10:17 KJV); and the other read, "For truly I say to you, if you have faith (that is living) like a grain of mustard seed, you can say to this mountain, Move from here to yonder place, and it will move; and nothing will be impossible to you" (Matt. 17:20 AMP).

In this "mailbox run," I felt God's presence as I ran with mustard-seed faith—timidly but stubbornly putting feet forward against the odds, so much so that it made every foot of that driveway come alive. The Word was there; therefore, God was there (John 1:1–14). I was actually in his presence. He was going to move my mountain! (Biblically, *mountain* is a synonym for *problem* or *challenge*.) My thoughts became expectant. Was he really causing his Word to be "sent out," to become "active and alive" as he "watched over (it) to perform (it)" for me? For the next four years, the Holy Spirit became my Coach. Again, he would cause the Word of God to counsel, comfort, help, teach, and convict me of what is true. He also brought to mind ideas for training—for example, to run on my toes when on level ground and up hills, to run with heels first when going down hills so as to avoid shocking my system, and to keep a long stride like a deer, which I found would automatically increase my pace. For four years, he trained me to run through the Blue Ridge Mountains in the southern end of the Shenandoah Valley to build up wind, stamina, and endurance and finally to run for seven months, doing the distance of twenty-eight miles up the steepest bike trail in North America with weights strapped around my ankles. When those weights came off, I felt like I had been given wings. Here, now, is how he trained me. (I had originally questioned titling Chapter One "The Body Marathon" because that wouldn't encompass my need to describe the additional "weights" pressing down from my mind and heart in addition to the ones strapped to my ankles.)

I can *run!*

The four years of training that followed the "mailbox run" were progressive and effective in my performance. I began to feel deep in my spirit that my Coach (the Holy Spirit) was mapping out a "wholistic" training program that would lead to achieving my longtime goal of running in the Boston Marathon. Being part Jewish, I love it when, at every Seder and when under the stress of captivity, Jews throughout history have prayed, "Next year in Jerusalem." So, in my captivity of training, I said, "Next year in Boston." The obstacles I faced were my continuing recovery and meeting the qualifying time.

The Holy Spirit led my thoughts: *Take what you are seeing about the mental and spiritual marathons and apply it to the physical.* I didn't understand. I set a plan in motion: from January through July, I would run with weights strapped around my ankles. On Monday and Wednesday mornings, I would do eleven-mile runs, and on Friday mornings, these shackled runs would be twenty-eight miles. The one day off between the eleven-mile runs and the two days following the twenty-eight-mile runs would give my body cells time to replenish. Later, I would painfully learn how the "weight training" would become a vivid, tangible parable for my spiritual condition.

The doctors had said my running days were over, but then I was coached to run with weights on. I couldn't see the mental–spiritual–physical connection. Then the Holy Spirit counseled me to keep the Word in mind:

"Therefore then, since we are surrounded by so great a cloud of witnesses (who have borne testimony of the Truth), let us strip off and throw aside every encumbrance—unnecessary weight—and that sin which so readily (deftly and cleverly) clings to and entangles us, and let us run with patient endurance and steady and active persistence the appointed course of the race that is set before us" (Heb. 12:1 AMP).

Training Note

In later years, following the events described in this book, I wrote a devotional book titled *Running Devotionals*. It contained monthly themes based on what had emerged from my four years of intense training. The following "months of training" in this book you are holding are my thoughts in dialogue with those planted in my mind, coached, by the Holy Spirit as I trained during those years. You may wonder as you read these conversations how I could remember all of this. The answer is that after each run, with sweat dripping, I would jot down words I had formed (acrostics), letting each letter stand for a thought, a point made, or an insight, which I would subsequently expand. Later in the day, with the help of my Thomas Nelson King James Study Bible, I would search for key words in the concordance—*run, endure, hope, sin, healing, forgiveness, peace*—and then pore over the Scriptures surrounding those key words in search of words that the Holy Spirit would choose to "speak" to me in that *rhema* fashion. When this happened, those words became programmed as I meditated upon and memorized them, much like a computer is programmed to perform its memory functions. Then, as needed in the following training runs, the Holy Spirit would do as Scripture says he would: "But the Comforter, which is the Holy Ghost, whom the Father will send in my name, he shall teach you all things, and *bring* all things *to your remembrance*, whatsoever I have said unto you" (John 14:26 KJV). Somehow, even then, I knew that the day would come when I would "recount" (Ps. 118:17) these training sessions in a book. A Bible concordance could assist you as you look over my shoulder in parallel training. A good footnote to this training exercise is to always read God's Word in context with the whole Word of God. It has been said, "Text taken out of context is only pretext." Let Word uphold and confirm Word! I strongly endorse the Nelson KJV Study Bible; its concordance is exhaustive and the biblical text contains expositions of key Hebrew and Greek terms taken from the very reliable *Strong's Concordance.*

God loves to use our wounds to build "wounded healers." Years after the events of this book, when I was working with drug addicts and alcoholics in the military setting (at Veterans Affairs Medical Centers), I learned to expand one of the twelve steps of recovery in light of this concept. I would sometimes say to the class, "Pretend you are in a large classroom and the teacher takes the chalk, goes up to the board, and writes in big letters, 'Wounded Healer.' He then comes to you, hands you the chalk, and asks you to go up and write out a definition for 'wounded healer.' If that should happen, what do you think you would put?" Sometimes they would scratch their heads and say, "I don't know." So I would ask, "Who is the best person to help an alcoholic?" Immediately, someone would say, "Another alcoholic." A wounded healer is someone who has been there, who has gone through the pain, problem, crisis, sin condition, weakness, habit, addiction, and so on. So, like an Army scout, he is the best person to come back and take the rest of the troops through the same territory. Those soldiers who could capture that vision as part of their recovery came back years later to tell the "guess what's been happening" kind of stories. They came also to see that they were in good company because Jesus was the greatest wounded healer of all times. "By his wounds, his stripes, we are healed" (Is. 53:5; 1 Pet. 2:24). What kind of wounds might you be carrying as we train? Feel free to adopt from these months what you sense to be helpful.

January: Month of Beginnings

Those weights were heavy and cumbersome as I stumbled in search of stamina. "They that wait upon the Lord shall renew their strength" (Is. 40:31), I recalled. I wondered how God would do that. And what does waiting on him entail? *Wait*, in Hebrew, means "to bind together by twisting." I was led to picture three ropes twisted together. John 1:1–14 reminded me that God is the Word and the Word is God. I needed to wait, therefore, on the Word—to let it bind and twist together, thereby becoming stronger to bring me the whole truth, setting me free. I began setting some seventy Scripture passages to music and would sing them in my mind as I ran (one of my bachelor's degrees was in music). The music accessed my left-brain motor skills in running and added good cadence. The Scriptures, housed in music, addressed my right brain, with its focus on feelings, memory, and perception. I began to have not just knowledge itself about his Word but an understanding in my heart of the boundaries of God's thoughts—thinking his thoughts after him. The pavement became a platform for Scripture to serve as a mantra or vehicle for deep meditation on what God was saying to me through his Word. I began to become protective of this time in running because of what he began to show me.

February: Month of Discontent

The weights were not getting any lighter; they were getting heavier, in fact, as though my feet were strapped to heavy-duty springs embedded into the pavement with some force underneath that was tightening them with every step. I couldn't see myself continuing with this; my heart wasn't in it. "Run in faith," I was coached. A spiritual dialogue ensued as the Holy Spirit coached me.

"I don't feel like it."

Faith is not a feeling; it is a decision.

"That decision is not in me."

Faith is not a human attribute; it is a God-given (1 Cor. 12:9) *ability to choose to trust him at his word, often against feelings, against circumstances.*

"Speaking of word, I've been waiting on *wait* and haven't seen anything yet."

As you run, center your mind on the rest of it.

I recalled "shall renew their strength" (Is. 40:31). "It's beyond me how I can have new strength in this condition."

After the training sessions, I was increasingly learning the value of studying his Word: "(God's) strength is made perfect *in* (focus on the word *in*) (your) weakness" (1 Cor. 12:9). When Jesus said, "Blessed are the poor in spirit," the original text reads, "Happy is the man who knows how much he needs God."

"So, when I see my weakness and how much I need him, that's not a step backward but a step forward?"

Carry on.

"Too much suffering with what I'm carrying in the run!"

For I consider that the sufferings of this present time are not worthy to be compared with the glory which shall be revealed in us (Rom. 8:18, emphasis added). Again, there was the word *in*.

"This grueling training program grinds my mind and beats my feet. I'm waiting for the divorce papers to be delivered. Today, as I run, the road looks long and lonely—unending."

Change it to a moment (1 Cor. 15:52), *and count it all joy when you fall into various trials, knowing that the testing of your faith produces patience. But let patience have its perfect work, that you may be perfect and complete, lacking nothing* (James 1:2–4).

"I'm carrying much more than these weights that are unrelentingly and unmercifully strapped around my ankles."

Tell me about it.

"Why should I have to tell you when you already know?"

Earlier, I had studied these words in the Amplified Bible: "Come to Me, all you who labor and are heavy-laden and overburdened, and I will cause you to rest—I will ease and relieve and refresh your souls. Take My yoke upon you, and learn of Me; for I am gentle (meek) and humble (lowly) in heart, and you will find rest—relief, ease and refreshment and recreation and blessed quiet—for your souls. For My yoke is wholesome (useful, good)—not harsh, hard, sharp or pressing, but comfortable, gracious and pleasant; and My burden is light and easy to be borne" (Matt. 11:28–30 AMP).

There was a long period of quiet in the run.

"I see my heart like a balloon strapped to a persistently dripping water faucet, each drop tearfully reminding me of what I have done to the 'wife of my youth' (Mal. 2:15)— two decades of marriage gone, family broken!" Of the four children, the one who had been on the motorcycle with me had expressed the most anger and hurt feelings following the accident and family breakup. In that day's run, I vividly recalled seeing him thrust his fist through the door to his bedroom immediately after hearing that our marriage was over. Another time, after witnessing an episode of severe depression and an angry scene on my part, he sobbed almost uncontrollably. After I apologized to him for yelling, gave him a hug, and assured him that both of us would be all right, he was able to recover.

It is the "dark night of my soul."

"Be still and know that I am God" (Ps. 46:10 New International Version, or NIV).

After another long stillness during the run, I picked up the dialogue again. "There's more." He was listening. "The Word is right when you say that those guilty of adultery will become a byword" (Ez. 23:10 AMP). And so I had become in the community and surrounding towns. During those early years following the divorce, I wondered if drivers who appeared to be trying to force me off the far side of the road and into the ditch during my training runs were simply saying, "Let's get this hypocrite off the road and into the ditch where he belongs." (See Prov. 6:30–33). I grew accustomed to walking into the local grocery store, bank, post office, gas station, and so on, only to catch the looks and the stares. I suppose if folks still remembered St. Paul as Saul, why should someone like me expect anything different? I thought of punishments for adultery through the course of time: stoning, crucifixion, hanging, shooting.

"But there is another weight that almost completely crushes my spirit." I discerned that he wanted me to spell it out, so, after the run I did. "I have become worse than those for whom Jesus had the harshest words when he was here. To the Scribes and Pharisees, the religious elite, he said, 'You hypocrites, white washed tombs' (Matt. 23:27 NKJV). And so, like those Greek actors (hypokrites), I have worn two masks, been two-faced, and lived like the walking dead, having a 'form of godliness but denying the power thereof' (2 Tim. 3:5 KJV)—a 'wolf (predator) in sheep's clothing' (Matt.

7:15 NKJV; 2 Cor. 11:14–15 NKJV). 'O God, you know so well how stupid I am, and you know all my sins' (Ps. 69:5 TLB). In summary, I have become a shame to your name!"

The next time I studied his Word, I realized that, yes, my sins had found me out (Num. 32:23), but I also saw this: "For if we would judge ourselves, we would not be judged. But when we are judged, we are chastened by the Lord, that we may not be condemned with the world" (1 Cor. 11:31–32 KJV).

In the next run, the weights shackled to my ankles were a moving picture of the weights tugging at my heart and spirit, each compounding the other; my unfaithful and adulterous heart—leading to divorce, the breakup of my family, and community shame—repeatedly beat my feet. It was impossible to keep lifting my feet and knees under this imploding heaviness. Even in the subzero weather I was sweating like a mule. But it was hard to tell the sweat from the tears. I thought, "Maybe if I make this run punishing enough, it will help my wife change her mind and come back." My mind held a debate: *"Change it to a moment"* and *"count it all joy."* "I can't just do that as though changing the channel." (The words for *change* and *count* are verbs calling for a faith-decision.) "My faith is too weak." *There is nothing faulty with the faith gift you've been handed to use; it's your use of it that is weak.* "God hath dealt to every man the measure of faith" (Rom. 12:3 KJV).

"That does it. That simply does it! Here I am trying to hold up under these horrible weights, and I can't even use the faith given me to bear up under them. This certainly has become the winter of my discontent!"

"For I have learned in whatever state I am, to be content" (Phil. 4:11b).

"How did Paul learn that?"

Accident, family breakup, loss of job, loss of home, facing bankruptcy, guilt, and so on—in the crucible of all of these stress factors, the Holy Spirit began to coach me in inexplicable ways on the most prominent Word in the Scriptures, the Word about *praise*. One day, as was my custom for a number of months while home alone, I was walking around the house aimlessly. Then, glancing over at the large bookshelf with some curiosity as to whether it held anything of meaning for me, there, as though it had been staring at me all along, asking when I was going to pick it up, was a small book titled *Prison to Praise* by Merlin Carothers, a retired Army chaplain. He had written three books on praise that had made the best-seller list, establishing him as one of ten authors in history to have three books on that list at the same time—one of them, *Prison to Praise,* being the international best-seller. The book highlighted the following Scriptures:

"Thank (God) in everything—no matter what the circumstances may be, be thankful and give thanks; for this is the will of God for you (who are) in Christ Jesus (the Revealer and Mediator of that will)" (1 Thess. 5:18 AMP).

And, as if to nail it in concrete, came the second:

"Through Him therefore let us constantly and at all times offer up to God a sacrifice of praise, which is the fruit of lips that thankfully acknowledge and confess and glorify his name" (Heb. 13:15 AMP).

I chewed my way through the above Scriptures and finally decided that since the first Scripture from Thessalonians said to give God thanks *in* all things, this did not mean to give him thanks *for* all things. Besides, that sounds too close to blasphemy or crediting God for Satan's work. So I wrote the author stating all this. He wrote back with one sentence, presumably to let the Word stand on its own two feet: "Giving thanks always for all things to God the Father in the name of our Lord Jesus Christ" (Eph. 5:20 NKJV).

This reinforcing third Scripture was perennially present. It splashed on the canvas of my heart where I was wading in a pool of self-pity. The Scriptures were concise: give thanks in and for *all* things. Matthew 4:4 tells me that "every Word that comes out of the mouth of God" is for me. Now the Word was saying to simply give thanks for all. I proceeded to read eleven more of Carothers's books to see for myself why there were over 19 million copies of them in print and in fifty-eight different languages. The Scriptures, cited, seemed to invite me—as into a living room—for conversation that searched me at the core of my being. The centerpiece of these conversations became the word *all*. I tried to ignore the specificity of those verses, hitting like bullets; however, the Word *all* loomed higher and higher, forming a panoply from under which nothing could escape. Although there was no way to dodge the directive of this Word about praise, nevertheless I started to praise God with sarcasm when I was wallowing in self-pity in the black of night. One day, I mentally shook my fist and said, "If I am going to give you thanks in and for *all* these things (I had a long list), then, by crackie, some of it will have to be through gritted teeth or tears or both." There was a long, still pause in both my mind and my surroundings. In that stillness, it seemed as though God were very near, sitting beside me, arms folded, slowly and firmly nodding agreement with what I had just said and thought.

God causes or allows. Shortly thereafter, during those bleak years following the accident, I was "tested" en route to home after a twelve-hour night shift in the nursing home where I was working as an orderly, with $3.75/hour pay and having done sheep shearing the previous day. A policeman clocked me at sixty-two miles per hour on a bypass exchange, without my seat belt fastened, and stopped me. As I tried to explain why I was driving so fast without a seat belt, it became clear to the officer that my state of exhaustion precluded me from driving safely. The series of infractions for which I was charged cost me almost one week of hard-earned pay.

You have probably heard it said that God will not allow more to be placed on us than we can bear (see 1 Cor. 10:13 for closest reference). I managed to give God "gritted teeth" thanks for his "being in this," not in the sense of making bad things happen—that was my doing—but to redeem or bring something good out of it. "And we know that all things work together for good to them that love God" (Rom. 8:28 KJV). I was the one responsible, of course, for my predicament. You will note that Scripture clearly outlines that just as light and darkness cannot exist in the same space, God can in no way endorse evil, nor will Christ, our High Priest, hear our wrong confessions that credit God as the source of sin or evil. My Coach was teaching me not to thank God in and for bad things as though he had somehow made them happen but to give him thanks with the understanding that he had *allowed* them for a reason and is the one who can reach in with his redeeming will and bring something good out of it all, much in the same sense of going to a "redemption store." As you will see, God can take the garbage Satan brings in through the "back door" and "work it toward good" so that it glides gracefully through the "front door" of our lives.

I would come to see God's twofold response to the "sacrifice of praise": 1) "The peace of God that passes all understanding"— like the eye of a hurricane. The Hebrew word for *peace* does not refer to peace in the absence of war or stress but peace in the *midst* of it. "And the peace of God, which passeth all understanding, shall keep your hearts and minds through Christ Jesus" (Phil. 4:7 KJV); and 2) miracle—where He rolls up his sleeves, so to speak, and works with those things you cannot do anything about.

In the meantime, I said, "If I'm really going to do this Word about thanks, then, some of it will be gritted-teeth thanks or tearful thanks." I was led to envision a day in which I gave joyful thanks instead of what used to be gritted-teeth thanks or tearful thanks. Why? The more I started thanking him, especially when it made no sense, the more I started, somehow, finding myself to trust him, giving him room to work in my life. "Will I see that day when these weights are lifted?" I thought. "What weights did Paul carry? Well, he had beatings, scourges, plots against his life, shipwreck, imprisonment, snakebite, betrayal , and so on, but you said your grace was sufficient (2 Cor. 12:9) when he asked you to remove them. I'm boldly coming before the throne of your grace (Heb. 4:16) to ask that they be removed anyway."

Training on the Word into the months ahead, I would find that time when the weights clinging to my feet and heart would lighten. Contentment would not be a matter of getting what I want but wanting what I got. So, how do we proceed? "Therefore do not worry about tomorrow, for tomorrow will worry about its own things. Sufficient for the day is its own trouble" (Matt. 6:34 KJV). Could I substitute the word *mile* for the word *day*? How do I approach the miles from this point? *"Be like a little child, let your faith become expectant."* So, I watched to see how each day might be the setting to "renew my strength."

March: Month of Wind

Is it just the principle of intentionality, a placebo effect, I wondered, or am I beginning to sense a slight lift in these weights? I recalled, again, the Old Testament Hebrew word for *spirit* (phonetically, *ru*-wach) means "breath, wind." In school, we learned that at the time of earth's formation, the wind was strong over it. "Was that you?" I asked.

"In the beginning of creation, when God made heaven and earth, the earth was without form and void, with darkness over the face of the abyss, and a mighty wind that swept over the surface of the waters" (Gen. 1:1–2 New English Bible, or NEB). *"The Spirit of God was moving (hovering, brooding) over the face of the waters"* (Gen. 1:2b AMP).

"Are you going to be the 'wind beneath my wings'?"

"The wind blows wherever it pleases. You hear its sound, but you cannot tell where it comes from or where it goes to. So it is with everyone born of the Spirit" (John 3:8 NIV).

On this particular day, I had to lean into the wind at almost a forty-five-degree angle because it was so forceful. I wondered how the Holy Spirit would train me during that month. I discern the answer: *Sprint the hills.* I had counted forty-six medium-sized hills and twenty-six big ones; just the few hills I sprinted in the beginning took all the breath out of me. I couldn't see myself doing it. Then, I sense a locker-room talk: *We will address your vision problem in May. My name also means "breath." Lift your hands high in the air as you approach this next hill and voice thanks and praise to me for the hill.*

"That's the last thing I feel like doing—to put even more effort into these hills. Nevertheless, at your Word. At the crest of the hill, with arms up, I had more air; my chest felt full and deep with air. "Wow! You knew this all along!" I felt led to breathe through my nose, to lean into and sprint the hills. I was desperately gasping for air, but thought, *Here goes.* At the next crest I felt more relaxed with this slower breathing through my nose and was less hungry for air. My body was thankful. Could I build up for those next hills by sprinting up and coasting down, taking air in through my nose and letting it out through my mouth so as to regroup? What had my coaches in school said? My football, wrestling, and track coaches would say, "No pain, no gain." That day, I sprinted more hills with hands raised high as I reached the top of each.

I received a summation: *I am the breath of life to* all *of your hills.* He began to coach me to see parallels between the physical hills and the "hills of temptation." He posed a question to me: *You were running a good race. Who cut in on you and kept you from obeying the truth?* Then we stepped up the pace. "Since we live by the Spirit, let us keep in step with the Spirit" (Gal. 5:25 NIV).

(In the original Greek text, the words "keep in step" have a depth of meaning far greater than just "being moved along"; they are a command that military logistics describe as "to get in line with, to make decisions, to take steps and initiate actions in accord with, continually.")

"Based on my weaknesses in the mental marathon (cognitive handicaps from the accident) and my failures in the spiritual marathon (unfaithfulness to God, family, community)," I said, "I will have to keep up with you by running in your grace." On the hills, for the first half of the run, I was running against the wind and leaning sharply into them. The hills and the wind were "God-allowed." Coming back, the wind was at my back and strong to the point of almost picking up my feet as I engaged the hills. Such resistance followed by such lifting force became a moving metaphor for me. I found inspiration in the perspiration as the Holy Spirit unfolded more of the Word.

I recorded some thoughts on the guidance my Coach gave as I ran:

> I can use the "nevertheless-of-faith" principle to offer words of praise as I begin to run the "hills of life" when I'm almost completely out of breath. Faith is not a human attribute or a feeling; it is a gift (1 Cor. 12:9) from God that enables me to make the decision to trust him to act. Therefore, there is nothing weak about faith; it's just my use of it that's weak. I'm being coached to dive back into the Word when my use of this faith gift becomes weak; then the Word addressing my impossibilities will strengthen my grip (Rom. 10:17). I just need to remember its origin. God does not give me, his child, something that is frail or unstable. It is his strength given to me that enables me to stand on his Word simply by making a decision to do so—sometimes against feelings

and circumstances. Just like I feel his pleasure when I break through the "wall" during my long training runs, would I feel it again when I break through the "wall" of temptation by using his gift? The Word flatly tells me that the only way I can be pleasing to him is to exercise that faith gift. So I need to run to please him. "And without faith it is impossible to please God" (Heb. 11:6a NIV).

This faith gift led me to face the hills with determination and say to them, "Nevertheless, I'm sprinting anyway." It became a vital organ, implanted within my being. "For whatsoever is born of God overcometh the world: and this is the victory that overcometh the world, even our faith" (1 John 5:4 KJV). A question coached me further: *Do you see what Jesus did when facing his hill?* "Because the Lord God helps me, I will not be dismayed; therefore, I have set my face like flint to do his will, and I know that I will triumph" (Is. 50:7 TLB). I asked for more coaching: "Can I 'set my face like flint' against the hills of temptation because Jesus runs with me? When he said from the cross, 'It is finished,' did he have the finish line in sight? Can I, too, run by faith to the goal, knowing there will come a point at which I see that *cross*over line?" "He that shall endure unto the end, the same shall be saved" (Mark 13:13 KJV).

I continually and more deeply saw the Holy Spirit as my coach. I said to him, "You are making the Word become the wind beneath my wings." I sprint the hills and coast downhill, lifting arms high as I approach the crest of each one and uttering words of praise and thanks.

This is a praise paradigm in which I sometimes utter certain Hebrew words: *shema*, meaning "hear," because I want God to hear my thanks; and *yadah*, "to worship with extended hands," because my hands are extensions of my whole person as my body, emotions, will, and so on give God praise even when I'm almost out of breath. Lifting my arms up, I discovered, also brings more air into my lungs. I also say *hallelujah*, "to boast or brag on God," which is the premiere word for praise that transcends the language barrier of the major cultures of the world and announces victory. In Scripture, it is spoken in heaven as the final victory shout over evil. I believe that when I speak it here, it acknowledges his mercy becoming his justice for my life. Something began to stir deep within me when my voice spoke praise for he who is greater than me. I not only got more wind; it lifted me up and caused me to, in some way, enter into the greatness that I was admiring. The pavement was becoming my sanctuary. This posture of praise affected those around me as they saw me delighting in him. He was showing me his remedy for the "month of discontent." I ask you to wrestle with the following and see how you are led: 1Thessalonians 5:18; Ephesians 5:20; Hebrews 13:15; Philippians 4:6.

April: Month of Water

"What will these April showers bring?" I asked. "I still feel the horrible weight of my sin."

"But you were washed clean (purified by a complete atonement for sin and made free from the guilt of sin); and you were consecrated (set apart, hallowed); and you were justified (pronounced righteous, by trust) in the name of the Lord Jesus Christ and in the (Holy) Spirit of our God" (1 Cor. 6:11 AMP).

"The guilt smothers the air out of my soul," I replied.

You have become "confessionally honest" with me. Read and heed my Word.

"If we say that we have no sin, we are only fooling ourselves, and refusing to accept the truth. But if we confess our sins to him, he can be depended on to forgive us and to cleanse us from every wrong. (And it is perfectly proper for God to do this for us because Christ died to wash away our sins)" (1 John 1:8–9 TLB).

What did I say—that 50 percent, 70 percent, some of your sin is forgiven and cleansed?

"No, all—100 percent."

Then accept it all by taking the step of forgiving yourself.

"I can't do that!"

Dig deeper into my Word.

(When I joined the Army Reserves as a chaplain in 1971, as I was also preparing to become a pastor, I had taken three years of Hebrew and two years of Greek in a seminary. A trip back through my notes brought to mind the words of my professors, who explained the four original words used in the New Testament for *forgiveness*. One, pronounced na-*me*-sius, gives us the word *amnesia*; the second, pronounced *eph*-e-say, gives us *to erase*; the third, pronounced *ther*-o-*pu*-o, leads to *therapy*; and the fourth, pronounced *tow*-lah, gives us *to cover*.)

What did you find?

"When God speaks the Word of forgiveness, he is telling me that he has forgotten, erased, healed, and covered my sin." Several Scriptures make the point:

- "For I will forgive their iniquity, and their sin I will remember no more" (Jer. 31:34b KJV).

- "He takes our sins farther away than the east is from the west" (Ps. 103:12 Jerusalem Bible, or JB).

- "Therefore confess your sins to one another, and pray for one another, and then you will be healed" (James 5:16a NEB).

- "Blessed and happy and to be envied are those whose iniquities are forgiven and whose sins are covered up and completely buried" (Rom. 4:7 AMP).

If I am doing all this in forgiving you, can you receive it by going the whole nine yards and taking that step of forgiving yourself?

"For me, that will be more like a hurdle."

"Your heavenly Father will forgive you if you forgive those who sin against you; but if you refuse to forgive them, he will not forgive you" (Matt. 5:15 TLB).

"Does this mean that if I do not forgive myself, I can, somehow, stand in the way of the Father's forgiveness getting all the way to and into me?"

Carry on.

In the first several years following the marital separation, when I would do my training runs, it was as though I was trying to conduct some sort of self-atonement program for the sins I had committed against my wife. I would sometimes think, "Maybe if I suffer enough, I can win her back." By making those runs punishing, I seemed to think I was somehow "paying" for the hurt inflicted. But then I saw that, if I did not forgive myself, I would sabotage the whole thing, pull the rug right out from underneath myself, as continued punishment and evidence that the leopard could not change his spots. It was such a physical lift of weight to realize that I didn't have to run the mental and spiritual "marathons" as well. There was magnificent power in letting the "Coach" conduct "spiritual exercise" during the actual physical exercise! Again, the pavement had become the altar upon which I could meditate. Meditate on what? The *rhema* Scriptures that had begun to stand tall during my times of Bible study. The trained focus I maintained on them while I ran, erased all the other stress factors trying to command my attention, ushering in God's peace and guidance. "Thou wilt keep him in perfect peace, whose mind is stayed on thee: because he trusteth in thee" (Is. 26:3 KJV). I began to understand that to have my mind "stayed" on God's Word is the same as having it "stayed" on him (see again John 1:1–14).

To let the Word truly address me during my April training runs caused the themes of forgiveness, washing, and renewal to pulsate through my entire system in the "month of water." David experienced this regarding his sins of adultery and murder. "Oh, wash me, cleanse me from this guilt. Let me be pure again. For I admit my shameful deed—it haunts me day and night.... Sprinkle me with the cleansing blood and I shall be clean again. Wash me and I shall be whiter than snow" (Ps. 51:2–3, 7 TLB).

> Then he saved us—not because we were good enough to be saved, but because of his kindness and pity—by washing away our sins. (Titus 3:5a TLB)

> That he might sanctify and cleanse her with the washing of water by the Word. (Eph. 5:26 KJV)

After completing an especially grueling training run up the steepest mountain around while visiting with my parents, my father said, "I don't think I'd punish myself like that." Later I thought about how good it is to train hard, not out of some sick idea that my atonement efforts were somehow needed along with Christ's but with the same understanding that the apostle Paul had in writing of how discipline and subduing the body parallels mental and spiritual discipline (see 1 Cor. 9:27). No pain, no gain.

Apply the same discipline of your soul on the spiritual pavement as you do your body on the physical pavement. Your training now becomes the tale of two pavements.

"How so?"

Just as I am the only one seeing you in secret as you run on those lone stretches of road, watching to see if you pay the price in the run, so I am the one who sees you in secret behind closed doors—again, watching for the price or sacrifice of obedience.

Later, in study, I contemplated the word *even* in the following Scripture, asking myself how training to a standard on the spiritual pavement could be reflected on the physical pavement. Would he reward me in secret? The old question, "If a tree falls in the forest and no one is around, is there any sound?" can be answered yes for God.

> Beloved, I wish above all things that thou mayest prosper and be in health, *even* as thy soul prospereth. (3 John 1:2 KJV)

> Speaking to Moses right after giving him the Ten Commandments, the Father said about Israel: "Oh, that they had such a heart in them that they would fear me and always keep all my commandments, that it might be well with them and with their children forever!" (Deut. 5:29 KJV)

This "month of water" was a time of cleansing and renewal by the Word. The words of forgiveness, mercy, and grace were filtering down through my spirit and mind and into my body, where they refreshed my whole system to run anew.

The days are coming when you will see how deeply the cross is planted in the ground of your being.

May: Month of Vision

> And it shall come to pass in the last days, says God, that I will pour out my spirit on all flesh; your sons and your daughters shall prophesy, your young men shall see visions, your old men shall dream dreams. (Acts 2:17 KJV)

"Will I perish without vision?"

What vision do you now have in your running?

"It has lifted me to, again, envision or actually see myself moving from one level of performance to another and forming specific goals, both on and off the pavement. I am to lift my knees higher, to see my toes like little Pac-man creatures, reaching out to grab the pavement, and to visualize my stride in front and behind in the form of a deer."

That is your body vision. What about your mind and spirit—your heart vision?

"I'm not sure what you mean."

> *That is what the Scriptures mean when they say that God made Abraham the father of many nations. God will accept all people in every nation who trust God as Abraham did. And this promise is from God himself, who makes the dead live again and speaks of future events with as much certainty as though they were already past.... But Abraham never doubted. He believed God, for his faith and trust grew ever stronger, and he praised God for this blessing even before it happened. (Rom. 4:17, 20–22 TLB)*

Do you see Boston? Do you see the hills of temptation being run and overcome?

Without vision, I will perish! Something Robert Kennedy once said has stuck with me through the years: "Some see things that are and ask why. I see things that are not and ask why not." I like that.

I call you to have an Abraham faith.

"So, in the world where 'seeing is believing,' you are asking me to say 'believing is seeing.'"

Carry on.

> I will stand my watch and set myself on the rampart, and watch to see what he will say to me, and what I will answer when I am corrected. Then the Lord answered me and said: "Write the vision and make it plain on tablets, that he may run who reads it. For the vision is yet for an appointed time; but at the end it will speak, and it will not lie. Though it tarries, wait for it; because it will surely come, it will not tarry. (Hab. 2:1–3 KJV)

> For I will work a work in your days which you would not believe, though it were told you. (Hab. 1:5 KJV)

June: Month of Fire

"What's going to burn?"

Your flesh.

"I don't like the sound of that."

My Word will burn out the lust from your heart.

> The heart is the most deceitful thing there is,
> and desperately wicked. No one can really know
> how bad it is! (Jer. 17:9 TLB)

> For everything in the world—the cravings of
> sinful man, the lust of his eyes and the boasting
> of what he has and does—comes not from the
> Father but from the world. (1 John 2:16 NIV)

There was no room to simply say, in Flip Wilson form, that "the devil made me do it" or that God was testing me through my trials with lust. His branding iron of the Word came to sear my soul with His truth.

> Never, when you have been tempted, say, "God
> sent the temptation"; God cannot be tempted
> to do anything wrong, and he does not tempt
> anybody. Everyone who is tempted is attracted
> and seduced by his own wrong desire. Then
> the desire conceives and gives birth to sin, and
> when sin is fully grown, it too has a child, and
> the child is death. (James 1:13–15 JB)

Every word of the above was being lived out before my eyes. A woman—the one discovered by my wife while I was in the hospital and who was perceived to be her friend—had made house calls during the year leading up to my accident to report on specialized school work with our children. She would come during the early afternoon, when my children were in school and my wife was at work. In my lust for her and in my envisioned and acted-upon sexual sin, I did not see a picture of death. Nevertheless, divorce, a broken family, the loss of my home, the loss of my career, community judgment, and a host of surrounding losses all came together to form a graveyard scene.

"I need a battle plan for the mind, to confront the hurdles of lust that stand up against me in the 'mental marathon.'" How could I break through that "wall"? What would help me begin to think my way into a new way of acting and to, subsequently, act my way into a new way of thinking?

1. *Honest confession. Allow me to sharply identify in your mind every area of wrong thinking. Look at it and then say, "Yes, Father, I see it. It is or was that bad. I confess it. In the name of Jesus, forgive me and deliver me."*

   "If we say that we have no sin, we deceive ourselves, and the truth is not in us. If we confess our sins, he is faithful and just to forgive us our sins and to cleanse us from all unrighteousness. If we say that we have not sinned, we make him a liar, and his word is not in us" (1 John 1:8–10 KJV).

2. *Prepare your mind to allow me to work: mentally/ spiritually place the* name *of Jesus* (name *being a New Testament synonym for* power; see Phil. 2:9– 11) *over every thought like an umbrella, covering the mental stresses and images that sometimes loom like those giant mushroom clouds, all the while claiming:*

Casting down imaginations, and every high thing that exalteth itself against the knowledge of God, and bringing into captivity every thought to the obedience of Christ; and having in a readiness to revenge all disobedience, when your obedience is fulfilled. (2 Cor. 10:5–6 KJV; see also 2 Cor. 12:9, Gal. 2:20, Rom. 8:13, Rom. 8:37, Phil. 2:13, 4:13)

"This will be more like daily pulling weeds from a garden."

Carry on.

"I know right from wrong but still end up doing the wrong!"

I cannot understand my own behavior. I fail to carry out the things I want to do, and I find myself doing the very things I hate. When I act against my own will, that means I have a self that acknowledges that the law is good, and so the thing behaving in that way is not my self but sin living in me. The fact is, I know of nothing good living in me—living, that is, in my unspiritual self—for though the will to do what is good is in me, the performance is not, with the result that instead of doing the good things I want to do, I carry out the sinful things I do not want. When I act against my will, then, it is not my true self doing it, but sin which lives in me. In fact, this seems to be the rule, that every single time I want to do good it is something evil that comes to hand. In my inmost-self I dearly love God's Law, but I can see that my body follows a different law that battles against the law which my reason dictates. This is what makes me a prisoner of that law of sin which lives inside my body. (Rom. 7:15–23 JB)

"I don't see how the Word will help me now when my parents took me to church and I read my Bible yet I still sinned terribly. I'm far worse than what Paul saw when looking at himself! If the Word has not done it yet, I don't see it doing it now."

For if we would judge ourselves, we should not be judged. But when we are judged, we are chastened of the Lord, that we should not be condemned with the world. (1 Cor. 11:31–32 KJV; see Prov. 3:11, 22:15; Heb. 12:5–6)

The hammer of God's law (see Gal. 3:24) was driving me to his amazing grace. His Word had sharply focused the spotlight on my hypocrisy.

> There is much more I would like to say along these lines, but you don't seem to listen, so it's hard to make you understand. You have been Christians a long time now, and you ought to be teaching others, but instead you have dropped back to the place where you need someone to teach you all over again the very first principles in God's Word. You are like babies who can drink only milk, not old enough for solid food. And when a person is still living on milk it shows he isn't very far along in the Christian life, and doesn't know about the difference between right and wrong. He is still a baby-Christian! You will never be able to eat solid spiritual food and understand the deeper things of God's Word until you become better Christians and learn right from wrong by practicing doing right. (Heb. 5:11–14 TLB)

I used to receive compliments on sermons and counsel I had given about marriage and family, but I was not living what I preached. The Word, not me, was performing ministry. Again, like those Pharisees, I had the appearance of godliness but was far from it—like a tree dying from the inside due to malnourishment but still giving the appearance of good fruit. I would sometimes say to myself that I needed to wrestle St.

Paul's title away from him, the one with which he labeled himself "chief of sinners." Paul wasn't a soap-opera sinner like me; God was showing Paul the bad things hidden from his view. My sexual immorality was blatant, and I had become a "byword" (Ps. 44:14) in the community as a result (see Matt. 5:27–28; Rom. 2:16, 22; Eph. 5:3; Rom. 6:12–14, 7:15–24; 1 Cor. 6:13b, 15–20; Eph. 4:17–24).

I thought, "I need to beat my mind back into shape. Yes, but I have to run with my whole being (body, mind, spirit), not just part." In my study time, I came across this passage:

> Do you not know that in a race all the runners run, but only one gets the prize? Run in such a way as to get the prize. Everyone who competes in the games goes into strict training. They do it to get a crown that will not last; but we do it to get a crown that will last forever. Therefore I do not run like a man running aimlessly; I do not fight like a man beating the air. No, I beat my body and make it my slave so that after I have preached to others, I myself will not be disqualified for the prize. (1 Cor. 9:24–27 NIV)

I reflect my understanding to the Holy Spirit: "You are dealing with my past by taking me 'back to the future'—leading me to forget the past, live in the present, and press on into the future (see Phil. 3:13). Is it like the training runs, as in thinking not about the miles ahead or behind but where I am now? You assure me that you are in my future now and in my past now; therefore, you can take care of both."

Good understanding.

"Is it a far stretch of the imagination for me to see that you can take my mind and work *it* like a computer? Could you cancel, save, delete, and even reformat my whole mental outlook through the commands of your Word?"

Could my life be reformatted? Could he work the past and the future in conjunction with my present? In the days of the Old Testament, the priest would trim the lamps in the Holy Tabernacle when needed. The used part was carefully placed into snuff-dishes, covered completely so there was no possibility of exposure or spilling, and then secretly and permanently destroyed. Would that be God's way with me? He gave me the following understanding: *I will never expose the waste items of your life, just trim them to a better testimony.* The sign for victory about all that has happened rests in this verse:

> Therefore if any person is (engrafted) in Christ, the Messiah, he is (a new creature altogether), a new creation; the old (previous moral and spiritual condition) has passed away. Behold, the fresh and new has come! (2 Cor. 5:17 AMP)

> No, dear brothers, I am still not all I should be but I am bringing all my energies to bear on this one thing: Forgetting the past and looking

forward to what lies ahead, I strain to reach the end of the race and receive the prize for which God is calling us up to heaven because of what Christ Jesus did for us (Phil. 3:13–14 TLB)

And he that sat upon the throne said, Behold, I make all things new. (Rev. 21:5a KJV)

These last words in our discussion spoke to me; I knew I was being addressed. We might ask, "How can this be?" Let's look again, this time a bit deeper, into those two words in the original Greek New Testament texts for the word *word*: *logos*, meaning "idea," "thought," "concept," or "creative energy that generated the universe," according to Strong's 3056; and *rhema* (see Rom. 10:17), meaning that the hearer is changed, moved, or motivated and personally and directly addressed by that Word (Jesus). For example, let's say that my wife raises the window and calls to the children playing basketball on the court I built, asking them to come in and wash up for supper. After ten minutes pass, she goes to the door and calls them in, saying, "Y'all come on in now and wash up for supper." Another ten minutes pass and no children come in. Finally, I go to the door and announce with an ominous voice, "Get yourselves in here right now or else!" Immediately, children are in the house, washed up, and sitting at the table with forks in hand, ready to eat. Now, that's *rhema*. They knew they were being addressed. My daddy would sometimes finish a corrective statement to me by saying, "Do you hear me?" He was asking whether or not I was hearing with the intention to obey. He was asking it in the same sense that God does in

Mark 4:9 (KJV) where Jesus says, "He that hath ears to hear, let him hear." (See also Rev. 1:3; 1 Tim. 4:13–16; 2 Tim. 2:15; see Training Regimen #7.)

In my studies at this juncture, the following words stood up: "For it is God at work within you, helping you want to obey him, and then helping you do what he wants" (Phil. 2:13 TLB). What do I do in the meantime about this sin within me? I was coached to train throughout the rest of the month on these words about God "helping me."

[Thoughts from the run: It is time to discipline myself to set self-centeredness, both bodily and mental forms, aside in order to make room to receive the strength and stamina of Christ, the Word, living in me. The apostle Paul stated that it was no longer "I" (ego), Paul, who lives but "Christ" within him; for me this meant I needed, like King David, to start hiding "God's Word in my heart that I might not sin against him" (Ps. 119:11).]

This month's theme strikes the cord of discipline. When the apostle Paul said, "I keep under my body and bring it into subjection" (1 Cor. 9:27a KJV), he was referring to the deliberate subduing of the mental appetites and bodily passions. Again, I hear, "No pain, no gain."

> No discipline seems pleasant at the time, but painful. Later on, however, it produces a harvest of righteousness and peace for those who have been trained by it. Therefore, strengthen your

feeble arms and weak knees. Make level paths for your feet, so that the lame may not be disabled, but rather healed. (Heb. 12:11–13 NIV)

Again, I began to summarize to God what I had understood: "To 'work out (my own) salvation with fear and trembling' (Phil. 2:12) means I am accountable to you and responsible for the way I use what you have given me in which to live, including my body." In my next time of study, he "spoke" the Word back to me:

> Haven't you yet learned that your body is the home of the Holy Spirit God gave you and that he lives within you? Your own body does not belong to you. For God has bought you with a great price. So use every part of your body to give glory back to God, because he owns it. (1 Cor. 6:19–20 TLB)

> For this is the will of God, your sanctification: that you should abstain from sexual immorality; that each of you should know how to possess his own vessel in sanctification and honor, not in passion of lust. (1 Thess. 4:3–5a KJV)

I must decide before and during each and every run in life whether or not I am going to agree with my creator that my body will indeed be his temple. Such discipline prepares me for greater tests. I recall from my early years of training a decision to always "run it out" when gravel or rocks got into my shoes. Those times of suffering toughened my feet with layers of skin to the point that, in later years, I never gave it a second thought. I was coached to see that I needed to toughen my feet in the same way on the spiritual pavement in handling the rocks of temptation. Athletes suffer, placing their bodies under stress to enter the greater Olympics. If I am to "cast down imaginations of the heart" (2 Cor. 10:5), "crucify (my)self" (Gal. 2:20), and "put to death the deeds of the body" (Rom. 8:13), then I will undergo training that will produce some suffering. As you will see, a few years later, this month's theme brought down on me the heat I needed to address issues of self-will versus God's will in the matter of lusting after women, a fire-kindled discipline.

The exercise of repentance during this month required discipline and sacrifice, much like that made in the training runs. A sacrifice entails a price paid; could I pay the price, which was denial of what I want? Eric Liddell, Scotland's greatest and best-loved athlete, whose story was told in the film *Chariots of Fire*, wrote the following:

> The Christian life should be a life of growth. I believe the secret of growth is to develop the devotional life. This involves setting aside time each day for prayer and Bible study.... We should come to it in an honest spirit, be prepared to face the challenge of God's Word as it lays down a way of life, and be prepared to face any inconsistencies in our lives which make them un-Christ-like.... One word stands out

from all others as the key to knowing God, to having his peace and assurance in your heart; it is *obedience*. Take obedience with you into your time of prayer and meditation, for you will know as much of God, and only as much of God, as you are willing to put into practice.... Obedience to God's will is the secret of spiritual knowledge and insight. It is not willingness to know, but willingness to do (obey) God's will that brings enlightenment and certainty regarding spiritual growth.... Obedience is the secret of being conscious that God guides you personally.... I challenge you. Have a great aim—have a high standard—make Jesus your ideal.... Make him an ideal not merely to be admired but also to be followed. (*The Disciplines of the Christian Life*, Abingdon Press)

The following Scriptures firmly nail down Liddell's point:

- "If any of you really determines to do God's will, then you will certainly know whether my teaching is from God or is merely my own" (John 7:17 TLB).

- "He replied, 'My mother and brothers are those who hear God's word and put it into practice'" (Luke 8:21 NIV).

- "Someone may say, 'I am a Christian; I am on my way to heaven; I belong to Christ.' But if he doesn't do what Christ tells him to, he is a liar. But those who do what Christ tells them to will learn to love God more and more. That is the way to know whether or not you are a Christian. Anyone who says he is a Christian should live as Christ did" (1 John 2:4–6 TLB).

Chosen to run the Paris Olympics in 1924, Liddell shocked everyone by refusing to run the 100-meter race because it had been scheduled on a Sunday. Sacrificially, he trained for the 400-meter race, in which he would go up against two men who had just broken the world records for that event in the semifinals earlier that week. Just as Liddell stood listening to the Highlanders band play, a man eased by him and slipped a note in his hand that said, "Them that honor me I will honor" (1 Sam. 2:30). In exactly 47.6 seconds, God did exactly that: Liddell set a new world record and became a legend in his own time for the quarter-miler. (A writer for the Billy Graham publication *Decision* asked Mr. Liddell's oldest daughter to share something about her father that was highlighted in her mind. She recalled a footrace in which she had not put her best foot forward: "I remember my father saying to me, 'Now, Tricia, when you're striving for something, you strive for the best. You don't just fool around with your energies and talents. You always strive for the very best in yourself'" (February 1995 issue).

My Coach convicted me during one of the training runs at the end of this month, showing me that when Jesus said that if I really love him, I will obey him, this means I need to get to know him better by having his Word live in me, leading me into obedience. He reminds me of King David's decision: "Thy word have I hid in mine heart, that I might not sin against thee" (Ps. 119:11 KJV). So, the old saying "Getting to know you is getting to love you" applies here. This month, he told me:

> Whatever your hand finds to do, do it with your might. (Ecc. 9:10 KJV)

> Therefore, prepare your minds for action; be self-controlled; set your hope fully on the grace to be given you when Jesus Christ is revealed. As obedient children, do not conform to the evil desires you had when you lived in ignorance. But just as he who called you is holy, so be holy in all you do; for it is written: "Be holy, because I am holy." (1 Peter 1:13–16 NIV)

July: Month of Endurance

The month of June had brought an ever-deepening conviction of how wicked and deceitful my life had been, and then, with one day's run, I said, "This heat and those pounding weights beat my feet and are punching me to death."

That's what we want.

I have been crucified with Christ: and I myself no longer live, but Christ lives in me. And the real life I now have within this body is a result of my trusting in the Son of God, who loved me and gave himself for me. (Gal 2:20 TLB)

For if you live according to (the dictates of) the flesh you will surely die. But if through the power of the (Holy) Spirit you are habitually putting to death—making extinct, deadening— the (evil) deeds prompted by the body, you shall (really and genuinely) live forever. (Rom. 8:13 AMP)

And he said to them all, "If anyone desires to come after Me, let him deny himself, and take up his cross daily, and follow Me. For whoever desires to save his life will lose it, but whoever loses his life for My sake will save it." (Luke 9:23–24 New King James Version, or NKJV)

"I'm just placing one foot in front of the other; I have no inspiration and see no hope in these shackled twenty-eight-mile runs."

Hope will come.

But he that endureth to the end shall be saved. (Matt. 10:22b KJV)

> For you have need of endurance, so that after
> you have done the will of God, you may receive
> the promise. (Heb. 10:36 KJV)

The "month of endurance" delivered me into a maze of continued heat, fatigue, boredom, and discontent. It captured all the negatives from the previous months of training and rolled them into one ball of fire that weighed down on my very soul. As I ran, I remembered the scenes filled with tears and anger as I felt the guilt of what I had done against God and family; I fretted over whether or not the strength to grow and change would come. The month of fire merged the theme of discipline into the theme of endurance. It was the seventh and final month that my Coach was leading me to run the distance of twenty-eight miles up the steepest bike trail in North America with the weights still on.

> Endure hardship as discipline. (Heb. 12:7 NIV)

Each mile had its own personality or life in relation to the practice of praise. I'm learning to respect what each mile could do. I was led to think not about the miles still ahead but to just give thanks (gritted teeth, tearful) for the one I was on at the time, to give thanks for the breath and heartbeat then and there.

> Take therefore no thought for the morrow: for
> the morrow shall take thought for the things of
> itself. Sufficient unto the day is the evil thereof.
> (Matt. 6:34 KJV)

I recalled words from my high school football, wrestling, and track coaches, who said, "Quitters never win, and winners never quit." I longed for the "month of hope." From the study of the Scriptures on hope, I remembered Galatians 6:9 (TLB): "And let us not get tired of doing what is right, for after a while we will reap a harvest of blessing if we don't get discouraged and give up."

> So brace up your minds; be sober—circumspect (morally alert); set your hope wholly and unchangeably on the grace (divine favor) that is coming to you when Jesus Christ, the Messiah, is revealed. (1 Peter 1:13 AMP)

(More thoughts as we run: Should God relinquish His control of my life for one heartbeat or one breath, I would be gone. When I try to live today *and* tomorrow or today *and* yesterday at the same time, I burn out fast—so with the miles *and* the weights.)

My sins shackle life's runs, weighing down the present through memories from the past—"For I acknowledge my transgressions: and my sin is ever before me" (Ps. 51:3)—and pressing down from an uncertain future. My heavenly Father is pleased when I raise up that "nevertheless of faith" and say to memories of the past, "I am forgiven and being redeemed"; to the temptations of the present, "I am making the 'sacrifice of obedience' because God's will and way is always best"; and to the *what if*'s of the future, "God is in my future, sending out his Word, now; therefore, he has the controls in his hands concerning matters of home, family, career, and so on." His Word sparks my faith to endure—to keep on keeping on. "So then faith cometh by hearing and hearing by the word of God" (Rom. 10:17 KJV).

That day, the initial miles of my longest training run were the most difficult. My mind tried to race over the miles yet to come and wonder how they would be exercised. The excruciating, shackled, twenty-eight-mile run was the crowning symbol of endurance for the marathons of the body, mind, and spirit. As I ran up a dirt road on the last steep hill through the woods, the enemy, lurking somewhere in those woods, whispered, "You think these weights and heat are heavy? Just wait 'til you feel the force of what I have left to throw on you. And look at the weight you have brought down on yourself."

> But he that endureth to the end shall be saved.
> (Matt. 10:22 KJV)

> The grass withereth, and the flower thereof
> falleth away: But the word of the Lord endureth
> for ever. (1 Peter 1:25 KJV)

I rehearsed the words that the Holy Spirit brought to mind and prayed prayers for forgiveness to clear the way for other prayers to be heard. Deep into the run that day, when the weight on my legs and mind felt heaviest, the Word lifted my burden. And coming around the last curve, I lifted my eyes at just the right moment to see the mailbox only a quarter of a mile down the road. I was home.

After a shower and breakfast, I came across this passage in my study:

> Moreover—let us also be full of joy now! Let us exult and triumph in our troubles and rejoice in our sufferings, knowing that pressure and affliction and hardship produce patient and unswerving endurance. And endurance (fortitude) develops maturity of character—that is, approved faith and tried integrity. And character (of this sort) produces (the habit of) joyful and confident hope of eternal salvation. Such hope never disappoints or deludes or shames us. (Rom. 5:3–5a AMP)

And to hold on to God's Word with faith is the same as holding on to him.

> But those who wait for the Lord—who expect, look for and hope in Him—shall change and renew their strength and power; they shall lift their wings and mount up (close to God) as eagles (mount up to the sun); they shall run and not be weary; they shall walk and not faint or become tired. (Is. 40:31 AMP; see also Heb. 12:1–4)

(From August to October, my Coach directed me to run on a course with more level ground for twenty-mile training runs leading up to the November 1991 Marine Corps Marathon in Washington, D. C., a qualifying run for Boston.)

August: Month of Hope

Remove the weights.

"I'm almost afraid to."

Take them off and slowly step out into your warm–up run.

"My feet certainly are lighter; I feel like I can almost pop myself in the chest with my knees."

What do you discern, at this point, about the spiritual pavement?

"When I confess my sins, receive forgiveness and then turn from my sins, the weights are lifted in the spiritual run."

Move out into your sprint when ready.

A half mile later, I said, "Wow! I feel like I have been given wings!"

> They shall mount up with wings like eagles. (Is. 40:31).

"I'm having to pinch myself; I feel like we're floating through the air! Will this last?"

They shall run and not grow weary. (Is. 40:31).

Begin to sprint all the hills.

"The crown of each hill still finds me breathless, but it is somehow different. I sense something in the wind. From where will the power come to renew my strength?"

Where do you think?

A few miles later, I reply, "The Word."

And who is the Word?

"Jesus."

Recall John, chapter one, and place the name Jesus for each instance of "Word." Ask yourself why the apostle Paul described him as the "express image of God" in his letter to the Colossians. Tell me what you have come to understand about the Word as you run.

Later in the run, I understood: "The more the Word lives in me and the more I live in the Word, that's the same as Jesus living in me. He becomes '(God's) strength made perfect in (my) weakness' (2 Cor. 12:9 KJV) so that 'I can do all things through Christ who strengthens me' (Phil. 4:13 KJV) and become 'more than a conqueror through Christ who loved (me)'" (Rom. 8:37). He gave himself up for me.

Answer my question again and state it more deeply.

A long stillness ensued as I ran. "When the apostle Paul said, 'It is no longer I, Paul, who live but Jesus within me' (Gal. 2:20), that's my deepest understanding, now, of what it means to be 'born again.' It means that Jesus becomes embryonic and cradled in the crucible—the womb—of my heart! Again, like David, I can say, "Thy word have I hid in mine heart, that I might not sin against thee" (Ps. 119:11 KJV).

Sounds like hope has come. Just like sin can be "conceived" in you by your entertainment of it in your mind, so can my Word be born/conceived in you.

"Yes, sir! But, this is just a step; the race has not been run, yet."

And so it is with your physical, mental and spiritual run; you need to exercise daily and 'hide (my) Word in (your) heart.

"Like the psalmist, I can say to you, "I hope in thy word (Ps. 119:114). "Dear Holy Spirit, my Coach, you have truly become the wind beneath my wings so I can 'mount up with wings like eagles'!"

September: Month of Memories

We continue running up that steepest bike trail in North America for one of my weekly training runs. Ten miles into the run, the upward trek above the small mountain town of Vesuvius, VA, begins. Almost halfway up the mountain, I see where the mailbox used to be—you guessed it, the one from the "Mailbox Run." The fact that it's not there is becoming symbolic to me—an agonizing reminder of the home I crushed with my sin of adultery.

Courtesy John Scott & Chad Conner

Today, in the run up the mountain, I can peer over into the valley and faintly see the outline of the house. A memory painfully stalks. One evening during the first year there with my three boys, I found myself sinking deeper into depression and anger. I had found some letters written by my wife, to whom I was still holding on like a clinging vine. The letters were to two men, and she was telling of her love for them. I was convinced that she had left them there just for me to find. That combined with the pressures of performing a dual-parish ministry with a failing memory caused me to lose control. Suddenly, when something went wrong at the supper table, I flew into a rage, shouting, pounding and turning things over—like someone who needed to be locked up for good.

The next thing I heard was Brooke jumping up from the table, and I caught a glimpse of his fist going through his bedroom door. Then, as the door slammed, I was sure I could feel the house shake. Then there was silence followed by the deepest sobs I have ever heard—the kind that sound as though they will never end. A minute later I composed myself, went in, hugged him, and said it would be all right. His crying began to subside. This has remained my most painful memory of the wounds I have inflicted upon my family. The other three children have carried their "broken-family" wounds over the years, silently borne. Their view, then, of two different houses—the good parts of our family history erased, separate school districts, unfamiliar associations, and so on— would one day resolve into a family portrait revisited. It will be an honor to tell you about it further into this recounting of his works!

Courtesy John Scott & Chad Conner

I reached the crest of the mountain and crossed onto the Blue
Ridge Parkway, looking over into the next valley. Now, it
was time for the trip back down, which is harder on me due
to the shock it causes in my system. The strategy of putting
my heels down first and rolling forward to my toes did not
prove effective; the mountain was too steep. Each step held
penetrating pain to my whole system. On the way down,
another memory stirred, this one still generating anger and
adding more "weight" to my feet. My former wife's boss, our
landlord, had called, saying that he wanted to raise the rent
from $350 to $1,500. This was his way of getting my three
sons and me to move out. I hopelessly looked for another
house while he badgered me with calls. Since we were having
difficulty making ends meet, this unwelcome news caused us
stressful moments at the time, many of which were almost

unbearable. I finally wrote the landlord a letter to say that I knew about his adultery. The calls stopped.

The memories kept playing like a movie as I ran. After much reflection and prayer, I had decided that the best course of action was to buy ten acres of land and a doublewide mobile home. After this purchase, much to my chagrin, I discovered that the power right-of-way would not be granted for fourteen months. Consequently, the Health Department would not allow my three boys to live with me since I was "camping out" in the mobile home, so they moved in with their mother. I firmly believe that my former wife demonstrated her love for me by encouraging the three boys to live with me as my daughter lived with her following the separation. She must have known that I would have a tremendous need to be with them during those years following the accident. And I also had a need to be needed by them. It was a healing venture for me to cook their meals, see them off to and back from the school bus, and take care of household tasks. I'll always remember the times that they would be ready to get up from the supper table by the time I was sitting down to eat. That was poor timing on my part in that I didn't have the meal completely ready; nevertheless, I enjoyed it when they would say, "That was good, Daddy." We made regular trips to nearby creeks for fishing; they would rather fish and hunt than eat. I deeply missed them those fourteen months while I was "camping" in the trailer.

The only amenities were a kerosene heater, a Coleman lantern, and water carried in from a nearby spring. One of my most vivid memories is sleeping under many blankets only to lift the upper cover and see my breath create fog as on a cold, dew-stilled morning in the outdoors.

A realtor in a nearby town allowed me to stop by every now and then to sponge bathe in the restroom sink. I was convinced that the reason my neighbors would not permit power right-of-way for me is that they were saying to themselves, *Let this hypocrite suffer a while and get what he deserves.*

More memories lingered. Soon after returning home from the hospital, I met with my children and their mother. All were gathered in the living room. My purpose was to make an honest confession and to ask for their forgiveness, which I desired partly because I desperately needed it from them. To ask that they forget would be to inflict further pain on them. They could heal in relationship with me only as they saw the transformation that God was making in me. Moreover, my doctoral studies had led me to a research in modern psychology, which firmly underscores what the Scriptures have said all along—namely that the reason children of alcoholics become alcoholics, children of abusers become abusers, and children of divorced parents become divorced is that they can't help but consciously and/or subconsciously judge their parents while riding the wave of severe hurt and emotional pain caused by tragic circumstances. Could this repetitive tendency manifest as a painful reflection on God's intense desire that forgiveness be exercised in our fallen condition of sin?

In my studying, the Word reinforced the following verses:

Judge not, that ye be not judged. For with what judgment you judge, you will be judged; and with the measure you use, it will be measured back to you. (Matt. 7:1–2 KJV)

The Lord is long-suffering and slow to anger, and abundant in mercy and loving-kindness, forgiving iniquity and transgression; but He will by no means clear the guilty, visiting the iniquity of the fathers upon the children, upon the third and fourth generation. (Num. 14:18 AMP)

The Word speaks the truth in saying that the "sins of the fathers" are passed on from generation to generation (Num. 14:18). Scientific research in deoxyribonucleic acid (DNA) has discovered that the footprint of the father remains in the genetic code until the third and sometimes the fourth subsequent generation (see above Scripture reference). This law of "being judged" as a result of our "judging" is as accountable and predictable as the law of gravity.

Modern-day psychological inquiry has established the fact that, as the Bible outlines, only forgiveness can break that generational curse. Of interest is the development of a new therapy that addresses this pattern; it is called "reconciliation therapy" and could be seen as a secular way of talking about forgiveness. I do not want my children to experience this "being judged"; my perennial prayer is that they take my request to heart and find a way to forgive me, for both my good and for theirs! Then, as I came back to the more conscious aspect of my run, I asked myself, *"What would hold the DNA for me to have a mind change, a heart change?"*

During the next training run, my memory flashed back to our "forgiveness discussion." I had felt led to share with them the story of Corrie Ten Boom as an example of how forgiveness can be given in harsh or extremely difficult circumstances. As you may know, Corrie Ten Boom was a prisoner of war in a Nazi concentration camp because she had aided Jewish personnel in their efforts to escape and hide. There she watched a German SS guard take her sister and others, whom she had grown to love, to the gas chamber. Had the war not ended at the precise point that it did, Corrie would have been next.

After the war, Corrie wrote about her experiences in books and toured Germany on speaking engagements. Following one particular tour, after speaking superbly on the subject of forgiveness (some of her books on the subject were best-sellers), she was greeting people and signing copies of her books when, suddenly, her eyes drifted up the aisle and locked onto the gaze of the German SS guard. He was marching down the aisle with his hand extended, saying, "Good evening, Fraulein. It's so good to see you again." Immediately, she dropped her head down and whispered, "Dear Father, I cannot forgive this man." And she had just gotten through delivering a speech on forgiveness that moved many people. While her head was still down, she turned her thoughts into this prayer: "Dear Jesus, you're going to have to give me your forgiveness to give to this man." As soon as this prayer was formed, she was able to lift her eyes to those of the SS guard, stretch out her hand to take his, and speak the words of forgiveness. In time, her emotions caught up with what her spirituality had done in making a decision, taking that step of faith, to forgive this man. A new book on forgiveness, even better than the others she had written on it, emerged from this experience.

My children spoke words of forgiveness, and, as the years have come and gone, I believe they have forgiven me. The wounds, at this writing, are still there, but they have healed enough that they believe they are not "parent-poor" but "parent-rich." My Coach also led me to forgive my former wife for divorcing me. I've come to see that it happened not for her need but for mine.

The Healing: My Marriage

In the next training run, I found that memories had merged into God's redeeming will. While on top of a mountain following the accident and its long gray line of losses—somehow I had identified the mountain as being the place where God would speak—I sat on a high ridge and asked the Holy Spirit to pray for me. I was resting on the promise that he prays for us when we do not know what to pray (see Rom. 8:26–27). After praying in the Spirit for over an hour, I knew that the Holy Spirit had covered all that was needed. My mind was at peace—nothing pulling or pushing through it. Then came four promises at about three-minute intervals: 1) "I am with you," 2) "I will continue to be with you," 3) "I will heal you," and 4) "I will heal your marriage." During those two years between the separation and the divorce, I held onto that last promise, thinking it meant that God was going to heal my first marriage. I was to discover that the promise meant that he was going to heal *marriage* for me.

After the accident and divorce, my new wife, Connie, was led by God's hand to comfort, counsel, and court me during those fourteen months that I was separated from my three sons due to my living conditions. In fact, during the last month, I started staying at her house. Due to these factors and unrest in the parish, my call to ministry was removed. This, I later discovered, would also place my call as an Army chaplain in jeopardy because it is required that I have a theological endorsing agency to remain under call. Nevertheless, I would come to see that sometimes God's grace comes through his law. During those "dark night of the soul" times, there was one time she just took my head in her lap and let me cry. We still court each other after a quarter of a century into the new "covenant."

So, as I ran that day, I rehearsed some of the truths formed through God's redeeming will in marriage. We can document those challenges to our primary pledge to one another as stepping stones of God's redeeming will. He caused them to help us grow closer and stronger in our bond than we would have if none of the drama had ever happened in the first place. We understand the psychological truth that indifference, not anger or hatred, is the opposite of love; however, we have also come to see the truth in the Word:

If you are angry, don't sin by nursing your grudge. Don't let the sun go down with you still angry—get over it quickly; for when you are angry you give a mighty foothold to the devil. (Eph. 4:26–27 TLB)

In your anger do not sin; when you are on your beds, search your hearts and be silent. (Ps. 4:4 NIV)

And, again, God's agape love is a decision, not a feeling. In the movie *Fiddler on the Roof*, one of the main characters, Reb Tevye, looks at his wife and asks, "After all these years, you reckon we love each other?" They look at each other and nod, and one of them says, "Well, after all we've been through together, we must." There was also a character called the "Match-Maker," and the people would gather in the streets and sing, "Match-Maker, Match-Maker, make me a match." I have prayed for God to be the matchmaker for my children's marriages. He knows their minds, hearts, personalities, and futures perfectly, as well as those of their mates-to-be. Therefore, he is the best one to place them together as marriage partners. Another good and encouraging chapter could be written on how God has been answering that prayer! How many fathers these days have a daughter whose boyfriend comes and asks for her hand in marriage and then gets to watch that bond grow stronger as the years go by? When they were kids, I sometimes reminded our children to pray for their mates-to-be. By doing this, they came to recognize those mates in their spirits before their minds and bodies got the message. And, yes, two of the children have already found out that true love is a decision, and they have been able to override certain feelings so they can honor that decision.

Countless times during the day, my wife and I will realize that we are thinking of or about to say the same thing, so one of us will say, "There we are, two peas in a pod." There is a strong by-product of God's redeeming will in our marriage. I call it "pure" knowledge, as opposed to "carnal" knowledge. My wife and I sometimes talk of the intimacy of "being known" and of being loved and accepted within the boundaries of that knowledge. "I will heal your marriage"—he has most assuredly kept his Word! And the relationship with my former wife has been healed to the extent that I know she loves me and she knows I love her. My children know that I will always love their mother, and my wife of God's "redeeming will" says she loves me more because of it. The day my first wife came back, following the separation, to move her things out of the house, I hugged her good-bye and said that, one day, we would know how to love each other in the kingdom. As this book was being made ready for publication, she agreed to proof it for accuracy and truthfulness. Her main comment was, "It's a very healing book." Now, all of that is God's doing!

Marriage and His Redeeming Will

At this point, my steeped study of the Scriptures about marriage led to the following understandings. After the door to marriage was closed, God opened another. This was with the understanding that divorce and remarriage are not

God's perfect will. God says he "hates divorce" and that remarriage following divorce is adultery, except in the case of unfaithfulness (see Mal. 2:16; Matt. 5:32). Marriage is so central and crucial to God's will that the apostle Paul compares it to the relationship between Christ and the church (see Eph. 5:31–32). However, remarriage following divorce *can* be his redeeming will (see Training Regimen # 5).

For me to be true to the truth of God's Word, I need to add two important caveats to the above commentary: 1) Divorce followed by remarriage is not the "unforgivable sin"; 2) yet I would never counsel someone to divorce and remarry, nor would I say, "There are more fish in the sea." I agree with the old adage, "Two wrongs don't make a right," and I would have to tell a couple who insisted on divorcing anyway that there is a price to pay when we step out of God's perfect will into his redeeming will. True, God's will is God's will, and his redeeming will is not a second-class will compared to his perfect will. But the question is, What did Adam and Eve miss out on by not remaining in God's perfect will in the garden of Eden? And look at what the people of Israel had to go through by rejecting God's perfect will. David's sin was forgiven, yet he still paid a price. If my former marriage and my current wife's first marriage had been healed and grown from there, God alone knows what might have happened. If the stories of Ishmael and Isaac and of Jacob and Esau had gone differently in terms of staying in line with God's best plan, would the generational division of nations that we have today between Jewish and Arabian lands still exist?

So what are some examples of the price paid by those who divorce and then remarry? If my children, for example, ever faced a possible divorce and said something like, "Well, Daddy, you and Connie have done all right," I would tell them that any success that they see in our marriage is not God's sanctioning of our sin of divorce and remarriage but his mercy and grace on our repentant minds and hearts. Then I would share some of the following general consequences experienced by those who divorce and remarry in general: we break a sacred vow made not only to each other but to God, and we get a reproach to our names. Guilt, being a function of our human spirit and not of the mind, cannot be relieved by reading books to justify divorce and remarriage, and we lower marriage standards for our children rather than letting our marriages be examples of Christ's love for the church (see Eph. 5:21–33). The divorce rate for second marriages is higher than that for first marriages because we carry over old behavior patterns into the new marriage without resolving them, thus compounding the problems in the marital communication process. Rivalry and rejection often arise in "Brady Bunch" families, insecurity among the children grows as they question whether step-parents really care about or love them, and the haunting question remains: "They did it before. Will they divorce again?" (You will profit by searching the following Scriptures: Malachi 2:14–16; Matthew 5:31–32, 19:3–12; 1 Corinthians 7.)

My new marriage bond is meaningfully symbolized when my wife paces me with her bicycle during my twenty-mile training runs. She is a great spirit! I see her as God's provision of a Proverbs 31 woman. She addresses me spirit to spirit as well as mind to mind and body to body; therefore, I "sing in the gates" (Prov. 31:28, 31). Her spirit is so close to the Father that all good things for the household flow from *that* bond. My former wife was also such a gift from God's hand, but I trampled that gift to death with my sin of adultery and workaholism. I have come to understand God's provision for fulfilled love in its microcosmic, as opposed to macrocosmic, form. The former "universe" is much more expansive, intriguing, and exploratory. One woman is God's creative, "universal" love connection.

But how much, you say, can one man really *know* one woman? Not much, compared to the lifelong exploration allowed for when the couple is committed to Jesus' being the only legitimate third party. With Jesus as the center, there is a partner of unfolding adventure to explore! I do not feel "limited" by one partner; rather, I feel privileged that she will share so much of herself with me. It's the difference between the naked eye and an electron microscope. One looks at "lovers" with naked eyes. In a marriage bond sealed by Jesus, we see each other spiritually and deeply, in ways no one else ever will. And what makes this happen? I see—come to know—Connie as she reflects God's Word living in her; she loves God's Word and, thereby, loves him. Herein lies the adventure of discovering *whose* we are and are becoming. I daily and joyfully thank God for his redeeming will in marriage.

As I turned to God for his comforting forgiveness, he used his redeeming will much like the man who, in a story, owned a beautiful diamond ring. My daddy gave me his diamond ring years ago; it isn't a very costly ring, but it's valuable to me because it belonged to him much of his life. But this other man's ring would have brought a lot on the market. Somehow the diamond suffered a deep scratch. The owner took the diamond to one dealer after another, but no one could remove the flaw. Finally, he came across an old master in the gem trade who took the ring back into his study for a good while, where he proceeded to paint a rose at the top of the scratch. The scratch became the stem of the rose, forming a most beautiful design in the diamond. In a similar manner, God began showing me how he can take the scratches in my life and redeem them into the stem of the rose.

I was on the last two miles of the day's run. My head lifted up in expectation of soon seeing the mailbox, the new one formed by his redeeming will in marriage and family. I could see it! My arms went up in joyful thanks for what he had done through his healing and redeeming Word—as it became "active and alive" (Heb. 4:12), "sent out" (Is. 55:10–11), and "watched over and performed" (Jer. 1:12).

September, like August, sustains my hope. Memories of past sins and tragedies begin to be healed and replaced by memories that joyfully linger. For example, "I thank God in every remembrance of my wife—the one sealed by his redeeming will and cradled in the palm of his hand." The Word says to "forget not all his benefits" (Ps. 103:2). And when my memory fails, signaling the time to offer up a "sacrifice of praise," he sends out the following Scripture:

[T]he Holy Spirit, Whom the Father will send in My name … He will cause you to recall—will remind you of, bring to your remembrance—everything I have told you. (John 14:26b AMP)

Remembering the magnitude of his grace showered upon me amplifies and motivates my will to line up with his will. Memories of past sins point my mind to that grace and the great gap he formed between what I deserved and where he placed me. And memories of failed attempts to qualify for Boston faded into dreams of things to come.

October: Month of Praise

"These days, as I look deep into the woods during this fall month of training, I clearly see that only you can bring something beautiful out of a dying situation."

As you 'deaden the deeds of the flesh' (Rom. 8:13), *'crucify the self'* (Gal. 2:20), *and 'cast down the imaginations of the heart'* (2 Cor. 10:5), *I can bring something beautiful out of you, as well.*

"Back in February, during the 'winter of my discontent,' you were right in telling me that I would see the day to offer joyful thanks over that for which I used to give 'gritted-teeth' or 'tearful' thanks. I'm looking at those days now."

What do you see?

"I see that giving you thanks when it makes no sense to or when I don't feel like it causes me to somehow trust you more; thereby, placing all things in your hands—giving you room to work them toward good and to give me peace of mind and heart in the meantime."

Look deeper into the pavement and tell me what you have learned from these months of training in relation to the practice of praise.

After several training runs, I recorded more thoughts: "From the 'month of fire,' it's clear to me that you don't want so much the obedience of sacrifice but the sacrifice of obedience. I recall your telling the people of Israel that you desire their obedience more than you do their sacrifices. From the months of endurance and hope, I see that you are not looking so much for the obedience of faith as you are the faith of obedience. All the months, collectively, tell me that you look not to the obedience of wisdom but the wisdom of obedience. And you are showing me during this month of praise that you look beyond the obedience of praise to the praise of obedience. From September, you tell me that I am to show you the love of obedience as I 'forget not all thy benefits' and hear you say, 'If you love me, you will obey me.' I'm making a sign that I will see every day from another *rhema* word, Psalm 91:14–16. It begins, "Because he has set his love upon me." I'm rewording it to read "Set my obedience upon you." Circling the letters *d*, *i*, and *e* in the word *obedience* reminds me that I need to "die" to self as a way of setting my love on him."

Carry on.

This was an expectant and joyful time of running. Each training run held the adventure of seeing how fast I could run. Psalm 103, each verse done for me, stood, for this runner, as a diadem of praise, merging all the themes for this "year of training." All of nature, during this month, joined in with praise as only God can bring forth beauty out of death. Sometimes during the training run, I would reach that point where my mind became "spacey," not knowing what to pray, so I would praise "in the spirit" by saying, "Dear Father, let my very breath praise you; let my thoughts praise you." My thoughts became like "prayer bullets," triggered by faith as I said, "Thank you, Father," with the understanding that the Father knows all that is needed for life's runs; "Thank you, Jesus," with the understanding that the Son has purchased all that is needed for these runs as he gave his last breath on the cross for me; and "Thank you, Holy Spirit," with the understanding that he is the one who delivers the timely Word needed in the marathon.

> And pray in the spirit on all occasions with all kinds of prayers and requests. (Eph. 6:18 AMP)

> Let the words of my mouth, and the meditation of my heart, be acceptable in thy sight, O Lord, my strength, and my redeemer. (Ps. 19:14 KJV)

My Coach was teaching me to make the "sacrifice of praise" on all levels of life by giving gritted-teeth thanks and tearful thanks. Now it was time to give *joyful* thanks as a lively hope and faith pronouncement of victory yet to come. A fellow runner suggested that I try the Army Ten-Miler, also in Washington. I had some doubts about doing that. Even the name, Washington, struck anxious cords in my heart as I saw all this time spent training centered on that one crucial Marine Corps Marathon trial in Washington. I had doubts despite the fact that the tempo training was going well and bringing me to surprising levels of performance. I began trying to recall shorter runs from the past and how they went. The only outstanding ones I could remember were the 440-yard run I had done in high school, with a time of fifty-seven seconds, and the mile run, which I completed in five minutes and eleven seconds. But that was so long ago and was done when I had no injuries. As I looked forward to the October 1991 ten-mile run, followed by the November 1991 Marine Corps Marathon, I was coached to rehearse what I'd been learning and experiencing since the earlier "mailbox run." I was seeing very tangible results in the training runs with this consistent approach: 1) keep the stride ("waiting on God" with deer-like form in my legs, with mind and heart holding onto his promise to renew my strength, help me mount up with wings, and let me run and not grow weary); 2) keep the pace (to continually see it pick up as I keep that stride and to understand this to be Jesus, himself, being my strength in the run); 3) keep the faith (repeatedly *decide*—over my feelings—to make sacrifice in the run with toes reaching out far to grab the pavement, knees high, and nose breathing in for more balance and peace in the run); and 4) run in his grace—use the renewed strength to reach for more. When the time came to get in formation for the ten-mile run, I was at peace and expectant at the same time. The gun fired. When it was all said and done, I had come in at 1,704 out of about 11,000 runners, a sign that training was, indeed, going well.

November: Month of Peace

I began settling into a most balanced and confident time of running. This was the month of the trial run for Boston. As Tevye says, "Life is a little like walking a tightrope, or like being a fiddler on the roof." My success depended on whether I maintained a proper balance in body, mind, and spirit. The Hebrew word for *peace* (*Shalom*) is best translated *balance*.

The Holy Spirit coached me: *Sing the Word in your mind as you run to the point of "running out."* I then set Psalm 121 and Psalm 23 to the tune of "Chariots of Fire." Also, a melody stayed with me for Isaiah 40:31, as did a song featuring the key names for Jesus. Singing the Word in my mind renewed my mind. It activated that hierarchy of spirit over mind over body and provided a steady, even cadence for running, the "balance" that I needed. Thereby, music became a vehicle to empower motor memory for my left brain. Singing the Word is the same as singing Jesus, the name above all names. Reading, meditating, memorizing, and singing the Word places it deeper inside me, moving from head to heart. The Word was becoming part of my body as well. Every step was, in fact, a step that was standing on his Word, for me, in a most literal way!

Those times during the November training when I am mentally and physically out of breath, struggling for stamina and endurance, my Coach says to run with the "nevertheless of faith." This brings forth the hierarchy or paradigm of God's Word, activating and equipping my spirit when mind and body are shaking hands in agreement to quit. Isn't it interesting that Jesus, when on this earth and with many people asking him to heal and help them, would say to them, "Be it done unto you according to your faith" (see Matt. 9:29). So, I begin to see a proportional relationship between my trust level and God's activity in my life. When the Scripture tells us that the only way we can be pleasing to God is through our faith (see Heb. 11:6), it means faith in the *person* of God the Father, God the Son, and God the Holy Spirit.

My longest physical training course, as earlier noted, has forty-six medium-size hills and twenty-six large hills. As much as I have coached people through the years about entering a *wholistic* running program, I still find myself often engaging my Coach in debate concerning his instructions to sprint the hills as I approach many of them. However, dear reader, each and every time I ignite that "nevertheless of faith" (the Word-faith connection), I discover tremendous renewal of my strength, stamina, endurance, and wind as I approach the crown of those hills, and my Coach is pleased. Do you remember the scene in *Chariots of Fire* where Eric Liddell talks of what it is like to put all he has into the run to the point that he feels God's pleasure? Liddell's head would then tilt back as he ran in God's grace.

The November theme of peace struck home. I began to become expectant, pregnant with the Word. To what would this give birth, and would that day come when I see corresponding great victory in facing the hills of temptation on the "spiritual pavement"? I recall the journey, the years of training, and the long-awaited goal. It is then that the run feels good. It gives me pleasure as I know that every step is moving toward him. In those final training runs in November, as I plug in my faith to his Word, he renewed not only my mind (Rom. 12:2) but also my physical strength to run. My confidence level rose. I disciplined and trained my mind (2 Cor. 10:5)—I was able to "cast down, deaden, and crucify" thoughts that were not in keeping with what he wants, and he rewarded me in the training run. During my long training runs, I was, therefore, enabled to "cast down" thoughts tempting me to slow down, quit, give in to the hills. In other words, my body parts and overall stamina began to celebrate and applaud the growing levels of performance achieved on the "mental pavement." The physical and mental pavements transferred the training to each other. Had he felt pleasure when seeing me make a faith-decision and push away lustful thoughts or actions? He rewarded my faith (see Heb. 11:6). My faith and hope became, once again, expectant.

As I ran, my Coach showed me when to "shift gears"—that is, when to increase my overall running tempo by keeping the *stride*, set by the Father's Word, while picking up the *pace*, the Son's "strength made perfect in my weakness." He also showed me when to step up both stride and pace by taking the "step of *faith*," ignited by my Coach through the Word, thereby overruling the cries of my body and mind to slow down. When, in the run, I placed my thoughts on what his Word was saying to me, that focus or concentration enabled me to put forth more effort and energy into the training run itself. To my continual surprise, my stride lengthened and my pace grew faster. I felt his Word filter down through my spirit into my mind and then pulsate through my body. As I ran in this formation of the Word, a quick look at my shadow told me that Jesus was with me and closer than my shadow. The Word (stride) and Jesus (pace) are the same. The Word is "alive." This three-fold advance—stride, pace, faith—resolves into a continual discovery: the balance of running in his Grace.

Let's summarize this running paradigm once more. I am being repetitious because my Coach was repetitious with me about it. In fact, all good training is repetitious. He is convincing me over these years to run with faith-vision, not sight-vision. That is, he tells me not to give in to the temptation to look down at my stride and pace to check them out but to see my stride and pace with the eyes of faith in my mind and spirit. So I remind myself of the coaching from the "month of vision" concerning my "deer-like" stride. And more important, I am to see that stride as standing on the Father's Word to "renew strength," "mount up with wings," "run and not grow weary" (Is. 40:31). I found without fail that my overall speed increased when I ran with this outlook. I know because I used to automatically look down to see how I was doing. For me, that downward look broke training. It is much more rewarding to "lift up mine eyes unto the hills."

If you remain in me and my words remain in you, ask whatever you wish, and it will be given you. (John 15:7 NIV)

Now faith is the assurance (the confirmation, the title-deed) of things (we) hope for, being the proof of things (we) do not see and the conviction of their reality—faith perceiving as real fact what is not revealed to the senses. (Heb. 11:1 AMP)

One discovery I made is that singing the Word in my mind not only practiced being in the presence of Jesus, keeping the pace for me, it also greatly assisted in keeping a steady and even tempo to that pace. My confidence to run was increasing as I chose to "forget not all his benefits"—that is, remembering as I trained all the mental, emotional, financial, interpersonal, and spiritual victories foretold and fulfilled by his Word. I set one of Connie's favorite psalms to the tune for "Born Free."

Bless the Lord, O my soul: and all that is within me, bless his holy name. Bless the Lord, O my soul, and forget not all his benefits: Who forgiveth all thine iniquities; who healeth all thy diseases; Who redeemeth thy life from destruction; who crowneth thee with loving kindness and tender mercies; Who satisfieth thy mouth with good things; so that thy youth is renewed like the eagle's. (Ps. 103:1–5 KJV)

The Word is alive (Heb. 4:12); life creates life. Jesus, the power that brought creation into being (Col. 1:15, 2:9; John 1:10; Heb. 1:1–4)—the Word made flesh (John 1:14)—is with us now in the Holy Scriptures. And our Head Coach, God's Holy Spirit, guides these words into the hierarchy of our existence (spirit, mind, body). They bring life and energy into our step. Train well on the Word.

> Bodily exercise is all right, but spiritual exercise is much more important and is a tonic for all you do. So exercise yourself spiritually and practice being a better Christian, because that will help you not only now in this life, but in the next life too. (1 Tim. 4:8 TLB)

The November 1991 Marine Corps Marathon in Washington, DC, had arrived. As I took my place in the formation of about forty thousand runners, I asked myself if the training would come alive on this pavement as well. The gun fired, and we were off. The large crowds did not capture my direct attention; instead, I began holding firmly to Isaiah 40:31, each and every word of it! There were no hills along the course; it was all on level ground and took us around all of the major monuments in Washington. That's why it is also called the Marathon of the Monuments. At about the halfway point, I had passed most of the immediate group that had formed ahead of me in the beginning. I saw a clock and determined that I was well under the time needed, so, as a faith-decision, I lengthened my stride and felt my pace lift to another level. Because I had made the "sacrifice of obedience" in the training I had undergone, he rewarded me. It is a most effective "condition-response" for me to keep on keeping on. I feel impressed at what I feel in the run; I feel not fear but pride—not in the sense of "pride before a fall," but proud of what God was performing in me. I don't add up the miles; I just let my feet glide over the pavement, and it almost seems like they don't even touch it. I thought, "Strength renewed, mount up with wings, run and not grow weary; this is really running in his grace!" Just as that thought formed, there it was, just a stone's throw away—the finish line. What did the timer say? As I crossed the line, it read, "3:21," three hours and twenty-one minutes. "He sendeth forth his commandment upon earth: his word runneth very swiftly" (Ps. 147:15 KJV).

December: Month of Victory— The Boston Experience

December, "month of victory," brought a letter confirming that my November ("month of peace") 1991 Marine Corps Marathon run of three hours and twenty-one minutes qualified me for the Boston Marathon. The qualifying time for forty-six-year-olds was three hours and twenty-five minutes. Symbolically for me, the Boston Marathon would be held on Easter Monday of 1992. As I found my place in the formation for the race, it filled me with great awe to have my family with me in Boston to watch this most prestigious of runs. That year, the Boston Marathon was hosting runners who were doing their qualifying runs for the Olympics. As stated at the beginning of this book, having my feet on the same pavement that was under the feet of world-class athletes was an honor all its own, a portrait of God's grace. As I mentally pinched myself to make sure that I was really here, the gun sounded and we were off. The basic theme running through my mind as I ran in this highly selective race was victory: how God's grace had ushered in his redeeming will in every area of my life. Where I deserved condemnation and death, he had placed me back in the saddle, sealed by his Word. As we ran, when my hands and arms go up with the posture of praise, a "V" for victory was formed in body, mind, and spirit. The legs that were to run no more have attained the long-awaited goal. The crowds, the weather, the symbolism of the event—all helped move me over the pavement; but nothing could hold a candle to his Word's ability to "renew (my) strength."

Well into the race, I began to notice more of the monuments and capture the cheers of the crowd. We were somewhere around mile seventeen, and I was beginning to feel hopeful that I just might qualify in this Boston Marathon for the next year's run. The clocks at miles ten and twenty each had good readings. At mile twenty-one, Boston's "heartbreak hill," I felt excruciating pain in my left heel. I had just pulled my Achilles tendon. "Ooh, Father, this hurts bad," I thought. I hobbled along to mile 22. I know the Bible says, "With the Lord a day is like a thousand years, and a thousand years are like a day" (2 Peter 3:8), but that mile certainly seemed to contain a lot of time. Between miles twenty-two and twenty-six, I let the Word sink in. The pain was still there with each and every step, but I knew it would come to an end; I could "change it to a moment" and choose to "be content in this state." But I couldn't seem to "count it all joy."

Just as I was whispering that last sentence in my mind, I heard a familiar voice, the voice of my oldest son, Brooke, who had been on that motorcycle with me. And there they were, yelling and waving their arms off—my wife, the children, the *joy*! It had all been worth it. *Thank you, Father! Thank you, Jesus! Thank you, Holy Spirit!* Mile twenty-six was a mile marker of God's Isaiah 40:31 Word.

The heel injury was a painful parable of my sinful condition, a mind prone to lust. While it prevented me from reaching the goal of qualifying for the subsequent year's Boston Marathon, I regarded the race as a personal victory programmed by God's grace. I will never forget the scene of my wife and children standing on the left sidelines at about mile twenty-six, frantically waving and shouting. In that moment, all I could do was point to my heel as the excuse for not qualifying for the next Boston Marathon. But that didn't make any difference to them; they were just happy that I had made it.

In writing this book, Brooke critiqued the earlier paragraph about my Achilles tendon and wrote in the margins: "Why do you think that a pulled Achilles tendon is symbolic of sin? Why is it not just physical strain?" I said, "That centers on the ongoing battle against my 'thorn in the flesh' (tendency to find myself mentally undressing women), or my spiritual Achilles' heel." Like the Hebrews who grumbled about the "heavenly menu" in the wilderness (Num. 11:1–34), I had to learn that what I determine to be the best menu is, in fact, poison compared to what's on God's table. My daily crucifixion of self (Gal. 2:20) and the strength of Christ working in me (Phil. 4:13) together win the race. When God says he "will cleanse (me) from all unrighteousness" (1 John 1:9), the Word *all* includes thoughts. The apostle Paul's words summarize the nature and substance of the battle:

> And he said unto me, My grace is sufficient for thee: for my strength is made perfect in weakness. (2 Cor. 12:9a KJV)

From the day of my "mailbox run," God's Spirit coached me. When depressed about my bodily wounds and when hung up on my memories of unfaithfulness and its consequent wounds/weights to the mind and heart, God's Holy Spirit directed his Word to my whole being. Today, at this writing, having completed forty-seven marathons, I can join ranks with the apostle Paul and "boast in Jesus." These runs were not my doing but rather his, every step of the way. The journey to run continues into still greater victory with focus on the "Mind Marathon."

CHAPTER 2
The Mind Marathon
1990–1998

In the same time frame as the "body marathon," the Holy Spirit was working to help me with a "mental marathon." You will recall that diagnostic and prognostic statements from clinicians in after-care status, several months after my hospitalization, noted, "severe long- and short-term memory deficits," "poor conceptual thinking," and "a 39 point lowered IQ; a follow-up test read 36." A subsequent series of tests resulted in a finding that read, "Visual memory severely impaired." Another interview statement stayed in my mind: "These factors preclude completion of your doctoral degree." I had been working on a degree in "wholistic" health care for several years before the accident, but therapists had to teach me how to talk all over again. My career looked dark and hopeless.

In the midst of these weights to my mind, as I read and studied the Scriptures, the Holy Spirit lifted up another *rhema* Word: "For I know the plans I have for you, declares the Lord, plans to prosper you and not to harm you, plans to give you hope and a future" (Jeremiah 29:11 NIV).

The original King James Version says "give you an expected end" rather than "hope and a future." It also says, "For I know the thoughts that I think toward thee, saith the Lord." That speaks to me on a deeper level because he is saying he has plans for me based on how he sees and knows me. I like the King James better: "An expected end." Did God want me to be expectant, pregnant with his Word, and, thereby through faith, thinking/speaking/acting according to that expectation? I began to think in that fashion. Thinking about him giving me an "expected end," which certainly would include "a hope and a future," led me to talk about it and then take steps— trusting, hoping they were in the right direction. Describing himself as "the God of all hope" (Rom. 15:13), he said he wanted me to *place* (gerund) my hope in him. As with faith, hope was a decision. He wanted me to take steps in line with his Word, to "run to the mailbox!" As I searched Scriptures addressing prayer, a passage underscored this understanding for me: "Now unto him that is able to do exceeding abundantly above all that we ask or think, according to the power that worketh in us" (Eph. 3:20 KJV).

Connie was led to raise the following Word to me:

> Because he has set his love upon Me, therefore will I deliver him; I will set him on high, because he knows and understands My name (has a personal knowledge of My mercy, love and kindness; trusts and relies on Me, knowing I will never forsake him, no never). He shall call upon Me, and I will answer him; I will be with him in trouble, I will deliver him and honor him. With long life will I satisfy him, and show him my salvation. (Ps. 91:14–16 AMP)

These words spoke directly to the need at hand. And as a commentary to the above Scripture, consider the following: "Blessed are all they that *put* their trust in him" (emphasis mine; Ps. 2:12b KJV). (The Scofield Reference King James Bible notes that the Old Testament word for *trust* parallels the New Testament word for *faith* in the sense of "taking refuge" or "to lean on" [p. 600].)

> And they who know Your name (who have experience and acquaintance with Your mercy) will lean on and confidently put their trust in You; for You, Lord, have not forsaken those who seek (inquire of and for You) (on the authority of God's Word and the right of their necessity). (Ps. 9:10 AMP)

The following came directly from my Coach.

> Every word of God proves true. He defends all who come to him for protection. (Prov. 30:5 TLB)

Around the same time of the Marine Corps Marathon qualifying run, there came a very focused mental victory. Like the journey to run on the physical pavement, the mental challenge during those same years was also great. The long- and short-term memory deficits caused me, initially, to have to look up the children's birthdays. At times, I would be inside and remember to check on something outside, but on the way out, I would forget where I was going or what I was going to do. Taking action, steps, toward this recovery required me to make more faith-decisions against the odds.

You may recall that I set about seventy Scriptures to music as part of my training regimen for running. My family began to discover that this music exercise not only provided good motor response to my left brain, helping me to run, but the Scripture—being escorted in a musical vehicle—renewed my right brain, where feelings, memory, and perception are housed. I am told by loved ones that during my time in the hospital, when my body and mind functions were their lowest, I would still recognize Scripture and participate in reciting it. God's Words not only gave my memory and feelings a vision for hope; they also exercised my perception of things, taking it to a new level. Furthermore, the acrostics I formed during the training runs and later expanded also exercised my memory and conceptual thinking abilities. Family and friends were amazed at how much I began to recall and perceive. At this writing, the visual memory factor is still a challenge. Connie will sometimes say things like, "Do you remember our trip last month to ..." and I will usually have to say, "No, I remember the idea of our doing it, but I do not *see* it." Sometimes the editors for this book would write in the margins comments like, "Telling, not showing." They were concerned for you, the reader, to be able to sense more deeply what was actually happening in my experience of things. I have, nonetheless, resisted the temptation to do creative writing to address my visual memory challenge.

I continued to exercise on the mental pavement to overcome the lowered IQ and conceptual thinking barriers to completing my doctorate. I began to surface and correlate the research data, and the degree was awarded in 1991 with the comment from the Lutheran Theological Seminary exam committee that the final research document in wholistic health care was "the best we have seen in the field." The committee member who said this had his doctorate in the same field. This, too, was God's doing. It was despite an earlier desire by the doctoral committee to release me from the program during those first couple of years after the accident, given my medical prognosis. Jeremiah 29:11 had been "sent out."

My doctoral research compared five wholistic health care centers in nonreligious, general practice settings with five general practice religious settings (churches) and one experimental center where Bible studies or theological didactics in healing were given to the interdisciplinary treatment team of health care providers (two medical doctors, two nurses, one pastoral counselor, one nutritionist, one biofeedback technician, one social worker and some church members trained in effective listening). The patient was included as a treatment team member, producing more ownership of treatment. The graph results regarding patient outcome went off the chart like an arrow into the clouds. And what was the independent variable? It was the experimental center's biblical intervention into the overall treatment process! Clinical results documented the power of the Word and good, whole-person health. Increasingly, major medical universities are requiring their students to consider the spiritual component in health care because of what they are finding out about the Word speaking to the human spirit.

From my final research document, *(W)holistic Health Care: A New Direction in Health Care/A New Mode of Ministry*, I quote the following paragraph:

> The term *(w)holistic medicine*, which has been used generally to cover all fresh approaches to health care, derives from the gestalt premise that (you) are a whole person—not just a physical body. (Your) mind (nous), body (soma), and spirit (psyche) interact. A change in one affects the whole. To be healthy in the (w)holistic sense is to maintain balance of mind, body, and spirit. So health (well-being) is not an end in itself, only a means to an end (personal growth). In a conference sponsored by the experimental WHC center's board of directors, a frontline leader in this new direction, Dr. Granger Westberg, said, 'Wholistic health care is based on the affirmation of body, mind, and spirit integrated in a whole that is greater than its parts. (Field notes, 1982).

As an interesting footnote to the above, Dr. Norman Cousins, author of *Anatomy of an Illness*, lay at the time of my paper's finalization at Walter-Reed Army Hospital with a diagnosis of terminal cancer. He read the Scripture that says, "Laugher works like a medicine" (Prov. 17:22). So, since he liked Charlie

Chapman movies, he ordered one after another to be brought into the hospital to watch. He laughed himself into recovery and was released with a new diagnosis: "Cured." And he wrote a best-selling book about it.

My mother, on what was pronounced to be her deathbed, was diagnosed with a condition very similar to a severe case of Alzheimer's disease, called Creutzfeldt-Jakob disease. It progresses very rapidly. While I was in Germany (1996) for Operation Joint Endeavor, doctors gave her one month to live. I called my dad in February only to hear him say that, at that time, they thought she had only one more week. So, there she was, no memory, in and out of consciousness, body dysfunctional. My two sisters would go every day and simply read Scripture to her. After a period of time of doing this, they had the idea—and I think God gave them this idea—to deliberately stop in the middle of a sentence. Long story short, whenever they would do this, our mother would pick it up and finish it. The doctors soon released her, saying she was "cured" and shaking their heads. When we would go home, visit, and play Scrabble, she would win. She had *memorized* the Scrabble dictionary! Anytime we would test her against it, she was always right. Over time, we found her to miss only one word, and that was a proper name in another language. Her memory had been dramatically restored. The hand of God, also, worked through the loving, never-stopping hands of her husband, nursing her back to health like a hundred Florence Nightingales—giving what medical care could no longer provide. (There is no known case of anyone ever recovering from this condition. When folks would say that she was probably misdiagnosed, I was able to say that one of the factors substantiating the diagnosis is that children will sometimes be born with Down syndrome. When our youngest son was born, the doctors thought he had it, but it resolved into a learning disability.)

I tell this about my mother as a platform for what happened next, another major proof point of God's hand in healing my mental faculties for conceptual thinking. A few years later, in 1998, Mama's experience with the Word became the catalyst for a research study—*Word (God's) Therapy: A Wholistic Approach to the Treatment of Alzheimer's Disease*—I conducted with forty-eight Alzheimer's patients (males and females) in a special unit of a Veterans Affairs Medical Center in Pennsylvania. I recruited forty-four volunteers from local churches, as well as family members, to come in and simply read Scripture to these patients several times a week, as my sisters had done with our mother. I also recruited five vocalists to sing the Scriptures to them. These volunteers gave up to seventy hours to this mission—truly servants of the Word. Could Scripture set to music do for these Alzheimer's patients what it had for me? We also played tapes of the same interventions as the participants slept. The bottom line is that, the interventions worked so well in improving memory, communication, mood, and behavior that, following their review of my research document, the Mayo Clinic featured it at their November 3, 2000, "Spiritual Care Research: Applications to Practice" conference in Rochester, Minnesota. The presentation by my associate (the most widely published researcher in his field) and me was rated the best presentation by conference attendees and declared to be "pioneering research." Why? Because no prior research had ever featured God's Word as the "independent variable," putting it under the microscope, so to speak. No follow-up studies, to my knowledge, have been done. The following paragraph was written by the Chief of Chaplains to the staff of the Coatesville VAMC, where the research was conducted:

> Chaplain Coffey has just received word that the Mayo Clinic in Rochester, Minnesota, will feature his research here at Coatesville with the Alzheimer's patients at its Fourth Spiritual Care Research Conference on November 3, 2000. Chaplain Coffey will be a featured speaker at the conference. Chaplain Coffey is to be congratulated on this prestigious recognition. In addition, appreciation is expressed to management, staff, volunteers, and patient families who have made this research possible. In a day when we are looking for alternative medicine and therapy, the research community is coming to an awareness of the place for spiritual therapy in treating the whole person. Chaplain Coffey's creative research will increase this growing awareness. We congratulate him on this significant honor.

His words underscored the miracle that God had done for me through his Jeremiah 29:11 Word: "For I know the plans that I have for you, says the Lord." When the Alzheimer's patients heard the Word—even in their sleep—Jesus, himself, was speaking to them ("And the Word became flesh and dwelt among us," John 1:14 NKJV). The Word addresses our spirits even when our minds and bodies are not receptive. And, for most of these patients, their minds and bodies were, like my mother's, about shot. When I, beforehand, asked God if he wanted me to conduct such a study, I checked the concordance for the word *word*. My studies about his Word led me to Psalm 138:2: "For thou hast magnified thy word above all thy name" (KJV). The Psalm 138 Word was like a tap on the shoulder, saying he wanted his Word to be exalted at the Mayo Clinic. It is now part of their archives.

God's Word recharged my spirit so as to direct my memory, IQ, and general thought processes against the odds. That recharging was done by a *rhema* word that addressed "a hope and a future" (see Jer. 29:11–13). Just as I kept the Isaiah 40:31 Word in the forefront of my mind as I took steps on the pavement, I applied the same exercise to the phrase "expected end," which certainly included "a hope and a future" but also addressed my faith as it was to become expectant—that is, to take real, concrete steps, accordingly. The placing of the doctoral cape and hood felt like God's arm around my shoulders.

But beyond my cognitive abilities, the Holy Spirit had deeper and ongoing training for me to do on this mental pavement. I had already found that what gets my mind gets me. Another Word came as *rhema*:

> And be not conformed to this world: but be ye
> transformed by the renewing of your mind, that
> ye may prove what is that good, and acceptable,
> and perfect will of God. (Rom. 12:2 KJV)

God's Word was clear and concise: what I had "sown," I was to "reap." Sin sees the bait but is blind to the hook. I had sinned by being unfaithful to my wife, having an adulterous relationship with her friend. Little did I know on that fateful day in June of 1986 what a grotesque plant this seed would germinate and that I was on the road to hell. Adulterers will not inherit the kingdom of heaven (see Gal. 5:21; 1 Cor. 6:9–10).

> Because the Lord was witness (to the covenant
> made at your marriage) between you and the
> wife of your youth, against whom you have dealt
> treacherously and to whom you were faithless.
> Yet she is your companion and the wife of your
> covenant (made by your marriage vows). (Mal.
> 2:14 AMP)

My former wife, God said, left *within* his will because of my unfaithfulness—unfaithful not only through adultery but also through the neglect that came from my being a workaholic. I misplaced my priorities and stole her time to push more ego-centered work into my time. As I worked eighty-five hours a week, people would pat me on the back and comment that they didn't see how I could do so much. This response propelled me even deeper into the sickness. She used to refer to the church (my work) as "the other woman." Both sin conditions on my part were more deeply rooted in a lack of honesty. I wasn't "eye to eye" with God or with my wife. I was not strong enough to be weak, to be confessional and honest with either her or God. My wife might have been able to cope with the affair; it was the lack of honesty in our overall communication and lives that wounded her spirit.

I vaguely recall her working on a complicated puzzle during that first month of separation. She had somehow gotten it all together except for one last piece that had gotten lost. It seemed a parable of what she was going through. I would sometimes say to myself, *God knows where that missing piece to the puzzle is.* "You were united to your wife by the Lord. In God's wise plan, when you married, the two of you became one person in his sight. And what does he want? Godly children from your union. Therefore guard your passions! Keep faith with the wife of your youth" (Mal. 2:15 TLB).

For several years after the separation, I emotionally hung onto a clinging vine, journeying through the "dark night of the soul." As I ran deeper into the darkness, a burning question flickered in the night: "Will daylight come?" The Scriptures show me the man in the mirror who walks away and forgets what he looks like. A passing glance in the mirror reminded me of someone who had miserably failed in the relational race (see James 1:8, 23–25; Romans 8:5–6; Ezekiel 33:31–32; Lamentations 3:39–40). For my children and the community, my life modeled not what to do but what not to do. My name was not only a shame in the community where I had served and lost my call as a pastor, but I had become a shame to his name, a disgrace to his grace.

> A good name is rather to be chosen than great
> riches. (Prov. 22:1 KJV)

Thrown into the "black hole" of despair, I desperately grabbed for bits and pieces to provide stamina to stay in the race. Running on the pavement became increasingly symbolic for maintaining endurance while heading toward a goal; could I run on the road to repentance? I prayed and asked national prayer ministries to pray for the healing of our marriage. I believed that God would work, using situations, circumstances, relationships, reasoning, and so on to give her every chance in the world to change her mind (see Phil. 2:13). However, no amount of prayer can ever force God to bulldoze his will over anyone, making that person go against his or her own will. It wasn't a matter of her "hardness of heart"; her spirit was broken, making the mending of our marriage bond impossible. I have come to believe that the broken spirit that occurs in marriage due to unfaithfulness is the reason Jesus upheld the Mosaic Law of divorce, Deuteronomy 24:1, when unfaithfulness is the issue of concern. The word *except* in the following passage clearly defines adultery as the exception, permitting divorce.

> Jesus replied, "Moses permitted you to divorce
> your wives because your hearts were hard. But
> it was not this way from the beginning. I tell
> you that anyone who divorces his wife, except

for marital unfaithfulness, and marries another woman commits adultery." (Matt. 19:8–9 NIV)

Good Grief

My refusal to sign a certificate of divorce began two long, sorrowful years of separation that finally ended in divorce, a relational death straight out of hell. When the sheriff came out to our house with a summons to appear in court, I felt like a fugitive from justice. During those two painful years, guilt paralyzed me. My heart was like a balloon wrapped around a dripping faucet of tears, making my heart heavier with each day. God's Spirit was doing the work of conviction, pointing out in intense detail the impact of my sin against everyone in my life.

> For God is closely watching you, and he weighs carefully everything you do. (Prov. 5:21 TLB)

> He knows about everyone, everywhere. Everything about us is bare and wide open to the all-seeing eyes of our living God; nothing can be hidden from him to whom we must explain all that we have done. (Heb. 4:13 TLB)

> For the Lord searches every heart and understands every motive behind the thoughts. (1 Chron. 28:9 NIV; see also 2 Chron. 32:31)

I the Lord search the heart and examine the mind, to reward a man according to his conduct, according to what his deeds deserve. (Jer. 17:10 NIV)

The philosopher Plato said, "The life which is unexamined is not worth living." Other famous writers have reflected the Scriptures: Faust said, "Self-mastery is a challenge for every individual"; Socrates said, "Let him that would move the world, first move himself"; and Aristotle said, "I count him braver who overcomes his desires than he who conquers his enemies; for the hardest victory is the self." God was showing me that my sin was not just a matter of "doing" but also a matter of "being"—a sin-condition. One of the Greek New Testament words for *sin* translates as *broken relationship*. My sinful condition separated me not only from people but from my heavenly Father.

Yes, divorce is a death straight out of hell. God says he hates it (see Mal. 2:16), probably due to his seeing the husband-wife relationship as analogous to the one between Christ and the church. Only here, in the "runner's" portrait he painted, could I feel the weight and vast underlying personal nature of sin, like those weights strapped around my ankles as my feet grew heavier on the pavement. Only here could the precise X-ray nature of God's vision reveal what needed to be purged from my thinking and perception of life. Words from St. Augustine's *Confessions* echo the portrait: "You set me there before my face that I might see how vile I was, how twisted and unclean and spotted and ulcerous. I saw myself and was horrified." My self-will and mind, held captive by lust, had to be crucified (Gal. 2:20, 5:24–25; Rom. 6:6), making room for a transformed (changed) will through the renewal of my mind. The Amplified Bible translation took me deeper into the Holy Spirit's coaching about a renewed mind:

> Do not be conformed to this world—this age, fashioned after and adapted to its external, superficial customs. But be transformed (changed) by the (entire) renewal of your mind— by its new ideals and its new attitude—so that you may prove (for yourselves) what is the good and acceptable and perfect will of God, even the thing which is good and acceptable and perfect (in His sight for you). (Rom. 12:2 AMP)

> You were taught, with regard to your former way of life, to put off your old self, which is being corrupted by its deceitful desires; to be made new in the attitude of your minds; and to put on the new self, created to be like God in true righteousness and holiness. (Eph. 4:22–24 NIV)

I had to learn what I call the Dead Sea Lesson. Water flows *into* the Dead Sea but not *out* of it. There, salt is seven times more concentrated than in any other ocean or sea; therefore, one can float on its surface as though in a hammock, as Connie and I have done while on tour in Israel. From a distance, it is most inviting, but nothing can live in it; it is the same with sexual sin or carnal knowledge. The Word hit with great force:

> Drink water from your own cistern, running water from your own well. Should your springs overflow in the streets, your streams of water in the public squares? Let them be yours alone, never to be shared with strangers. May your fountain be blessed, and may you rejoice in the wife of your youth. A loving doe, a graceful deer—may her breasts satisfy you always, may you ever be captivated by her love. Why be captivated, my son, by an adulteress? Why embrace the bosom of another man's wife? (Prov. 5:15–20 NIV)

Due to my "deceitful heart" (Mark 7:20–23) and the camouflage tactics of our number one enemy (Satan), "crucifixion of self" was a hard death. However, as you will see through the journey of this run, my own heart had become the real enemy. The root of my problem was not sexual passion; God's Word says that misdirected passions are a form of idolatry.

> Set your mind on things above, not on things on the earth. For you died, and your life is hidden with Christ in God. When Christ *who is* our life appears, then you also will appear with Him in glory. Therefore put to death your members which are on the earth: fornication, uncleanness, passion, evil desire, and covetousness, which is

idolatry. Because of these things the wrath of God is coming upon the sons of disobedience, in which you yourselves once walked when you lived in them. (Col. 3:2–7 NKJV)

For be sure of this: that no person practicing sexual vice or impurity in thought or in life, or one who is covetous (who has lustful desire for the property of others and is greedy for gain)—for he (in effect) is an idolater—has any inheritance in the kingdom of Christ and of God. (Eph. 5:5 AMP)

Whoever commits adultery with a woman lacks understanding; he who does so destroys his own soul. (Prov. 6:32 KJV)

Strip yourselves of your former nature—put off and discard your old unrenewed self—which characterized your previous manner of life and becomes corrupt through lusts and desires that spring from delusion; and be constantly renewed in the spirit of your mind—having a fresh mental and spiritual attitude. (Eph. 4:22–23 AMP)

The Word was clear concerning the standard to which my mind was to be trained:

Therefore, prepare your minds for action; be self-controlled; set your hope fully on the grace to be given you when Jesus Christ is revealed. As obedient children, do not conform to the evil desires you had when you lived in ignorance. But just as he who called you is holy, so be holy in all you do; for it is written: "Be holy, because I am holy." (1 Peter 1:13–16 NIV)

Kierkegaard once wrote that one's life is the expression of one's dominant thoughts. Yet, what about those "bad thoughts"? How are their needs met? As captives, our minds are slippery eels. Perhaps we should take no prisoners and simply circumcise our minds (see Jer. 4:4) of bad thoughts. We present our thoughts to a judge, not a jailer. The brain cells in my right brain, where feelings, perception, and memories reside, were the trickiest. I needed to ask Jesus to systematically capture each and every one of those cells! This really was an all-out battle. My mind was like a computer programmed by what I put into it. "For as he thinketh in his heart, so is he" (Prov. 23:7 KJV). What captured my mind captured me. Adulterous thinking made me an adulterer. "But I say to you that whoever looks at a woman to lust for her has already committed adultery with her in his heart" (Matt. 5:28 NKJV).

My mind can be dragged away from God's will. In computer language, this is expressed as "garbage in, garbage out." Computerized sex, promoted as cybersex, is instrumental in launching the fulfillment of the following Scripture:

"Furthermore, since they did not think it worthwhile to retain the knowledge of God, he gave them over to a depraved mind, to do what ought not to be done" (Rom. 1:28 NIV).

I identified with all of the following words that the apostle Paul wrote to the church in Rome, outlining his battle for the mind:

> I cannot understand my own behavior. I fail to carry out the things I want to do, and I find myself doing the very things I hate. When I act against my own will, that means I have a self that acknowledges that the law is good, and so the thing behaving in that way is not my self but sin living in me. The fact is, I know of nothing good living in me—living, that is, in my unspiritual self—for though the will to do what is good is in me, the performance is not, with the result that instead of doing the good things I want to do, I carry out the sinful things I do not want. When I act against my will, then, it is not my true self doing it, but sin which lives in me.
>
> In fact, this seems to be the rule, that every single time I want to do good it is something evil that comes to hand. In my inmost-self I dearly love God's Law, but I can see that my body follows a different law that battles against the law which my reason dictates. This is what

makes me a prisoner of that law of sin which lives inside my body.

What a wretched man I am! Who will rescue me from this body doomed to death? Thanks be to God through Jesus Christ our Lord!

In short, it is I who with my reason serve the Law of God, and no less I who serve in my unspiritual self the law of sin. (Rom. 7:15–25 J. B. Phillips New Testament, or JB)

The apostle Paul was describing to the letter how I was "breaking training." To mentally undress a woman despite what I knew this could lead to caused me to look in the mirror and just shake my head in unbelief. I could vow in my mind to faithfully follow the training to "cast down," but I continued to dream on. At this reading of the Word, I knew that I needed to not only make my thoughts captive to God but also surrender my deceitful heart, asking God to take it and mold it, as a master potter, the way he wanted it to be because "A man's conscience is the Lord's searchlight exposing his hidden motives" (Prov. 20:27 TLB). The "potter" prayer was a good and right prayer because it set the stage for God to get at my heart through my mind and spirit; but how could I retain that renewed mind and perception? How could I see people and situations the way God wanted me to see them? I already knew from my doctoral studies that feelings are actually thought choices, and I was seeing that God backs that up. But understanding was not enough. This called for an intense conditioning and training program for the mind. The "spiritual pavement" beckoned.

> Those who live according to the sinful nature have their minds set on what that nature desires; but those who live in accordance with the Spirit have their minds set on what the Spirit desires. The mind of sinful man is death, but the mind controlled by the Spirit is life and peace. (Rom. 8:5–6 NIV)

I asked point blank for a picture of what this exercise would look like for me, and in the next run, he painted it for me. The scene unfolds, showing our farm and me working on the beds in the greenhouse I built. As I turn the dirt for planting, my hand picks up a clump of fresh cow manure; instantly, I throw it down—not wanting to see it in my hand another second. Then, I see myself brushing my hands together as to remove any remains. Immediately, in this vision, I'm coached to "cast down" improper looks at women with the same disgust and zeal, recalling what it could cause me. Next, I see someone on a life-support system in a hospital; the decision is made to remove the supports and let the person die. I'm further coached to understand this picture to mean that when I stop entertaining daydreams of sexual exploits, I'm "deadening the deeds of the flesh." Toward the end of the run, one more picture comes—this time of someone drowning. I begin to see the connection with "crucify the self." Most crucifixion deaths were caused by suffocation. Just like water replaces the air in the lungs when someone drowns, I needed to replace my wrong thinking with right thinking (see Phil. 4:8). So he gave me the exercise of replacing the junk in my mind with what the four gospel writers had to say about the passion of Christ. This was a vivid picture of how God wanted me to "crucify the self," a "renewing of the mind."

I needed to let the following Word be my training guide, especially the words italicized here: "… that I may know Him and the power of His resurrection, and the *fellowship of His sufferings*, being *conformed to His death*, if, by any means, I may attain to the resurrection from the dead" (Phil. 3:10–11). Is this part of what it means for me to be "found in Christ," to be a "new creation," or to "have the mind of Christ" (see 2 Cor. 5:17; Phil. 3:9; 1 Peter 4:1)? I believe that you, at this point, would say, "Yes, you're progressing in your training on the Word, but I sense that there remains a still-deeper root system for the ground of your being as you run on the road to repentance." How would the "cast down, deaden, crucify" exercise connect me to "the fellowship of his sufferings" and being "conformed to his death?"

What we "see" is what we get. If I continued to see myself locked into the same sinful mode of operation, I would remain in bondage to what I see. You have heard the expression "Seeing is believing." Let's rearrange it to say "Believing is seeing." For example, when I go to town and step out of the car as the wind lifts the skirt of a beautiful woman on the street, guess who is going to be the first to look? But now, there is a difference. I have come to understand that "seeing" is not lust; "looking" is. When tempted, I pray the words of the Psalmist: "Turn away my eyes from looking at worthless things, and revive me in Your way" (Ps. 119:37 KJV; see in context of verses 33–40). I had started to title this chapter "Training of the Eyes."

Again, what captures my mind captures me. My thoughts, as Martin Luther wrote in his treatise, *On Bondage of the Will*, can place me in a state of bondage to sin, or I can place them in bondage to Jesus by "bringing into captivity every thought to the obedience of Christ" (2 Cor. 10:5 KJV). My freedom lies in the exchange of one bondage for the other. Without this exchange, I remain in bondage to sin and death and cannot free myself. But, given the exchange, I am in bondage to Jesus and His holy ways. "And being found in fashion as a man, he humbled himself, and became obedient unto death, even the death of the cross" (Phil. 2:8 KJV).

I have come to see that temptation itself is not sin. However, temptation that is allowed to dwell in and be entertained in the mind (see "Sermon on the Mount," Matt. 5:17–48) and that proceeds out of my mind, marching into wrong words and wrong actions, is sin. The old mountaineer adage, borrowed from Martin Luther, then applies to my "lust looks": "You can't stop the birds from flying over your head, but you sure can keep 'em from building a nest in your hair." I had allowed too much "nest building." In the early years of my second marriage—at this writing, now approaching twenty-five years—my wife would be walking next to me in a store, see my eyes wander, look sternly at me, and say, "Well, did you get a good look?" I was hurting with my unfaithful eyes.

A Scripture that outlines this progression stared me down again, as I failed to "cast down" the imaginations of my heart, follows:

> Happy is the man who doesn't give in and do wrong when he is tempted, for afterwards he will get as his reward the crown of life that God has promised those who love him. And remember, when someone wants to do wrong it is never God who is tempting him, for God never wants to do wrong and never tempts anyone else to do it. Temptation is the pull of man's own evil thoughts and wishes. These evil thoughts lead to evil actions and afterwards to the death penalty from God. (James 1:12–15 TLB)

But what, I asked him, can I do when it just seems impossible for me to do this exercise of overcoming? He said, "There hath no temptation taken you but such as is common to man: but God is faithful, who will not suffer you to be tempted above that ye are able; but will with the temptation also make a way to escape, that ye may be able to bear it" (1 Cor. 10:13 KJV). So when I said, "I can't," he who knows me better than I know myself said, "Yes, you can." Just like he said he would "renew my strength" in the physical marathon, he would do likewise in the mental one.

Luther said, "My temptations have been my masters in divinity." True repentance is what will enable me to grow and change without being haunted or prodded by circumstances from the past and present. I, therefore, find myself being "transformed by the renewing of (my) mind" (Rom. 12:2). (Note, again, that the verb *renew* ends with *ing*; it is a gerund, stating an ongoing process or exercise.) It is also the powerful preventive medicine that allows me to "shoot down" future temptations, "having in a readiness to revenge all disobedience" (2 Cor. 10:6). The US military standard is, also, "readiness training." Temptations would become a training ground, moving me to a new level of performance.

I need to read God's message to Israel as if it were spoken directly to me:

> If a righteous man turns from his righteousness and commits sin, he will die for it.... But if a wicked man turns away from the wickedness he has committed and does what is just and right, he will save his life. Because he considers all the offenses he has committed and turns away from them, he will surely live; he will not die.... Therefore, O house of Israel, I will judge you, each one according to his ways, declares the Sovereign Lord. Repent! Turn away from all your offenses; then sin will not be your downfall. Rid yourselves of all the offenses you have committed, and get a new heart and a new spirit. Why will you die, O house of Israel? For I take no pleasure in the death of anyone, declares the Sovereign Lord. Repent and live!

(Ez. 18:26–32 NIV; see Training Regimen #1.)

During the early years of my emotional turmoil, Rev. Larry Christenson, an internationally respected theologian, responded to my letters of desperation. He wrote that he had prayed about my situation and was led to direct the following Word to me:

> Trust in the Lord with all your heart and lean not on your own understanding. (Prov. 3:5 NIV)

This Scripture didn't say not to *have* any understanding but simply not to lean on it.

> Commit everything you do to the Lord. Trust him to help you do it and he will. Your innocence will be clear to everyone. He will vindicate you with the blazing light of justice shining down as from the noonday sun. Rest in the Lord; wait patiently for him to act. (Ps. 37:5–7 TLB)

God's Spirit coached me to see that the day would come in which the public would see not just a "soap-opera sinner" but one on whom God had chosen to pour down his amazing grace in superabundant proportions. I suppose this is one major reason for this book, to show what he did as promised in his Word.

> "Come now, let us reason together," says the Lord. "Though your sins are like scarlet, they shall be as white as snow; though they are red as crimson, they shall be like wool." (Is. 1:18 NIV)

During the first years of shock and depression to my entire system, my Coach kept saying to me, "You need to let Jesus become your closest person; to seek the kingdom first (Matt. 6:33) is to seek him." To leap ahead in this story, you will see that as I began to let that happen, all other relationships—including mine with myself—became simply a bonus, not life or death. This closeness meant getting into the Word and the Word into me. Jesus *is* the Word.

> Yes, everything else is worthless when compared with the priceless gain of knowing Christ Jesus my Lord. I have put aside all else, counting it worth less than nothing, in order that I can have Christ, and become one with him, no longer counting on being saved by being good enough or by obeying God's laws, but by trusting Christ to save me; for God's way of making us right with himself depends on faith—counting on Christ alone. (Phil. 3:8–9 TLB)

It has been said, "A Bible stored in the mind is worth a dozen stored on the shelf." I have never seen a worn and torn Bible owned by a person who was worn and torn.

God was teaching me that I needed to be faithful also with my eyes. One friend who is also an author, in reviewing the manuscript for this book, commented,

> Another thing that helps with this is to remember that Jesus views us as brothers and sisters. Would you think that about a brother or sister? Looking at the opposite sex as God's "workmanship" separates the physical aspects of the person from the soul. We *must*, as God's workers, be so consumed by our zeal for souls that the physical appearance doesn't enter into our minds from our eyes. In other words, our interest in fellow humans is so focused on helping them to God's glorious heaven that what they look like is completely a secondary or trivial matter. This is looking at people with "our Father's eyes." I think that you can see that this principle improves our relationships not only with "the beautiful" but also with "the ordinary" or even "the ugly."

From this statement, I saw that I must start to stop even before the "looking." Was I ever out of shape! I recalled times past when people would ask me how I ran a marathon, and I would often answer, "One step at a time." So it would be on the road to repentance. In the days of my youth, why hadn't I, like Job, "made a covenant with my eyes" not to "look" with lust "upon a young woman" (Job 31:1 KJV)? I would have asked not, "How can I get this woman into bed?" but "How can I help her be in the kingdom?"

Perhaps a good acrostic for *ego* would be "easing God out." I began to see that behind my physical desires, acted out in two cases of adultery—one against my former wife, the other as I courted someone when her divorce was not yet final—was a deeper spiritual appetite dining on a starvation diet. The real fire igniting my uncontrolled sexual desire was the belief that I could secure my own heart's passion and need for God through sexual pleasure. St. Augustine, a fourth-century bishop, experienced this struggle and wrote about it in his book, *Confessions*. His words have stood the test of time: "Every man's heart is restless 'til he finds his rest in God." In my weakness, instead of turning more deeply to God, I tried to dull pain with pleasure that was within my power to control. The only thing that scratched my heart's surface was sensuality. But the need for intimacy with God ran too deeply to be silenced. The spiritual pavement began to call more loudly.

CHAPTER 3

The Spirit Marathon

1990–2000

"For godly sorrow produces repentance leading to salvation, not to be regretted; but the sorrow of the world produces death."—2 Cor. 7:10 NKJV

The third type of run I engaged in was spiritual because it involved my heart. Since, like Israel, I tried to exchange the one true God for a false god, I had to pay the price. A scene in the famous movie *The Ten Commandments* comes to mind. It's where Aaron takes the fine jewelry among the waiting tribes at the foot of the mountain that Moses had gone up to meet God. He gathers it all together to make an idol for the people to worship. Each time I've seen that scene, I say to myself, *How could his hands do such a thing, especially after all that the true God has done for Israel?* Now, my Coach tells me to look at my own hands. My adultery was idolatry. Like King David, I needed to acknowledge that my adultery was against God (see David's Psalm 51). I was putting what I wanted before what he wants; that, in a nutshell, has been mankind's history of idolatry.

Instead of controlling my desires, my desires controlled me. My enemy wanted to control me, and he had won. This "run" left me breathless. I broke training by not sprinting the hills of temptation. Struggling to "cast down," "deaden," and "crucify" my thoughts and imaginations pushed me to the wall in my spiritual marathon. Did God have a design for desire just as he has designed everything else? My heart was beginning to come into a truthful attitude. God was preparing to "revive the spirit of the humble, and to revive the heart of the contrite" (see Is. 57:15). For there was a way back *home!*

During those first few years after the accident, no one could have been harder on me than I was on myself. The glares and whispered comments that I witnessed as I walked into a local store could not compare to my own deep stare into my sin-sick soul. I simply could not forgive myself for my sin. Self-atonement formulas, dreaming up ways to punish or sabotage myself, to make the training course steeper and harder, would not relieve my guilt. He spoke clearly:

> For if we searchingly examined ourselves (detecting our shortcomings and recognizing our own condition), we should not be judged and penalty decreed (by the divine judgment). But when we (fall short and) are judged by the Lord, we are disciplined and chastened, so that we may not (finally) be condemned (to eternal punishment along) with the world. (1 Cor. 11:31–32 AMP)

> As many as I love, I rebuke and chasten: be zealous therefore, and repent. (Rev. 3:19 KJV)

Then he explained to me that without repentance there is no remission or forgiveness of sin and, thereby, no salvation—only hell to pay. "I tell you, No; but unless you repent—(that is,) change your mind for the better and heartily amend your ways with abhorrence of your past sins—you will all likewise perish and be lost (eternally)" (Luke 13:3 AMP; see Mark 1:4, Acts 2:38, Ps. 25:7, Rom. 6:1–16, Matt. 26:28, Luke 24:47, Rom. 3:25). Here it was—the wall.

Not self-induced suffering but God's discipline is what I needed (see Heb. 12:5–11; Ps. 119:67, 71, 75, 92). The Rev. Jamie Buckingham paraphrased Revelation 3:19, saying, "Those whom God loveth, He beateth the hell out of." As I look down the long road to repentance, it seems like it is almost past the eleventh hour to the midnight call. Then, another *rhema* Scripture started burning in my mind:

> For Godly grief and the pain God is permitted to direct, produce (Old King James: 'worketh') a repentance that leads and contributes to salvation and deliverance from evil, and it never brings regret. (2 Cor. 7:10 AMP) (Note: *Worketh* means that repentance is a work in process.)

The Road to Repentance

Again, he said to me, "No repentance, no forgiveness." The wisdom literature (Psalm, Proverbs) of the Old Testament and its reflection in the New Testament tell me that "the fear of the Lord is the beginning of wisdom" (Ps. 111:10, Prov.

1:7). I was to find that this "fear" is essential to the pursuit of obedience. I had to learn three distinct meanings or levels of "the fear of the Lord," in ascending order:

1. The first level addressed my fear of the consequences of my wrongdoing; it was "wise up or else." I needed to fear the one who could cast both body and soul into an eternity of hell fire.

2. The second level moved me to fear missing out on God's best provision (health, peace, prosperity) for this life.

3. The third level melted me into a deepening awareness of who God is as I stood in awe of his name—the silence of anonymity—and his amazing grace; this level led me to fear wounding his heart anymore with my sin. This was "godly sorrow."

Levels one and two by themselves will not win over my deceitful heart. For example, if I'm sorry just for the pickle I get myself in when I step away from God's will, then when the dust settles, I'm right back to my old ways. Or if I'm sorry only for missing out on his best provision, the "me" takes over again. I, as St. Paul said, will fall back into my old pattern and choose to "settle for less" (one of the Greek New Testament meanings for *sin*). True repentance, for me, started to mean far more than a mind change; it involved a heart and will change that moved from mind change to changes in my actions, decisions, and behaviors. It makes sense that John the Baptist and Jesus would begin their messages with the word *repent* (*metanoia*). The Greek prefix *meta* means to "turn around," and the suffix *noia* translates as "mind." Doesn't there have to be a change of mind before the other changes take place? True, what gets my mind gets me; but efforts to repent from sins have been more like New Year's resolutions—made only to be broken. I needed to want repentance to the same level of a drowning man wanting air to demonstrate "fruits worthy of repentance" (see Luke 3:8). Not until I reached that point did Jesus throw me a rope. God's Spirit, our head coach, began training me, not so much with the question "What's on your mind?" but "What's in your heart?" (See Training Regimen #10.)

Most of the Greek New Testament words expressing grief indicate weeping, crying out, wailing, beating the breast in anguish, and other outward expressions of grief. But the "godly grief" of 2 Corinthians 7:10 says I needed to mourn intensely within my heart. So, I asked, from where does that "godly sorrow" come? Several years back, I was going through some things stored away in an old Army trunk that contained some of my earthly father's records. In the search, I found something that made me even more proud to be his son. It was a newspaper article yellowed with time, some of which read,

> He was awarded the Bronze Star medal for heroic
> action in connection with military operations

against the enemy on 25 December 1944, in Belgium. In the face of heavy artillery, mortar and small arms fire, completely disregarding his personal safety, he advanced 300 or 400 yards across open field to establish communications with the forward command post. Although wounded by enemy artillery fragments he completed his mission and aided in removing the wounded. (One communiqué stated, "wounded who were less wounded than he.") Displayed extraordinary courage and devotion to duty, reflecting credit upon himself and the military service.

My father was stationed at the theater of the fiercest and biggest battle ever fought on the face of this planet, the Battle of the Bulge. The words "completely disregarding his personal safety" jumped out at me. I had to salute him for his selfless heroism. I want to be pleasing to him as my earthly father, not wound his heart with disobedience. Now, my coach, the Holy Spirit, said, *Think about Jesus, waging war against the forces of evil throughout the universe and for all of time. Look deeper into the selfless price he paid in the battle against sin, death, and disease. How much more do you want to respect, obey, and be pleasing to your heavenly Father?*

From where does the power come? I read the apostle Paul's message to the early church, saying that the cross is the very heart of God's power for salvation (1 Cor. 1:18). What does this mean? And would the cross somehow hold the DNA necessary for me to get on the road to repentance, that is, to creatively give me a new mind and heart with which to make real-life changes? Then I learned that medical science now says that crucifixion is the most agonizing and cruel form of death ever invented by man. I heard, while on duty in Germany as backfill for Operation Joint Endeavor, one soldier tell how he suffered having 60 percent of his flesh burned off by a phosphorous grenade in Vietnam and how that was no suffering compared to what Jesus went through. He used the example of a wine press, slowly and deliberately turning to squeeze and, then, without loosening its grip, tightening up again and again. The press never lets up till all is drained out (crucifixion, like a wine press, would often crush the prisoner's bones). Then my coach reminded me that Gethsemane, which means "place of the oil press," is where Jesus agonized over his decision; he knew what was coming!

Having taught courses on stress management in the military and in community colleges, I was able to teach that medical science tells us that it is humanly possible to be under so much stress that one could sweat drops of blood (the Greek words *hematidrosis* and *agonia* are used only once in the Scriptures to describe such stress and agony). At this point in my thinking, my coach has me ponder the fact that Jesus, being also fully human as well as fully God, did exactly that—sweated drops of blood—in the garden of Gethsemane. I began to see how *deadly* serious Jesus is about wanting to help me grow and change through the Father's grace. Yes, agape love, like faith, is a decision, not a feeling.

I knelt, while on a tour in Israel, as close as possible to the rock in that garden where those drops fell. I was close enough to touch it, but I didn't feel worthy. Instead, I began rehearsing some of the major prayers prayed during the past several years. And each time I would finish a prayer, I would glance at that rock and say, "Thank you, Jesus, for the decision you made *here* so that this prayer could be answered." Later, at the Wailing Wall, I wrote on a piece of paper and placed it in one of the wall's crevices; it contained prayers for God to bring me and our whole household closer to him through his Word and into his kingdom. Decades after the divorce, I told my former wife that since St. Paul likened the husband's headship of the wife to that of Jesus and the church, I should have sweated blood, if that's what it took, to keep from being unfaithful to her. I told her that I had come to see that God's kind of love is not a feeling; it is a decision. Now, decades after being beside that rock in the garden of Gethsemane, I still hold that time as the most symbolic and significant point in getting my feet on the road to repentance. It is not the rock that moves me; it is the Word surrounding the rock. (One does not have to go to Israel for God's Word to be effective.) The Holy Spirit, like a master artist, painted a picture of Jesus in that garden, making a death-defying decision for me: I don't need a picture of him from the canvas of some other artist to see him there.

On this tour in Israel, while standing at the site of Golgotha ("place of the skull"), I could see how the rock structure does look like a skull as I listened to the guide explain the crucifixion event. A shortage of wood called for prisoners to carry a crossbeam that would be fastened to a tree. Bulky nails went into his hands; executioners twisted his body to the side as they nailed through the sides of his ankles to the tree. Twisted and, thereby, having less capacity for air, he would suffocate faster. The guide explained that people in those days were shorter than modern people are and that Jesus was probably eye level with his mother, John, the soldiers, and other bystanders as he hung suspended on the tree, slightly above ground level. So his mother could see into his eyes as he asked her to look at John and then said, "Behold your son" and, to John, "Behold your mother." It would have been easy to thrust a spear into his side. With his lungs screaming for air, the only way to open the cavity was to sit back on a plank nailed to the tree. But as soon as he did, his body weight caused pain to shoot like bullets from the nails in his hands and run throughout his body. So after a split second, he would have to push back up with his feet, where there was no air. So it went throughout the whole crucifixion process, for six hours. In the midst of that agony, the spitting, the insults, and so on, the bystanders could hear him say, "Father, forgive them, for they know not what they do."

Scripture, the guide reminded us, tells that he died in the ninth hour (three o'clock), the time normally set for killing the lamb during Jewish Passover. (I find that significant!) It was customary to break the legs of those hanging on the cross in order to speed up the suffocation process, but Scripture says that God's lamb (Jesus) would not have his bones broken (see Ex. 12:46; John 19:36). They did not break Jesus' bones because he died before the others. Why? He had been scourged during his trial. This, explained the guide, meant the Roman soldiers whipped him with a long leather-type strap with metal hooks or pieces of bone placed at intervals. He was beaten on his back and front; each time, those hooks tore out chunks of flesh. He probably almost bled to death before he got to Golgotha—beaten beyond human recognition (see Ps. 22:6 and Is. 53). Yes, I said, this explains why he fell with that heavy crossbeam on the way to Golgotha.

> As many were astonished at thee; his visage was
> so marred more than any man, and his form
> more than the sons of men. (Is. 52:14 KJV)

My Coach asked, *Can you see him stripped, bound, and scourged, with a crown of thorns forced into his skull, long square nails pounded into his palms and feet, and a spear thrust into his side, hoisted onto the cross, where his nerve centers flashed the most excruciating pain a human can experience—and, all for you, personally?"*

My Coach helped me look deeper into Matthew's, Mark's, Luke's, and John's accounts of this event. (Those words hold the power to place us there.) At the point of unfathomable agony and despair, a cry came from the cross: *"Eli, Eli, lama sabachthani?"* Jesus uttered this in Hebrew, which means, "My God, my God, why have you forsaken (original meaning: "forgotten") me?" (Matt. 27:46). This was not evidence of a lack of faith on his part; I came to see that this means that Jesus, being fully human as well as fully God, suffered every dimension of pain and agony that you or I would have on that cross. Plus, he was not only receiving into himself everything that the enemy had been allowed to do through the Roman soldiers and bystanders, he was also taking all the punishment and wrath from God the Father for all the sins of humanity, past, present, and future. And Jesus surely had seen the Father look away from him because God will not look upon sin. This "looking away" by the heavenly Father gave Jesus a severe taste of hell in the truest definition of that word: "separation from God." Furthermore, he had said earlier, "The Father and I are one" and "He who has seen me has seen the Father." Does this mean that Jesus actually felt his identity or spirit being torn in two?

> For he hath made him to be sin for us, who knew
> no sin; that we might be made the righteousness
> of God in him. (2 Cor. 5:21 KJV)

Medical science, I have found, now has a possible explanation of why Jesus died after only six hours as opposed to the usual day and a half or two. Psalm 22 states much that occurred on the cross; Jesus had spoken many of those words about himself. He spoke verse six when he said, "I am as a worm." The word *worm* used there is from the Hebrew word *Tolah*, which is the name of a worm that is round in shape like a beetle. When it is pregnant and ready to give birth, it will climb to the top of a tree. When there, its heart will explode and it gives birth. Medical science now raises the possibility that, given all that came down on Jesus in body, mind, and spirit, his heart may well have exploded while hanging at the top of his tree. Could I let what happened to his heart give birth to change my heart?

As I stood there at Golgotha in the midst of the above understanding, God had me picture myself standing in front of the cross as though I were the only one there. He then said to my heart, *You need to see that all of this is done for you as though you were the only person on this earth!* God, the Father, above all things, being a *just* God, demands that my sin be punished. "That is, that God was in Christ reconciling the world to Himself, not imputing their trespasses to them, and has committed to us the word of reconciliation" (2 Cor. 5:19a, 21 NKJV). "To the praise of the glory of his grace, wherein he hath made us accepted in the beloved" (Eph. 1:6 KJV; see also Ps. 66:18, John 9:31).

I began to see that his love reaches that far for me. Jesus endured the cross for me personally in total empathy, not sympathy. It would be tantamount to blasphemy for me to give in to the suggestions of the enemy and thereby believe that God can't forgive someone so wretched as me. This understanding is what started to move or motivate me, more than any other force, to want his will to be done in my life. Herein lies the power of God from the cross.

Can I glance at my temptation (form of a beautiful woman) and then look firmly at the cross, glance again at the temptation and turn again to see the cross, and recall that I was on his mind then and there. That "cross look," I have found, is the power to overcome; it is the way to "cast down imaginations of the heart" (2 Cor. 10:5), "crucify (my) self" (Gal. 2:20), and "put to death the deeds of the body" (Rom. 8:13). Overcoming, then, for me, came as I was enabled to start shifting my focus from the body (house) this person lived in to seeing a person in that house who needed the counsel and comfort of God's Word to give meaning, healing, and hope to her future here and in God's heaven. While this shift, initially, was a faith-decision, my feelings would catch up to what I had done on a "spirit" level. God was surely doing in me what I could not do on my own! The "cross look" is crucial! The Word is most certainly true:

> For the message of the Cross is foolishness to those who are perishing, but to us who are being saved it is the power of God. (1 Cor. 1:18 NKJV)

> But God commendeth his love toward us, in that, while we were yet sinners, Christ died for us. (Rom. 5:8 KJV)

Just like Moses repeatedly said, "Behold the mighty hand of God" in delivering the children of Israel out of Egyptian bondage and through the Red Sea, there at Golgotha God was saying to me, *Behold the mighty outstretched arms of my Son in delivering you out of bondage to sin, your Red Sea.* Think about His bodily wounds; they form the outline of a door. We are to enter heaven by the "narrow door" (Matt. 7:13–14). In one of my training runs while in Israel, I thought about Golgotha ("place of the skull"), Calvary ("cranium"), and the crown of thorns, and I thought about how my head is the first place to sweat during a run. Then it makes sense that I can be transformed (changed) by the renewing or training of my mind on what happened to Jesus then and there. From his head to my head, is there a meeting of the minds—the "mind of Christ"?

Pilate had placed a board on the cross saying, "Jesus of Nazareth, the king of the Jews." The Hebrew consonants formed the word *Yhwh*. That, this writer believes, is the reason the Jewish authorities asked Pilate to take the sign down. Because Pilate answered, "What I have written, I have written," I believe the sign reflected God's handwriting. When Moses asked God who he should say sent him to Egypt to free his people, God said to tell them that Yhwh, "I Am," had sent him. Jesus and these words hanging on the cross were saying—as he had already said when asked about his identity and origin—"Before Abraham was, *I Am*." The soldiers who had come to arrest him fell down when Jesus answered their question, "Are you the Christ?" by saying, "I Am." (I was tempted to print Colossians 1:15–23 to address the identity of Jesus in being the great "I Am," but a better idea is for you to search it out in your own Bible.) The above word, *Yhwh*, from which we take the English word Jehovah, is written from right to left in Hebrew. The letter *Y*, Hebrew Yod, means "hand"; the next letter, Hei, means "grace"; the next letter, Vav, means "nail"; and then, again, Hei is "grace." The name means, "I am who I am." Jesus on the Cross, hands outstretched with nails in them, was saying, "I am God!" (See

John 19:19–22.) The Father was saying: "Here I am, *in* Christ, reconciling all to myself."

When Jesus said from the cross, "It is finished," that was not a cry of defeat but a statement of victory. The Hebrew words used were what someone would write on a bill when it was paid in full. The original Greek word for that text reads, "It is accomplished." In Bible days, if you heard someone running through the streets shouting *"Tetelestai! Tetelestai!"* it meant their marketplace bill had been paid in full. My sin and God's forgiveness—mission impossible, accomplished!

Jesus, upon being questioned by religious leaders ready to stone a woman caught in adultery, said, "He that is without sin among you, let him first cast a stone at her" (John 8:7b KJV). After each dropped his stone and the crowd slowly dwindled, Jesus asked the woman where her accusers were. When she stated that they had left, Jesus said, "Neither do I condemn thee: go, and sin no more" (John 8:11b KJV). It's the going and sinning no more (repentance) that would give me trouble. Little did I know that one day, like her, I would be standing in the midst of a circle of officials ready to throw stones at my life and career.

Later, Mary Magdalene grew to "love much because she had been forgiven much" (see Luke 7:47). And she was delivered from the evil consequences of her sin on all three levels; level one, because her accusers dropped their stones and walked away; level two, because she began to want what Jesus had to offer in life. She then discovered the same motivating force (level three) that the apostle Paul had when he asked his fatal question:

"O unhappy and pitiable and wretched man that I am! Who will release and deliver me from (the shackles of) this body of death?"

His answer was spontaneous:

> O thank God!—He will! Through Jesus Christ, the Anointed One, our Lord! (Rom. 7:24–25a AMP)

Never lose hope, says my Coach. *The Father, who wants you to exercise self-control, will find a way to give you victory, to provide a way out of your weakness of sexual temptation.* The Greek New Testament word for *self-control* translates literally to "holding myself within myself." I need to tell my own head the truth, that Jesus has become my strength. To quote an old and well-loved children's song of worship, "I am weak, but he is strong." Even though I need to exercise self-control, God needs to initiate it in me. Like every step of a training run, I must choose to exercise that particular step in space and time. Read how Job performed this exercise (Job 31:1–12). A famous Pharaoh's assistant, named Joseph, exercised this gift from God as he literally ran from the advances of Potiphar's wife (Gen. 39:6b–12).

Modern expressions such as "self-actualization, human potential, and self-esteem, which are by-products of the New

Age "religion," have set a minefield of deception around the great commandment of love. The camouflaged falsehood lies in the teaching that to hate one's flesh (see Gal. 5:24; John 12:25) is to not love oneself. The truth lies in the teaching that, to love God in the sense of the great commandment, I must crucify the desires of the flesh, of the self. This act is, in reality, an act of love for oneself. When I am self-centered and out of control, I have the problem of *not* loving myself. "Renewing my mind" on the cross gives me the grounds for loving myself so as to kill wrong thoughts and actions. I begin to see the "person" who lives in the body, not just the "house" she lives in. My "self" is controlled; the crest of the hill looks reachable as I lean into the stride.

> Loving God means doing what he tells us to do, and really, that isn't hard at all; for every child of God can obey him, defeating sin and evil pleasure by trusting Christ to help him. But who could possibly fight and win this battle except by believing that Jesus is truly the Son of God? (1 John 5:3–5 TLB)

So I ask, "What's *on* your mind?" We can summarize the above battle plan for the mind by the following prayer:

> Dear Heavenly Father, I confess ———. Yes, it is that bad; I deserve only condemnation and death. I ask, in the name of Jesus, for your forgiveness (to cover me with the blood of Jesus; to choose to remember my sins no more; to heal

me; to erase my sin) and your deliverance from my bondage to sin with its evil consequences on all three levels—that I might find the way of escape from temptation.

You will receive my "broken and contrite heart"; therefore, I ask that you help me to have the "godly sorrow that *produces* a repentance (turning around of the mind) which leads to salvation!" Build in me the great "Shema (commandment)." Let me be like St. Paul and come to say, "It is no longer I (self-centered me) who lives, but Christ within me" and "God's strength is made perfect in my weakness."

I call for the "name that is above all names" (Jesus) to reside over my mind like a huge umbrella—making *all* my "thoughts captive to the obedience of Christ"—again making "a way of escape." Thank you that right thinking produces right speaking and right acting— (transforming me) "by the renewal of (my) mind."

Now, Father, move me deeper into level three in "the fear of the Lord" that I might not cause your heart any more pain. Thank you for reminding me that each of these requests is firmly based on the pedestal of your Word and is therefore *heard* by You. For you to hear is for you to answer (1

John 5:14–15). Thank you that forgiveness clears the runway for your hearing of my prayers! Help me always see myself standing at the cross when confronted with Satan's garbage (deceptive appeals). I know that right prayers bring right results, so I thank you for your answers even before my eyes see them. And yes, Father, it will be neither by might nor by power but "by my Spirit, says the Lord!" Amen.

Psalm 51, King David's repentant words concerning his unfaithful act with Bathsheba and the plotted murder of her husband, spoke the depth cry of my spirit, particularly in verses 3–4:

> For I admit my shameful deed—it haunts me day and night. It is against you and you alone I sinned, and did this terrible thing. You saw it all, and your sentence against me is just. (Ps. 51:3–4 TLB)

You recall Jesus telling Peter that he would deny him three times. Upon the third denial, the rooster crowed. "And the Lord turned and looked at Peter. Then Peter remembered the word of the Lord.... So Peter went out and wept bitterly" (Luke 22:61 KJV). I have felt his look! He called me to love and be the head of the "wife of my youth"; just as David expressed in Psalm 51, my adultery was a sin against him.

When I came to grips with my stabs to God's heart, that's when "godly sorrow over (my) sins began to *produce* a repentance that leads to salvation." Without that "godly sorrow," my efforts to repent evaporated like those broken New Year's resolutions. I had no appreciation for how deep the *sorrow* ("godly grief") is for the sin against him. I could do nothing to erase my sin, to pay *that* price. As I relate later in this book, we (parents and step-parents) had to counsel our children at times to pay the price for their behavior, as this would help them take ownership of their "growing edges" for maturity. But for this sin against God, there was no "paying the price." There was nothing I could do to make it right with him. The ultimate price had already been paid, and the decision to pay that price was agonizing (see Heb. 12:3–4).

Herein lies the power in godly sorrow over sin. How would it be if you went out tomorrow and robbed the local bank, got caught, were tried, and were found guilty, but just as the judge's gavel was coming down to pronounce a sentence, Joe, a friend of yours in the back of the court, raises his hand and says, "Judge, let me take his punishment for him"? The judge, then, turns to your friend and says, "Done" and punishment is delivered. What would your friend's action do to motivate you to not go out and rob any more banks? Before you answer that, the world we live in would say, "Well, if Joe is going to do that, let's just go out and rob some more banks 'cause Joe's gonna take care of it." That's what folks said to St. Paul when he described God's grace "always abounding to cover the sin." Paul answered them with the equivalent of our "Hell, no!" The best the King James scholars could find in translating the Greek and Aramaic text is "Certainly not! God forbid!" (See Rom. 5 and 6.) I found confirmation of God's plan for my repentance in the following verses:

> The goodness of God leads you to repentance. (Rom. 2:4 NKJV)

> Don't you realize how patient he is being with you? Or don't you care? Can't you see that he has been waiting all this time without punishing you, to give you time to turn from your sin? His kindness is meant to lead you to repentance. (Rom. 2:4 TLB)

> The Lord is not slack concerning his promise, as some men count slackness; but is longsuffering *to* us-ward, not willing that any should perish, but that *all* should *come to repentance*. (emphasis added; 2 Pet. 3:9 KJV)

> "Now, therefore," says the LORD, "turn to Me with all your heart, with fasting, with weeping, and with mourning." (Joel 2:12 NKJV)

> "The Lord is close to those who are of a broken heart and saves such as are crushed with sorrow for sin and are humbly and thoroughly penitent." (Ps. 34:18 AMP)

If I tell myself that I have no sin, I'm only fooling myself and refusing to accept the truth. But if I confess my sins to him, I can trust him to forgive and to cleanse me from every wrong (see 1 John 1:8–9). And it is perfectly proper for God to do this for us because Christ died to wash away our sins.

I accepted that God forgave me; but, like King David, "my sin was ever before me." The Holy Spirit, in my Bible studies on forgiveness, had gradually persuaded me to accept the Father's forgiveness to the point of taking that step, mentioned earlier, to forgive myself. Not forgiving myself would keep me in my bondage; it was a way of punishing myself, as I would continue to say, "A leopard cannot change his spots." One day I was looking, again, at that Scripture where Jesus said that if you do not forgive *others*, neither will your heavenly Father forgive you (Matt. 6:15). "Am I an 'other'?" I wondered. It was a sobering question.

Following the insurance settlement from the accident, I was at the county courthouse and hugged the lady who had been driving the Cadillac with which I had collided. I told her about the need to receive all of God's forgiveness by taking that step of forgiving herself. She thanked me. God was using the Word to wash and cleanse: "by the washing with water through the Word" (Eph. 5:26 NIV). And the "cleansing" journey came into focus. God wanted me to be as his Word says: "and to cleanse us from every wrong." His Word stated the thoroughness of the goal:

> Don't you know that a little yeast works through the whole batch of dough? Get rid of the old yeast that you may be a new batch without yeast—as you really are. (1 Cor. 5:6–7a NIV)

> Cleanse your hands, you sinners; and purify your hearts, you double-minded. Lament and mourn and weep! … Humble yourselves in the sight of the Lord, and He will lift you up. (James 4:8b–10 KJV)

I recalled the words of a song I wrote while in seminary; the seminary choir sang it for graduation exercises. It is entitled "Celebrate Christ," stemming from the words "Christ's Mass" (*mass* means "celebration")—which has been shortened to *Christmas*. The first verse I was led to write begins, "Under the cover of new-fallen snow is hiding the meaning of Christmas." One of the things my coach (God's Holy Spirit) began telling me is that, though my sins are like scarlet, the blood of Jesus washes them white as snow (see Is. 1:18, Ps. 51:7). Also, as stated earlier, one of the New Testament Greek words for *forgiveness* translates to "cover." So, for me, the real meaning of Christmas *is* hidden not only in a manger but under the cover of new-fallen snow—a very real and living parable of God's grace to me. See the Christmas cradle with the sign of the cross draped through its center.

I knew that the English-language translations of the four New Testament Greek words for *forgive* were *forget, erase, cover,* and *heal.* So, I asked myself how God could do those four things regarding my sin and the harm it had caused. The Holy Spirit reminded me of a debate that occurred during the Middle Ages in which one side tried to postulate the nonexistence of God by raising questions like, "Can God make a rock so big that he can't lift it?" When I asked myself whether God could really forget my sin, it dawned on me that I was raising the same kind of doubt as the Middle Ages debater. The answer to both questions is "Yes, if that is what he wants to do!" The Word came to me:

> I, even I, am he that blotteth out thy transgressions for mine own sake, and will not remember thy sins. (Is. 43:25 KJV)

> For I will be merciful to their unrighteousness, and their sins and their iniquities will I remember no more. (Heb. 8:12 KJV)

> He then goes on to say, "And their sins and their lawbreakings I will remember no more." (Heb. 10:17 AMP; see also Heb. 8:12)

This Word also convinced me that God could choose to "erase" my sin. Since God will not look upon sin, I needed for it to be erased from his vision of me. He could then listen to and hear my prayers with no obstruction. And, like the Hebrew people who sprinkled blood over their doorposts in Egypt so the angel of death would pass over their dwellings, Jesus became the blood covering my doorpost, my Passover.

This righteousness from God comes through faith in Jesus Christ to all who believe.… God presented him as a sacrifice of atonement, through faith in his blood. (Rom. 3:22, 25a NIV)

In him we have redemption through his blood, the forgiveness of sins, in accordance with the riches of God's grace that he lavished on us with all wisdom and understanding. (Eph. 1:7–8 NIV)

Once you were alienated from God and were enemies in your minds because of your evil behavior. But now he has reconciled you by Christ's physical body through death to present you holy in his sight, without blemish and free from accusation—if you continue in your faith, established and firm, not moved from the hope held out in the gospel. (Col. 1:21–23a NIV)

The word for *forgive* that translates into our word *heal* means that God uses forgiveness between us and him and between us and others to bring healing to our brokenness; again, one of the main words for *sin* in the Greek New Testament means "broken relationship."

The story is told of a young boy who, when he would disobey his parents, had to drive a nail into a thick piece of wood for each offense. After a few days, he would be told to go out to this plank and pull out the nails. One day he asked his father why he didn't cover up the nail holes, and his father replied that it was so he could see and remember where he had done wrong by the marks that had been left. God's Holy Spirit will allow, or perhaps help, me to bring it to my remembrance when I need to see the great gulf between what I deserve and where his grace has placed me. "Remember...from whence thou art fallen, repent." (Rev. 2: 5 KJV) Whether someone is a president, pastor, or policeman, the road to repentance is a journey of the heart. I needed to run in his grace, to let the power of the cross move my heart on the road to repentance, with mind and heart set like flint to the goal of overcoming.

> Blessed is the man that endureth temptation: for when he is tried, he shall receive the crown of life, which the Lord hath promised to them that love him. (James 1:12 KJV)

The apostle Paul put it this way:

> Therefore I always exercise and discipline myself (mortifying my body, deadening my carnal affections, bodily appetites, and worldly desires, endeavoring in all respects) to have a clear (unshaken, blameless) conscience, void of offense toward God and toward men. (Acts 24:16 AMP)

The key word in that Scripture about godly sorrow (2 Cor. 7:10), to which God's Spirit had drawn me, is the word *produce.* Yes, godly sorrow over my sins would produce a repentance that leads to salvation. True repentance, therefore, is God's work *performed* in me by the "cross-look," not any successful "Spartan" efforts on my part. God's Holy Spirit would keep pointing me to the cross. It was way past time to stop associating any of my running regimens with somehow trying to lay an atonement burden back on myself. My issue of control would only be resolved through what the Holy Spirit showed me, through the Word, about the cross.

> Not by might, nor by power, but by my spirit, saith the Lord of hosts. (Zech. 4:6 KJV)

> For if you live according to the sinful nature, you will die; but if by the Spirit you put to death the misdeeds of the body, you will live. (Rom. 8:13 NIV; see also Gal. 6:7–9)

> David wrote, "In the day when I called, You answered me, and strengthened me with strength (might and inflexibility) (to temptation) in my inner self." (Ps. 138:3 AMP)

God's Holy Spirit had used the Scriptures to bring not only conviction of my sin but also conviction of his forgiveness. Again, my study of the four gospel accounts of the passion of Jesus placed me there, making it real and convicting me that this was for me—personally! I began to realize that the only opinion I needed to be concerned about was God's. During those years that I was the "talk of the town," I, because I am possibly part Cherokee, projected the old Cherokee prayer to those who continued to judge, saying, "Dear Father, do not let me criticize my brother 'til I have walked at least two moons in his moccasins." I would also remind myself that often we judge because of what I call the "seesaw effect": the only way to feel up is to put someone else down. There were times, however, that my only escape appeared to be walking into the local small-town gas station where gossips gathered like flies on a donkey and engage in a knock-down-drag-out. But, again, my coach convinced me that there was one, and only one, opinion with which I had to be concerned (see 1 Cor. 4:3–5 and Rom. 2:16). Retaining such an internal, emotional posture about the town gossip, for me, required singing Flip Wilson lyrics: "Here come de judge, here come de judge. Ev'rbody rise 'cause here come de judge." The Holy Spirit, as the one who convicts of truth (John 16 8), and Jesus, as the judge, are the only ones who can judge a person being judged and the person doing the judging without wounding either. However, I found it hard to resist quoting an old folk saying: "A reputation once broken may possibly be repaired, but the world will always keep their eyes on the spot where the crack was."

I started praying for those whom I sensed were still judging me so that they would not find themselves "being judged." It is meaningful to me to see Jesus, in his resurrection appearance, redeem Peter by asking him *three* times if Peter loved him—matching Peter's three denials. Notice the strength and conviction in Saint Peter's words to the New Testament church after Christ had placed him "back in the saddle" as a "circuit rider" of the Word, asking him to "feed my sheep":

> And Peter answered them, "Repent (change your views, and purpose to accept the will of God in your inner selves instead of rejecting it) and be baptized, every one of you, in the name of Jesus Christ for the forgiveness of and release from your sins; and you shall receive the gift of the Holy Spirit." (Acts 2:38 AMP)

Paul summed it up:

> For we do not have a High Priest Who is unable to understand and sympathize and have a fellow feeling with our weaknesses and infirmities and liability to the assaults of temptation, but One Who has been tempted in every respect as we are, yet without sinning. Let us then, fearlessly and confidently and boldly draw near to the throne of grace—the throne of God's unmerited favor (to us sinners); that we may receive mercy (for our failures) and find grace to help in good time for every need—appropriate help and well-timed help, coming just when we need it. (Heb. 4:15–16 AMP)

I identified strongly with Peter. My sin of adultery was tantamount to denial of Jesus; it took "boldness" on my part to ask for repeated forgiveness of repeated sin! I have prayed often for God to help me be a "man after God's own heart," like King David, despite his sins of adultery and murder. See, baths were taken on the roofs of houses back in Old Testament days, and as David stood watching from his palace, Bathsheba took her bath. He arranged the murder of her husband by telling the troops to pull back in the heat of the battle (see 2 Sam. 11:1–27), leaving Uriah exposed so that he would be killed—leaving Bathsheba for himself. At that wicked moment, did God see a future David and know that one day he could say about him, "I have found David son of Jesse a man after my own heart; he will do everything I want him to do" (Acts 13:22 NIV)?

Did God—"understanding and sympathizing with my weaknesses" (Heb. 4:15)—look at me in the years leading up to my accident and see that I would one day be a man after his own heart? I have prayed for this through the years. My Coach once again brought up the following Scripture as an interpretation and confirmation of his grace's ability to make me "innocent" and, yes, be a "man after (his) own heart":

> Because he hath set his love upon me, therefore will I deliver him: I will set him on high, because he hath known my name.
>
> He shall call upon me, and I will answer him: I will be with him in trouble; I will deliver him, and honour him.

With long life will I satisfy him, and shew him
my salvation. (Ps. 91:14–16 KJV)

Someone once wrote, "He is no fool who gives up what he
cannot keep to gain what he cannot lose."

> For it was through reading the Scripture that
> I came to realize that I could never find God's
> favor by trying—and failing—to obey the laws. I
> came to realize that acceptance with God comes
> by believing in Christ. I have been crucified
> with Christ: and I myself no longer live, but
> Christ lives in me. And the real life I now have
> within this body is a result of my trusting in the
> Son of God, who loved me and gave himself for
> me. (Gal. 2:19–20 TLB)

Jesus, while on the cross, asked the Father to forgive those
who were tormenting him "for they know not what they do."
But you will see in this book that I knew what I was doing.
I realized that I was not only to continue with his training
program that outlines the "crucifixion of (my) self" so that
"it is no longer I who live but Christ Who lives within me,"
but also, in the practice of truth therapy, I am to tell myself
the truth, which sets me free. For example, I am to remind
myself of what Satan's deceptions and devices have gotten me
in the past—and what they could get me in the future—and
recall the victories crowned through God's Word. I need to
give Satan no more ground on which to stand against me.

No one serving as a soldier gets involved in civilian affairs—he wants to please his commanding officer. Similarly, if anyone competes as an athlete, he does not receive the victor's crown unless he competes according to the rules. (2 Tim. 2:4–5 NIV)

Anytime I would slack off or break my physical training program, it took a major effort and additional time to get back on course. This is equally true of my spiritual training program to exercise my mind and heart on his Word. Again, for me to adopt the Flip Wilson joke "The devil made me do it" would be to deny the reality of my deceitful heart and the fact that I indeed do need to "make (my) thoughts captive to the obedience of Christ" (2 Cor. 10:5 KJV). The "enemy" tempted, but I creatively cooperated in a big way. I cannot entertain the deceptions (temptations) offered to my mind by the enemy for even a quick moment. I get out of shape faster there, in my spiritual training, than I do from any slack-off in physical training. God wants me to consistently train in order to be in shape for trials and tests—those occasions that trigger daydreams of seduction. The "crucifixion" of my "self-will" is a daily process, successfully done only with the power of Christ, God's Word, living within me (see Rom. 6:3–11). The unsaved do not have this help. Indeed, it *can* be said that the devil made them do it, as they are slaves of this world. Herein lies the difference between a Christian and a *Christ*ian. The latter has Jesus as Lord, or King, of his or her life. The former has a "form of godliness but denying the power therein" (see 2 Tim. 2:4). Sometimes I would tell soldiers, "I wouldn't give you a plug nickel for being religious, but I'd give you a whole lot for wanting a heart close to God's heart." I asked my coach to help me avoid breaking training. I knew that I must run with the goal always in mind. If I didn't, I would find a reason to slack off. As I dreamed of Boston, I needed to also maintain the vision of winning the mental and spiritual marathons.

> You were running a good race. Who cut in on
> you and kept you from obeying the truth? (Gal.
> 5:7 NIV)

My training then stepped into the same arena in which Jesus was led when tempted in the desert. Hungry from forty days without food, alone, and—being fully human as well as fully God—perhaps wondering about his mission, the enemy tempted him at every point of his "weakness." As from the time of the garden of Eden to the present day, Satan's tactic is to camouflage falsehood with truth. With Jesus, he did it by quoting Scripture, but Jesus met this sword with his own sword of the Word. Those swords clashed more dramatically than *Star Wars* could ever depict. Could I let Jesus be the Word of truth living in me, hanging like panoply over my mind, the ultimate power enabling me to "cast down the imaginations of the heart" or the feelings lodged in my right brain that constantly tried to gain control? The enemy's sword strikes me, saying, "Look at that woman's beautiful figure. Wonder what it would be like …?" The sword of the Word clashes, saying:

Keep your eyes on Jesus, our leader and instructor. He was willing to die a shameful death on the cross because of the joy he knew would be his afterwards; and now he sits in the place of honor by the throne of God. If you want to keep from becoming fainthearted and weary, think about his patience as sinful men did such terrible things to him. After all, you have never yet struggled against sin and temptation until you sweat great drops of blood. (Heb. 12:2–3 TLB)

Despite my past sins of lust and adultery, God now enables me to see the *person*, not just the body. The pervasive question in my mind is, "How can I see the *spirit* who has a *mind* and lives in a *body*?" More powerfully than this, God's Spirit coaches me to "run" from the bondage of sin as he continually helps me see myself at the foot of Jesus' cross. The hymn "Were You There?" takes on new meaning with such an image. As I look upon that scene and ask myself how people could do such a thing to Jesus, my coach points out a horrible picture—a picture of me, standing there with a hammer in my hand. Could I stand there and continue on with an unrepentant mind, entertaining the lusts of the heart? It is then that I understand that Jesus, being fully God, cast his eyes into the past, present, and future while on the cross. He saw me and my sin of adultery two thousand years ahead of time, and I was on his mind as he hung there. Again, in the face of every temptation, can I turn and take that long, cold stare at the cross and see that it was personal and for me, glance back at the temptation, and then look still deeper at what he suffered for me? Here, again, is where the power for true repentance comes in. Apart from that look, all efforts to repent fail. Again, could this be the reason Paul told the early church that the "cross is foolishness to those who are perishing, but to those who are being saved it is the power of God." Paul was the intellectual of his day and could debate any subject far beyond his contemporaries' capabilities, but he is the man who said, "For I determined not to know any thing among you, save Jesus Christ, and him crucified" (1 Cor. 2:2 KJV).

I identify with the thief on the cross who looked at Jesus and saw an innocent man taking on the sins of the world, acknowledged his own guilt, and asked to be saved (see Luke 23:39–43). We relate to what we "see." What's on your mind?

> For the preaching of the cross is to them that perish foolishness; but unto us which are saved it is the power of God. (1 Cor. 1:18 KJV)

> It was through what his Son did that God cleared a path for everything to come to him— all things in heaven and on earth—for Christ's death on the cross has made peace with God for all by his blood. This includes you who were once so far away from God. You were his enemies and hated him and were separated from him by your evil thoughts and actions, yet now he has brought you back as his friends. He

has done this through the death on the cross of his own human body, and now as a result Christ has brought you into the very presence of God, and you are standing there before him with nothing left against you—nothing left that he could even chide you for; the only condition is that you fully believe the Truth, standing in it steadfast and firm, strong in the Lord, convinced of the Good News that Jesus died for you, and never shifting from trusting him to save you. (Col. 1:20–23a TLB)

The cross becomes the platform for what it means to be "born again"—that is, to have God's Word conceived in my heart, giving me a personal, trusting relationship with Jesus Christ as Lord and Savior. Note how the Word clearly tells that it is the Spirit who "baptizes" us with the Word and who, in turn, becomes born in us.

Jesus replied, "With all the earnestness I possess I tell you this: Unless you are born again, you can never get into the Kingdom of God.... Men can only reproduce human life, but the Holy Spirit gives new life from heaven; so don't be surprised at my statement that you must be born again! Just as you can hear the wind but can't tell where it comes from or where it will go next, so it is with the Spirit. We do not know on whom he will next bestow this life from heaven." (John 3:3, 6–8 TLB)

The Spirit gives life; the flesh counts for nothing. The words I have spoken to you are spirit and they are life.... He went on to say, "This is why I told you that no one can come to me unless the Father has enabled him." (John 6:63, 65 NIV)

For you have been born again, not of perishable seed, but of imperishable, through the living and enduring word of God. (1 Peter 1:23 NIV)

God is *always* as good as his Word, and he watches over his Word to see what it will perform in my heart. When I pray, therefore, is God watching to see if I will exercise the faith of obedience so as to answer my prayer "according to my faith"? The only way I can avoid hearing Jesus, as my judge, say to me, "Depart from me; I never knew you" (Matt. 7:21–23), is to have the Word living (Heb. 4:12) and abiding (John 15:7) in me. That gives him a picture of my heart being moved by him. Because he himself is the Word, if he sees that the Word has made a mark on my heart—producing changes—then he can say, "I know you." Like the apostle Paul, I need to "press on to the mark" (Phil. 3:14). Assurance of salvation, from where does it come? (See Training Regimen #3.)

And because of what Christ did, all you others too who heard the Good News about how to be saved, and trusted Christ, were marked as belonging to Christ by the Holy Spirit, who long ago had been promised to all of us Christians. His presence within us is God's guarantee that he really will give us all that he promised; and the Spirit's seal upon us means that God has already purchased us and that he guarantees to bring us to himself. This is just one more reason for us to praise our glorious God. (Eph. 1:13–14 TLB)

These things have I written unto you that believe on the name of the Son of God; that ye may know that ye have eternal life, and that ye may believe on the name of the Son of God. (1 John 5:13 KJV)

Jesus' answer regarding who can be saved was, "What is impossible with men is possible with God." The King James note to this says, "Jesus answered this question by explaining that the change of heart one must experience in order to know God is possible only through him. Any person who enters the kingdom does so only by the marvelous grace of God" (see Luke 18:26–27; see also 1 Peter 1:1–9, especially verse 4; John 17:11–12; Ps. 37:28; John 10:1–18; 2 Peter 1:3–4, 2:5, 2:9; Lamentations 3:21–24; Ps. 130).

The new birth is a must if I want to be in his kingdom. At the judgment, it will do me absolutely no good to say, "Well, I preached some good sermons, helped people with effective counseling, received some high recognition, and wrote a book about what you did in my life." The thief on the cross did not get baptized, go through confirmation, attend church every Sunday, receive merit badges for good deeds, or hold any ecclesiastical office, yet he was born again through acknowledging his sin and stating that Jesus has a kingdom and, thereby, is Lord. Jesus said to him, "Today shalt thou be with me in paradise" (Luke 23:43 KJV).

This promise was given to him because of his penitent heart, evident in his admitting his guilt and asking to be saved. With "godly sorrow" in his heart, he turned directly to Jesus on the cross. God says he is "no respecter of persons" (see Acts 10:34). Therefore, it is fair to say that he respects Abraham, King David, and St. Paul no more than you or me. However, it is also fair and true to say that he is respectful of Abraham's "faith," King David's "broken and contrite heart," and St. Paul's "godly sorrow"! Again, he looks on the heart (1 Chron. 28:9; Jer. 17:10).

My enemy doesn't care if I hear or preach sermons or if I am baptized or confirmed. Religion does not deter him in his effort to keep me in bondage to my sin. But he has to let me go each and every time I turn to the cross and let it determine my motives (see Is. 64:6 and Rom. 8:1). My mother bore me in pain. She would have died, if necessary, to allow me to arrive. For me, it was simple—no suffering. The same is true of my new birth and the suffering Jesus endured to bear me.

So there was a "way back home." The road signs became clear.

First, "delight yourself in the Lord and he will give you the desires of your heart" (Ps. 37:4 NIV). How do I do this? The

Holy Spirit continually coached me to be hungry for what God's Word would say to me about any kind of temptation to move away from his best. When I would take my Bible in hand—with the aid of its concordance—and read, meditate, and sometimes memorize, a Word would "stand up" and speak deeply within me (to my spirit). I then found myself delighting in him with both mind and heart. This is what began changing me from lusting after a woman to desiring God's best for the one before my eyes. My heavenly Father told me that he does not want me to deny or repress my passion. Desire is what he placed in motion to bring me to himself. "Whom have I in heaven but you? And I desire no one on earth as much as you!" (Ps. 73:25 TLB). For me, to desire God is to worship him, to behold the passion that brought his Son to the cross. When I consider my sin—willingness to "settle for less"—in the face of what God had been trying to offer me, "it would seem that our Lord finds our desires not too strong, but too weak," as C. S. Lewis put it in *The Weight of Glory*. "We are half-hearted creatures, fooling around with drink and sex and ambition when infinite joy is offered us, like an ignorant child who wants to go on making mud pies in a slum because he cannot imagine what is meant by the offer of a holiday at the sea. We are far too easily pleased" (pp. 1–2). And, as for the goal, here is what he says: "But as it is written, eye hath not seen, nor ear heard, neither have entered into the heart of man, the things which God hath prepared for them that love him" (1 Cor. 2:9 KJV).

Second, do not follow my example of making my own efforts at control through sexual pleasure for it is nothing more than the dark side of desire. My heart was restless because I had not found my rest in God. Am I to be more passionately moved by an affair or sexual fantasy than by Jesus' suffering so that I might live? Again, as King David said, God's Word hidden in my heart is what empowers me to overcome any form of rebellion against God's will. For me, the most powerful part was and is the Word telling and showing me the cross. There is no substitute for having a power that will mold, mentor, and move my heart.

Third, turn to the right and ask God to redirect my desires (see Phil. 2:13). As with every substance that can be abused, sex can become a god that needs to be cast down. Satan had been killing, not building, my passion. My repentance and broken and contrite heart actually marked the renewal of passion. Saying no to the dark side of desire becomes a pleasure as I remember the growing intimacy of God's presence and the vast power of his grace to motivate me into his will. "The Lord is near to those who have a broken heart, and saves such as have a contrite spirit" (Ps. 34:18 KJV). Again, my "spirit" is that *person* who has a mind and lives in a body. It is the "me" who knows when God is speaking a Word to me and my life condition.

The word *help* (see Ps. 33:20, 46:1, 121:1, 124:8; Heb. 4:16) takes center stage in a good prayer my coach has formed in me:

> Dear Father, *help* me to get increasingly in really
> good shape in my spirit and mind so that I

won't have to train or learn the hard way. *Help me, therefore, not to grieve your heart or ever cheapen your grace through deliberate sins. Help me to continually grow and change*—like King David who moved from adultery and murder to the composition of Psalm 51, like Saul of Tarsus who became the apostle Paul, like St. Peter who grew from denial of Jesus to bold proclamation of him—by an act of repentance performed in me by Christ living in me.

(For the reader who desires or needs to journey further into the "battle-for-the-mind-mission," train, step by step, on the following Scriptures: 1 Tim. 1:12–17; 1 John 3:4–24; Rom. 5:6–21; Is. 30:15; Rom. 4:1–25; Rom. 7:11–25; Rom. 8:1–2, 13; Ps. 42:11; John 15:16; 2 Cor. 5:17; 2 Cor. 10:5; 2 Cor. 7:10).

The year following the removal of my call and the venture of knocking on 147 job inquiry doors, Connie and I joined hands one night in prayer and asked God to somehow intervene in that "job marathon." After we finished praying, she looked at me and said, "I believe the job God has in mind for you will come knocking on your door." Her poise and posture made it seem that she knew something.

I held on to Scriptures addressing my need for a theological endorsing agency to continue as an Army chaplain. One in particular says, "Let us then, fearlessly and confidently and boldly, draw near to the throne of grace—the throne of God's unmerited favor (to us sinners); that we may receive mercy (for our failures) and find grace to help (in good time for every need—appropriate help and well-timed help, coming just when we need it) (Heb. 4:16 AMP).

A fellow Army Reserve chaplain told me during a weekend drill that I should talk to Independent Baptists. One of their churches was within sight of our house on the hill. I was interviewed by a panel of three Independent Baptist pastors concerning a call to ministry. Following the interview, in which questions of faith and honest confession were the topics, they agreed to issue the call with the understanding that it was not to be a pastor but to continue as an Army chaplain. God's grace works through their hands, and I awaited endorsement of their call. Full Gospel Chaplaincy Fellowship International endorsed the request as an official call to ministry, which then needed to be made a matter of record at the Pentagon. A retired artillery commander who used to work at the Pentagon made the "knock" on this ominous-looking door, a knock that thundered through the halls. He proved to be an instrument of God's provision. As Ray and I drove to Washington, DC, we talked much of God's grace. I "boldly drew near" to that throne.

While there, I was interviewed again, and the discussion centered on confessional honesty, repentance, and the call to serve. The *following* day, I received a telephone call from the Chief of Army Reserve Affairs, asking me to take sequential tours of duty as post chaplain for Fort Indiantown Gap,

Pennsylvania—a most "timely help," coming just when I needed it (Heb. 4:16)!

The greatest "mover" now of my human will is God's Grace. Once I thoroughly viewed the disgusting condition of my human nature, I was able to recognize the great gulf between that nature and where his grace had rescued me. He made a way where there was no way, according to the Pentagon, the church body, and the military chaplaincy chain-of-command.

God's grace birthed this endorsement! I now see the wisdom of giving God thanks for "closed doors" and what appear to be unanswered prayers—there are none, in fact, as even "no" or "not yet" is an answer. I came to realize God's protective and wise hand in closing certain doors that I tried to open. Connie will sometimes see a young deer and want to coax it to just lie down and be still so that it won't run away from her and into the sights of hunters. We, like that deer, need wisdom to "be still and know that (God is) God" (Ps. 46:10). She had the words "In his time" engraved in my wedding ring. She knew I counted on God's answering prayer in his time (Ecc. 3:11; Heb. 4:16). I find myself, sometimes, touching that ring as I pray.

God's "redeeming will" continued to fashion a "wounded healer." For example, when working with soldiers and families at Ft. Bragg, Ft. Jackson, Ft. Dix, and Ft. Indiantown Gap on matters of communication, stress, and faithfulness, God sometimes used my repentance journey, from conviction to forgiveness to overcoming, as a "wounded healer" vehicle (see 2 Cor. 1:3–7, 1 Cor. 10:11). It helped open up their ears to listen on a deeper level, to see how that journey might proceed and to hear it from someone who has been there. When clients displayed addictive behaviors, I could tell them how the cross moved me to make changes. When they had brokenness in relationships, I could show them how I did what the Scriptures say about praying for and seeing the other person differently and the healing that brought to my family. When a client had circumstantial challenges, again I could give testimony of how God's Word made the impossible possible through a faith-decision I had made to trust his Word over feelings and circumstances. When stressed out, I would give them "the praise prescription."

Why Praise

In addition to the fact that God deserves our praise as creator and redeemer, he has also placed a powerful reciprocal blessing on us as we give him praise! Just like reading a good conversational book can make me feel like I know the author, reading God's book (the Holy Scriptures) brings me closer to him. What I keep learning and relearning is the wisdom of making the "sacrifice of praise." For this author, it's like the "treasure hidden in the field" (Matt. 13:44)—so great, said Jesus, that the one who stumbled over it went out and sold everything he had and bought that field. What is the substance of that treasure? It is this: by getting smack-dab in the middle of my stress and concerns, where they make no sense, and giving God that gritted-teeth and/or tearful thanks, my trust level is raised, giving God room to go to work. The rest becomes good history.

I have been learning the hard way that this sacrifice is both good psychology and good theology. Through *ex*pression, it keeps the evolving cycle of *sup*pression, *re*pression, and *de*pression from attacking the emotional system, not to mention the body's natural immune system for good physiological health, as well. To Israel, God said he would "appoint unto them ... the garment of praise for the spirit of heaviness" (Is. 61:3).

Some comparative studies in my doctoral research in wholistic health care revealed stunning results in both nutrition and heart-related illnesses. Research in the former showed that it is not so much a matter of what you eat that makes you sick or well but what's "eating you." I venture to say that a similar study could be conducted regarding the practice of praise as it addresses depression, pain management, and stress management. My coach conducted such tests with me when I had a herniated disc that produced so much pain that three medications did not phase it. But each and every time, I would take his "praise prescription" and say with eyes watering, "Thank you for allowing this pain to be exactly like it is, and thank you for what you can do with it," that's when the pain would shift to the back burner, moving from a level 7 to a level 3. Yes, his Word is "medicine to all our flesh" (Prov. 4:22).

There is an old saying that says, "If someone has a hammer, they think the world is made out of nails." I have yet to see a stress concern that the hammer of praise does not hit squarely on the head. No soldier or civilian has ever come back to say, "Chaplain, this praise stuff doesn't work. Nothing happened." At some point, I became so ingrained in this "prescription" that, when one soldier happened to mention that some of his stress related to the time his wife threw a bowl of grits at him, without thinking, my immediate response was, "Give some gritted-teeth thanks." Through the years, I have repeatedly, following counseling with soldiers about stress concerns, been led to simply hand them a one-page sheet with the key praise Scriptures printed out for them and then counsel them to wrestle and pray their own way through (see Training Regimen #4.) Then, when they are led to take up the gauntlet of praise, they know it is real, not just some chaplain saying they should do it.

I served as mobilization and demobilization chaplain, counseling soldiers and their families, during Desert Shield and Desert Storm. From the outset, I was mobilized to counsel 140 soldiers at Ft. Bragg who were experiencing certain stressors (marriage, family, career, the mission, the unknown—sometimes all of these at once). Initially, I gave them counsel that love is a decision they can make, overruling feelings, in their marriages and family relationships. I, sometimes, would tell them how Jesus proved, while praying in the garden of Gethsemane, that God's kind of love is a decision and that Jesus gave us a new commandment to love as he has loved. For the duration of the Gulf War and through the eventual stress of reunion, those soldiers and hundreds more—especially those addressing PTSD—received the spiritual prescription for the *"practice* of praise." The reason I have been led to coach soldiers to do the practice of praise—that is, to thank God for allowing things to be as they are and then thank him for what he can do with it—lies in the fact that we do not naturally think to do it. For example, I might counsel a soldier to say, "Thank you for allowing my wife's disposition toward me to be exactly as it is" and then go one step further—"Thank you for being able to do far more about the way she is seeing me than I can even ask or think, and thank you for helping me make changes that you know need to be made." I have to learn and relearn all the time to take my own medicine. Also, ingrained into the *sacrifice* of praise theology is the premise that God is not calling us to find a reason to give him thanks; it is a faith step, sometimes over and against logic and feelings.

Furthermore, I coached them to put on the back burner the possibility that the enemy may hit harder as they begin to wage warfare with praise. Why? Satan flees the praises offered to the Father. Satan was in charge of praise when he was still in the kingdom. He cannot stand it; it is his sore spot. Therefore, when we offer up praises to the Father—especially when those praises are for the garbage Satan has been "allowed" to deliver into our lives, which God can wonderfully redeem into the stem of the rose—Satan is compelled to retreat. Scripture does tell us that God "inhabits" or lives in the praises of his people, so we have Satan running away and God moving in. I advised the soldiers that *if* things got worse following their entrance into the "practice of praise," they should give even more thanks because the right force will be upset. It's a good battle strategy because Satan eventually gets the message that we are not going to lay down this heavy artillery weapon, and he leaves us alone. It is spiritual warfare of powerful and intense magnitude!

> Therefore put on the full armor of God, so that when the day of evil comes, you may be able to stand your ground, and after you have done everything, to stand. Stand firm then, with the belt of truth buckled around your waist. (Eph. 6:13–14a NIV)

One dramatic moment of spiritual warfare, the nature of which has never been witnessed before by this writer, occurred one year later at Ft. Jackson during a subsequent tour-of-duty. Drill sergeants began coming up to me from one particular battalion. They said something had to be done! They were shaken; and Drill Sergeants don't get shaken. In one of the Star Ship classroom/billeting areas, strange things were happening:

1. Many of the soldiers had cold chill sensations as they would walk past certain areas.

2. One soldier was hoisted out of his bunk bed in the middle of the night, when no one was awake.

3. Some would see the light turned on underneath the door to a storage room, which was locked.

4. Another was awakened in the middle of the night only to see a cross, upside down and in red, on the same door.

5. In front of a urinal in one of the men's restrooms, a dark spot formed and grew larger; no amount of scrubbing helped.

6. The soldiers were out of sorts with one another to an abnormal pitch.

Instinctively, I requested that the troops gather in the large bay area of the Star Ship. Immediately, I asked them to join hands and sing with me some praise songs, one being "Jesus, Name Above All Names." After singing for a while, I talked to the troops about that name, Jesus, being a power or force above all other powers or forces and then asked them to place that name in the chilled areas they would pass and also to sing songs of praise. Also, I went into the restroom and stood on the spot in front of the urinal. I gave God thanks and placed the Name over that spot.

Two days later, the Drill Sergeants started coming up to me and saying: "Chaplain, you won't believe what's happening." They said:

1. The chill places are gone. No one feels them anymore.

2. The soldier who was shoved out of his bunk from underneath could finally relax and rest at night.

3. Lights did not come on anymore in the storage room.

4. The soldier who saw an upside-down red cross on the storage door was awakened once again only to see a lighted, right-side-up cross on the same door.

5. The spot in front of the urinal was fading away.

6. A new spirit of communication and order moved among the troops.

When a dog starts chasing me while I'm running, I stop, turn toward him, and sometimes run at him. Instinctively, I act on a tip from my daddy; he said for me to turn directly toward pursuing dogs and make good eye contact with them. Once, some large Dobermans broke loose from a chain and ran after me. When I stopped and ran toward them, they retreated. God's Word frequently tells us that Satan runs when we resist him (see James 4:7–8). The practice of praise, I would tell soldiers during Desert Shield, Desert Storm, and Operation Joint Endeavor, is like the "Truman Decision" to use the bomb; it not only wins the battle, it ends the war.

Debates over the origin of evil have gone on throughout history, perhaps the most noted one being between St. Augustine and Pelagius in the fourth century. In this debate, Pelagius tried to cite God as the origin of evil if, in fact, God had made *everything*. Augustine argued back that, no, God had made everything true to his nature—free—and that this meant man was free to obey or rebel. Pelagius came back with the view that God, then, had created the *potential* for evil in providing such freedom, and Augustine countered by stating that God had not created a potential for evil but rather a plan to redeem and allow individuals, with their fallen nature, to freely choose to come back to him. And this plan involved Jesus and a cross. Hence, we see God not only as all powerful and all just but also as all loving. His justice becomes his love, and vice versa. Of all the "gods" of history, only the God of the Old and New Testament Bible gives his life for his creation. Again, "that is, that God was in Christ reconciling the world to Himself, not imputing their trespasses to them, and has committed to us the word of reconciliation" (2 Cor. 5:19a NKJV).

Satan reviews our lives and "walks about like a roaring lion, seeking whom he may devour" (1 Peter 5:8 NKJV). The fact that Satan will actually ask others to do his own works of evil was illustrated when Jesus told Peter that Satan had requested to "sift him like wheat" (Luke 22:32). His boastfulness and request to use calamity to turn Job's allegiance away from God is also a case in point. God is in the business of redeeming and completely turning around the evil and bad things that Satan generates. Is it not interesting that the crowds asked

Jesus about the man who was born blind, saying, "Rabbi, who sinned, this man or his parents, that he was born blind?" (John 9:2 NIV). Jesus answered, "Neither this man nor his parents sinned, but that the works of God should be revealed in him." (John 9:3 NKJV).

Why did God allow Satan to do so much to Job? Regarding the practice of praise, do you recall the words of Job after he had lost and suffered so much that not even his friends could console him and his wife had finally told him to just curse God and die? He said, "Though He slay me, yet will I wait for (trust, hope) in Him" (see Job 13:15). "The Lord gave, and the Lord hath taken away; blessed be the name of the Lord" (Job 1:21 KJV). God honored that posture of praise and trust with his peace and the seven-fold restoration of everything Job had lost in every category of his loss and suffering.

> From the lips of children and infants you have
> ordained praise because of your enemies, to
> silence the foe and the avenger. (Ps. 8:2 NIV)

Practicing such praise builds trust and faith, giving God room to act. There is, therefore, a vital link between giving God thanks in *all* things, the exercise of faith, and God's activity. Why else would Jesus sometimes say, "Be it done unto you according to your faith," "Your faith has made you well," or "Your faith has made you whole" (see Matt. 9:29; Mark 10:52; Matt. 15:31)?

The "sacrifice of praise" is not a psychological gimmick such as the "power of positive thinking;" neither is it a leverage pole to somehow pry God's hand into action. It is a *trusting relationship*. Read with the "eye of a trainee"—hungry for a Word that endures to the end—these three Scriptures that I handed to soldiers over the past two decades. See if they lead you to give God a "sacrifice of praise" in relation to your life circumstances, watching to see if this spiritual exercise begins to condition you into a deeper trust walk with God— giving him room to act in your life. (See Appendix: Training Regimen #4.)

The Marathons and the Word about Praise

What about all those other "marathons"? I had managed to give "gritted-teeth thanks" for the accident, my bodily and mental condition, and the prognosis about running and the completion of my doctoral program. I then gave tearful thanks when driving home from the divorce court, more gritted-teeth thanks when we lost the house, both gritted-teeth and tearful thanks when I had to part with my children due to living conditions and job circumstances, gritted-teeth and tearful thanks when the ministry and I parted ways, and gritted-teeth thanks in almost becoming bankrupt. In each and every category of stress (a score on the Holmes and Rahe Stress Scale would have shown me to be "going off the deep end"), I lifted up a sacrifice of praise.

Again, this sacrifice of praise was not in any way my attempt to make God the author of evil. Satan came to steal, kill, and destroy. My perennial question and expectant hope centered on what God would do to "work all things together toward good" (Rom. 8:28). How could he bring something good out of so much bad?

> Now unto him that is able to do exceeding abundantly above all that we ask or think, according to the power that worketh in us. (Eph. 3:20 KJV)

God's Response

Again, the Bible shows us that Satan runs from the praises offered to the heavenly Father and that God actually inhabits (lives in) our praises (see Ps. 22:3). This unveiling was like walking into a dark room and flipping on the light switch. Darkness and light cannot exist in the same place. I discovered that God initially honors the sacrifice of praise by granting peace of mind.

In *every* situation, God rewarded this practice of praise by providing what the Bible calls "the peace of God that passes all understanding" (Phil. 4:7)—a peace of mind amid the storm, very much like the eye of a hurricane. During the initial years following my exercise on praise, people in the community would approach me at a store, the bank, post office, or wherever they happened to see me and say, "I know you have had (this, that, and the other) happen to you, but you seem to be so much at peace. How can this be?" When I looked them in the eye and answered, "Because I'm giving thanks," they would do double takes, providing me the opportunity to talk about the sacrifice of praise—the faith-decision step outlined in the three Scriptures (1 Thess. 5:18; Eph. 5:20; Heb. 13:15) on which our head coach was training me.

One summer, when pulling weeds in the garden and greenhouse, I found myself trying to find faster and faster ways of pulling. It proved an exercise in building stress. God did something different with me; he said, "Stop! Give me thanks for each and every weed as you pull it, and say it slowly as though you mean it." So I forced my fingers and mind to slow down. As I carefully and meticulously pulled each individual weed, I said, "Thank you, Father. Thank you, Jesus. Thank you, Holy Spirit." After a while, I started to enjoy pulling those weeds, and the work got done with my mind and shoulders not tight or stressed. Had he just given me a parable?

I had worked with a therapist in outpatient status because of the mammoth amount of stress incurred in those early years after the accident. At the end of that work, the therapist looked at me rather strangely and said, "Given the stress load you've had, you should be hospitalized, under heavy medication, or both, but, here I am ready to release you. You must be doing something right with your religion." He doesn't know how close he was to the truth! Shortly after a sacrifice of praise concerning college costs for three of the children, my former wife informed me that the college where she was working had a policy that, after an employee has accumulated six years of continuous employment, it will pay 90 percent of the tuition for each child in the family, no matter what college they attend. It eased the financial burden on me for my children's education. This was a godsend in the truest sense of the word. The children's mother had also sacrificed through the years by turning down opportunities for advancement in other jobs. The family salutes her in this!

The word *peace* comes from the Hebrew word *shalom. Shalom* does not necessarily refer to peace in the absence of war or peace in the absence of stress; it most often means peace in the midst of war or in the midst of stress. Imagine a tightrope walker, walking along a very high wire, carefully placing one foot in front of the other. What is the most important instrument this person has in his or her hand? The *balance* pole. Again, the English word *balance* is the best translation of the word *shalom*. God does not always remove the stressful conditions in my life, but he does provide the balance to move through them. *Shalom* does not refer to a spiritual endorphin; it refers to the balance that it takes to weather a storm and come out a winner.

> Be anxious for nothing, but in everything by prayer and supplication, *with thanksgiving* (emphasis mine,) let your requests be made known to God; [7] and the peace of God, which surpasses all understanding, will guard your hearts and minds through Christ Jesus. (Phil. 4:6–7 NKJV)

I began to see what the apostle Paul meant in saying, "For I have learned, in whatsoever state I am, therewith to be content" (Phil. 4:11b KJV). It was significant to me that Paul, in the midst of his own ongoing stressful conditions, was the author of those Scriptures coaching me to give thanks. God's response of peace to the practice or exercise of sacrificial praise creates this learning process of contentment in all circumstances. God is the "author and finisher of our faith" (Heb. 12:2). Be assured that this word of praise is true and will help you weather life's storms like nothing else can!

The Family Portrait Revisited

The seven children (one adopted) of our "Brady Bunch" now look at their homes, parents, and stepparents with an eye that sees themselves not as "parent poor" but as "parent rich." My sin had excised a heavy cost to my family, but the hand of God's "redeeming will" still heals, shapes, and renews them. For all of us, the broken family portrait of God's perfect will is being healed by the great grace flowing through his redeeming will. Such healing from God's hand uses the tragedies of our lives, whether outwardly or inwardly caused, to show the connection with forgiven sins—forming the "stem of the rose"—and to bring glory to his name (see Matt. 9:2–8 and John 9:1–3). One of my daughters-in-law gave me a coffee coaster with the words, "Every saint has a past; every sinner has a future."

From time to time, people ask us, "How can divorced parents and stepparents get along so well in caring for the children?"

For a quick and powerful answer, read the following prayers of the apostle Paul for the early church. I handed these in laminated form to soldiers during Desert Shield, Desert Storm, and Operation Joint Endeavor with instructions to substitute the name of an alienated family member every time they saw the word *you* or a form of it. Then they were to pray these prayers until the day they became real or heartfelt. God's Spirit, working through a world-renowned minister, Kenneth Hagin, had already coached me to do this for my former wife.

> I have never stopped thanking God for *you*. I pray for *you* constantly, asking God, the glorious Father of our Lord Jesus Christ, to give *you* wisdom to see clearly and really understand who Christ is and all that he has done for *you*. I pray that *your* hearts will be flooded with light so that *you* can see something of the future he has called *you* to share. I want *you* to realize that God has been made rich because we who are Christ's have been given to him! I pray that *you* will begin to understand how incredibly great his power is to help those who believe him. (Eph. 1:16–19 TLB)

> When I think of the wisdom and scope of his plan, I fall down on my knees and pray to the Father of all the great family of God—some of them already in heaven and some down here on earth—that out of his glorious, unlimited

resources he will give *you* the mighty inner strengthening of his Holy Spirit. And I pray that Christ will be more and more at home in *your* hearts, living within *you* as *you* trust in him. May *your* roots go down deep into the soil of God's marvelous love; and may *you* be able to feel and understand, as all God's children should, how long, how wide, how deep, and how high his love really is; and to experience this love for *yourselves*, though it is so great that *you* will never see the end of it or fully know or understand it. And so at last *you* will be filled up with God himself. (Eph. 3:14–19 TLB)

These prayers, persistently prayed, brought me to the place in my mind where I no longer possessively held on to my first wife. A new love developed, one in which I truly wanted God's best for her. When she found it, these prayers lifted my mind from daydreams of "winning her back" from the guy who had what used to be "mine" to an honest appreciation for God's redeeming will being worked out in her life. The missing puzzle piece had shifted from my *want* to her *need*. Today, should someone try to undo her marriage, they would have me to contend with, too. In all actuality, the love I have for her now is a much deeper love than that I had in former years.

For the Word that God speaks is alive and full of power—making it active, operative, energizing and effective; it is sharper than any two-edged sword, penetrating to the dividing line of the breath of life (soul) and (the immortal) spirit, and of joints and marrow (that is, of the deepest parts of our nature) exposing and sifting and analyzing and judging the very thoughts and purposes of the heart. (Heb. 4:12 AMP)

In March 1991, during my doctoral degree award ceremony at the church in which I grew up, another outstanding victory was highlighted. My spirit almost exploded when I noticed my daughter, Julie, get up from a pew, walk up to the lectern, and proceed to tell how she had been watching me over those several years after the accident as I grew closer to God, moving deeper into honest confession and repentance and learning to trust him more. Julie concluded by stating that witnessing my journey had shaped and strengthened her own.

After her own struggles and growth, Julie decided to be baptized again as an outward expression of her new birth in the faith. Her expression when rising up out of the water was even more joyous than the one she had when she walked down to the platform to receive her degree in counseling and psychology from a major university. Both were "high water marks"! I give continual heartfelt thanks for this shining evidence of God's redeeming will.

Our household takes joy in yet another victory that occurred in the life of our oldest boy. Brooke, the son who was on the motorcycle with me, had been engaged in honest doubt and questions about God and his Word, especially since the accident. Remembering the words of St. Augustine, "There is more faith in honest doubt than all the creeds of Christendom," I resisted the urge to preach too much to him. Instead, silent prayers went up without ceasing.

On Easter Sunday 1993, the Baptist church we attend had a guest missionary. Following his message and an invitation to come forth to profess Christ, I caught a glimpse of someone tall moving past us. I almost fainted with joy as I watched Brooke march up the aisle, stand tall, and profess his faith in Jesus and agree to be baptized as an expression of his faith. My prayers for him had been centered on Philippians 2:13, placing everything between Brooke and God. Shortly after the baptism, I shared with him the following Scripture:

> But what saith it? The word is nigh thee, even in thy mouth, and in thy heart: that is the word of faith, which we preach; that if thou shalt confess with thy mouth the Lord Jesus, and shalt believe in thine heart that God hath raised him from the dead, thou shalt be saved. For with the heart man believeth unto righteousness; and with the mouth confession is made unto salvation. (Rom. 10:8–10 KJV)

This passage and the very familiar John 3:16 formed the platform for educating him on God's promise of salvation by grace through faith. Once again, the working of God's Holy Spirit, in conjunction with the Word, raised high the *V* for *victory.* The Word is what convinces us of the truth that sets us free.

> So faith comes by hearing (what is told), and what is heard comes by the preaching (of the message that came from the lips) of Christ, the Messiah (Himself). (Rom. 10:17 AMP)

> I write these things to you who believe in the name of the Son of God so that you may know that you have eternal life. (1 John 5:13 NIV)

> For my Father's will is that everyone who looks to the Son and believes in him shall have eternal life, and I will raise him up at the last day. (John 6:40 NIV)

All four children had spirits that were not broken, just bridled—bridled in the sense of the biblical word *meek* as it refers to one who allows him- or herself to be shaped and molded by the Father's Word. It is much like a water hose that has more power to it when one squeezes the end of the hose as the water pours forth or a wild stallion captured in the wilderness that is bridled but whose spirit is not broken. One editor, reviewing this book prior to publication, happens to be a horsewoman. She wrote in the margins of this section, "When we use the bridle properly in advanced horsemanship, it is only a tool of communication, not an instrument of torture or pain. We use the bridle in conjunction with our weight, balance and legs to direct the horse in the most beautiful way to express itself with a rider on its back. But truly beautiful rides are on horses that are submissive, but not broken." Julie graduated from a major university, excels in homeschooling her children and found time and creative energy to set up a wholistic health care business, helping folks live in a more balanced manner. Brooke overcame his dyslexia so well that he graduated from a major university and became a resource manager in an outstanding industry—I think it helped him in those early years at home when I told him one day that Einstein was also dyslexic. Isaac and Adam overcame learning disabilities to the point that Isaac also graduated from a major university and became a gifted WMCA director; Adam's gift of being able to "think with his hands" has earned him promotions in carpentry and mechanics. Our children were turned out to the world as beautiful and stronger stallions, bridled and guided by the Word. The Word had made a strong impact on both my mind and my heart, giving me the legitimacy to address the children with some sense of loving authority and assuredness.

I wrote a letter to them a few years ago that included the following paragraphs:

> I know that you sometimes wonder why I write things like the contents of this letter instead of just telling you. It has always been more meaningful for me to write deeper or vital things than just speak them. I take comfort in the fact that God must have felt the same way in communicating important or crucial things

to us—so as to have them written down. When they are simply spoken, they can be simply and soon forgotten; when they are written, they can be reviewed or received many times over.

Not too long ago, as Isaac and I were building a fence, we stopped for a moment and I told him that one thing has grieved me greatly over the years. It is the fact that psychologists have found, to some extent, children's perception or understanding of God is shaped or formed by how they experience earthly fathers. I told Isaac that when you children could not see in me a father who is trustworthy or faithful and dependable, it constantly worried me how I may have damaged your faith relationship to God. As usual, Isaac's response was to listen and maybe nod his head in an understanding way.

Here's how I see God's rescue of each one of you from this snare:

Julie, your rebaptism was and remains a testimony of your trust in God to perform His Word in your life. You have set your face like flint toward seeking His will in marriage, family, and service. Congratulations on God's entrusting you with more children to raise in His care.

Brooke, do you remember your initial impression of Philippians 4:19? The Word seemed to speak to you; and so it has. Your hunger for His presence and Word in your life has gone through growth spurts that will mature into an advancing and strong faith. Your journey up the aisle-way at church many years ago, leading to your rebaptism, has a "water-mark" place in my book. I can still feel the brush of someone tall stepping forward to make that profession of faith.

Isaac, I believe you have suffered in silence more than any. I greatly respect your creative initiative—stepping out into life's work and securing your own house and vehicle. You have "gone it alone" a lot and become "Mr. Tough-Man" in more respects than just the recent contest (marathon) of toughness. Our faith relationship to God is very personal and internal. I'm sure the waters run deep in your search for truth.

Adam, your rebaptism is also a testimony to your ongoing ability to lean on God and trust Him. I have told soldiers through the years of how God has worked His Philippians 2:13 Word in you. It has given them encouragement to hear of it. Through the years, you have remained jealous of your time with the Scriptures. This is nothing short of wisdom. I tell soldiers to pray for God to help them become hungrier for His Word. When they do, the rest is good history.

I ended the letter by summarizing for them some of the major messages I wanted to place in my book.

On the one hand, God—

Is just, demanding punishment of evil. (Deut. 32:4; Is. 45:21; Acts 3:14)

Is an angry God when viewing sin. (Ex. 32:22; Num. 32:13–14; Deut. 7:4)

Is one who will not be mocked. (Gal. 6:7)

Chastens [trains, teaches, compels] and disciplines.

Speaks fearfully in Hebrews 6 and 10 about sin.

Grants no remission without repentance. (Matt. 3:7–9; Luke. 3:3, 8; 24:47; Acts 2:38; 26:18–20; 2 Cor. 7:9–10; Heb. 6:1, 6)

Will not hear prayer when iniquity is regarded in the heart. (Ps. 66:18)

Says if I love Him I will obey Him. (John 14:15, 21, 23)

I can seem close to him and appear to know him and still be a "Judas."

On the other hand, he:

Has paid for it all. (1 Cor. 6:20; 7:23)

Makes his strength perfect in my weakness. (2 Cor. 12:9)

Helps me see that faith is a decision, not a feeling. (Luke 22:42)

Is a rewarder of my faith. (Col. 3:24; Heb. 11:6; 2 John 1:8; Rev. 22:12)

Says that if I judge myself, I will not be judged. (1 Cor. 11:31–32)

Helps me do what he wants (Phil. 2:13; 4:13; 1 Cor. 1:18; Rom. 12:2)

Says that sorrow for what I have done against him leads me to repentance (2 Cor. 7:10)

Coaches me, saying: (1.) he is not so concerned about my *obedience of wisdom* as about the *wisdom of obedience* (protecting me from the bad consequences of going against his will). "Casting down the imaginations of my heart" accomplishes this. (2.) He is not so concerned about the *obedience of faith* as about the *faith of obedience* (protecting me from missing out on God's best because I make a decision against feeling to "deaden deeds of my flesh"). His Word says, "Be it done unto you according to your faith." (3.) He is not so much interested in my *obedience of sacrifice* as he is in my *sacrifice of obedience*, in my giving up my sin desire as I *"crucify my flesh"* (protecting me from wounding his heart). He told the people of Israel that he wanted their obedience more than their sacrifices. (4.) He is not centered so much on my *obedience of praise* as he is my *praise of obedience*. (5.) He wants me to show him the *love of obedience* (often telling us that if we love him, we will obey him).

The children's healing and growth will continue as we never let up on praying and being emotionally and physically available to them. The depth of my wife, Connie, is once again reflected in her idea for Adam's mother to pool resources with us and buy him a class ring to replace the original one that he lost. He loved and was proud of that ring. Having it replaced was one more act of healing for him, instigated by the love of his stepmother. The children will be shielded from the spiritual gravitational law of "judging and being judged" because honest confession and honest communication and prayer will open the door wide to forgiveness (God's healing and reconciliation). They will love the sinner and hate the sin. I sense deep within my spirit that what they need to see now is the continual and persistent "working out" of God's grace in my life, shaping me into his image and will.

Stems of the Rose

Our heavenly Father continues to form "wounded healers," making his strength "perfect in (our) weakness." The following writing by an unknown Confederate soldier puts it in perspective:

I asked God for strength, that I might achieve,

I was made weak, that I might learn humbly to obey.

I asked for health, that I might do greater things,

I was given infirmity that I might do better things.

I asked for riches, that I might be happy,

I was given poverty, that I might be wise.

I asked for power, that I might feel the praise of men,

I was given weakness, that I might feel the need of God.

I asked for all things, that I might enjoy life,

I was given life, that I might enjoy all things.

I got nothing that I asked for but everything I had hoped for.

Almost despite myself, my unspoken prayers were answered.

I am, among all men, most richly blessed.

So how can prayer become a major exercise in the healing of our families? Scripture tells me that I can pray but miss the mark. Military forces use lasers or infrared beams of light that can fix on a target at night, making it possible for soldiers to always hit it. Likewise, when I ask the Holy Spirit to pray for me (see Rom. 8:26–27), the prayer is always right on target. Why? Because he fully knows the mind (will) of the Father as well as my mind. Therefore, he is the one best suited to line up the two minds in prayer; with his prayers, I cannot lose. I start sometimes from scratch, as did the disciples of Jesus, and simply ask him to teach me to pray. This renewed exercise also helps guide my prayers on to the target. I like to think of prayers as beams of light, extending from "prayer cells" that are charged by the "nevertheless-of-faith" indicator; perhaps God looks down at earth and sees some prayers only flickering like flashlights with weak batteries. But others shine with the intensity of a laser beam. Those prayers that stand firmly on the Word, are heartfelt, and seek after God's name being glorified in the answers are the "laser beam" prayers. (See Training Regimen #7.)

Right Prayers Bring Right Results

And this is the confidence—the assurance, the (privilege of) boldness—which we have in Him: (we are sure) that if we ask anything (make any request) according to His will (in agreement with His own plan) He listens to and hears us. And if (since) we (positively) know that He listens to us in whatever we ask, we also know (with settled and absolute knowledge) that we have (granted us as our present possessions) the requests made of Him. (1 John 5:14–15 AMP)

It is interesting to note that when God receives a prayer that is in his will and in the name of his Son, Jesus, the above Scripture says that, in his eyes, it is already done and answered. For me to pray his Word is to pray his will!

And this promise is from God himself, who makes the dead alive again and speaks of future events with as much certainty as though they were already past. (Rom. 4:17b TLB)

If you live in Me—abide vitally united to Me—and My words remain in you and continue to live in your hearts, ask whatever you will and it shall be done for you. (John 15:7 AMP)

The earnest (heartfelt, continued) prayer of a righteous man makes tremendous power available—dynamic in its working. (James 5:16b AMP)

The effectual fervent prayer of a righteous man availeth much. (James 5:16b KJV)

"Righteous man" doesn't mean "goody two-shoes." It refers to someone who has a faith like Abraham's, and he had the kind of faith that led him to believe God could make something out of nothing. The apostle Paul described Abraham's faith as believing in "the God who gives life to the dead and calls things that are not as though they were" (Rom. 4:17b NIV). Abraham believed to the point of acting on that belief. When God told Abraham that he had made him the father of many nations (Rom. 4:17), Abraham and Sarah didn't know anyone was in the womb. For God, when he speaks, it is already a "done deal," simply to be worked out in his way and in his time. So has his Word been for me!

I heard Billy Graham give an illustration one time to describe faith. He told of a famous tightrope walker who walked across Niagara Falls on a wire, turned around, and walked back. The crowds went wild. Then he got a wheelbarrow and pushed it across the cable, turned around, and came back. Again, the crowds couldn't stop cheering. Next, he filled the wheelbarrow with bricks, enough to equal an average person's body weight, and pushed it across and back. The crowds grew silent in awe. At this point, the man asked the crowd if they believed he could push one of them across in the wheelbarrow. The crowd shouted, "Yes!" The man asked one of them who was calling out the loudest, "Will you, sir, volunteer to get into the wheelbarrow?" All of the sudden, the man grew silent and pale, backed up, and shook his head. What kind of faith would I need on the road to repentance?

Abraham had "wheelbarrow faith." Again, we cannot please God other than by our faith (see Heb. 11:6).

> But Abraham never doubted. He believed God, for his faith and trust grew ever stronger, and he praised God for this blessing even before it happened. He was completely sure that God was well able to do anything he promised. (Rom. 4:20–21 TLB)

The Word

If the Word of God says it, it is true; it is done! When the Holy Spirit guides the *logos* Word from the Bible into our hearts and minds as *rhema*, then we know that we know that we know. Jesus also said, "It has been written, Man shall not live and be upheld and sustained by bread alone, but by every word that comes forth from the mouth of God" (Matt. 4:4 AMP). I've seen his Word become activated:

> Yes, as the rain and the snow come down from the heavens and do not return without watering the earth, making it yield and giving growth

to provide seed for the sower and bread for the eating, so the word that goes from my mouth does not return to me empty, without carrying out my will and succeeding in what it was sent to do. (Is. 55:10–11 JB)

Whatever the challenges, tests, or difficulties, the *V* for *victory* can always be raised when we choose to stand on God's Word—that's right, *choose*. Again, if we wait until we feel forgiven or saved, we may be waiting for a long time. Sometimes, like sprinting a hill, faith has to be exercised with abandon.

Recall the account of Peter trying to walk on water. He was the brashest and most outspoken of the disciples. When the disciples saw Jesus walking on the water, Peter was the one to speak out and say, "If that is you, Master, bid me come to you." Jesus gave his Word and directed Peter, personally, to come forth from the boat on to the water. At first, Peter stepped out in faith, and the impossible happened: liquid held up as solid. But when Peter began to become aware of the wind and the waves, feelings and circumstances took over, overriding his faith. He could not stand on feelings, and he sank like a rock. Jesus reached out to him and reminded him of his "little faith." Faith is a decision to stand on God's Word regardless of what feelings and circumstances try to dictate in us.

In earlier days, Jesus had questioned the disciples about who people thought he was, and after the disciples gave him a list of responses, Jesus asked, "Who do you say I am?" Read Peter's confident response and Jesus' encouraging reply:

> Simon Peter answered, "You are the Christ, the Son of the living God." Jesus replied, "Blessed are you, Simon son of Jonah, for this was not revealed to you by man, but by my Father in heaven. And I tell you that you are Peter, and on this rock I will build my church." (Matt. 16:16–18a NIV) (Research into the original text reveals that Jesus might have been building on the word *peter* when he drew the analogy to the "rock" (*petros*) of faith that will build his church.)

I, as already noted, struggled greatly in those first years after the accident, divorce, and all that came with them regarding the issue of forgiveness for my sin of adultery and the "battle plan for the mind" outlined by my coach through the Word. Finally, I had to, during those depressive years, "come to grips" with a faith-decision. Did I have enough faith to make a decision to *be* forgiven? That decision was based firmly on the Word. One Scripture in particular begins with the Word *therefore,* and one of my seminary professors once said that the word *therefore* is so important in the Bible that it would be wise to look and see what it is "there for."

> Therefore (there is) now no condemnation—no adjudging guilty of wrong—for those who are in Christ Jesus, *who live not after the dictates of*

the flesh, but after the dictates of the Spirit. For the law of the Spirit of life (which is) in Christ Jesus (the law of our new being), has freed me from the law of sin and of death. (Rom. 8:1–2 AMP)

He who believes on Him—who clings to, trusts in, relies on Him—is not judged (he who trusts in Him never comes up for judgment; for him there is no rejection, no condemnation; he incurs no damnation). (John 3:18a AMP)

Therefore being justified by faith, we have peace with God through our Lord Jesus Christ: By whom also we have access by faith into this grace wherein we stand, and rejoice in hope of the glory of God. (Rom. 5:1–2 KJV)

Winds blew strong, as you recall, in the medical prognosis that precluded any hope for me to run again; they gusted in tornado fashion against any hope of a career; and they formed deep drifts along the road to repentance. Nevertheless, God's Word about "renewed strength" to run (Is. 40:31), "hope and a future" concerning my career (Jer. 29:11), and "godly sorrow" over my sins (2 Cor. 7:10) weathered those winds.

The Lord will work out His plans for my life. (Ps. 138:8 TLB)

Prayer grew to such intense proportions that my Coach would help me hunger and look for his Word to "speak" in the mental and spiritual "marathons" of life with the same expectations I have during physical training, where I have learned to truly hang on to those words. When I read God's Word, I'm reading the same power that brought creation into being; I'm reading Jesus! His words to me have been and are *events*; therefore, there was a growing expectation for a crowning event to demonstrate that his Word is "active and alive" (Heb. 4:12). Faith is a *decision* to stand on God's Word despite whatever feelings and circumstances prevail—to get out and "run to the mailbox" anyway.

The Hallelujah Factor

I found a vital link between praise and faith. Giving God the sacrifice of praise in the midst of pain and difficulties—where it makes little sense—*developed* trust in him, which is the response he wanted from me so he could go to work. Therefore, the real miracle that was not written about in those seven newspapers and the international magazine is the one that has made me closer with the Father, the Son, and the Holy Spirit than I have ever been in my life. Praise is the training field on which I came to exercise, thereby becoming more wrapped up in a trusting, personal relationship with him.

> What I want from you is your true thanks; I want your promises fulfilled. I want you to trust me in your times of trouble, so I can rescue

you, and you can give me glory. (Ps. 50:14–15 TLB)

The praise-faith connection was not a mechanism, but a relationship. My praise to God established a trusting, personal relationship (faith) that was the runway God used to rescue, save, and deliver me in a masterful manner. And there came a plateau of time in which God allowed me to look back over my shoulder to see what he has been doing through the sands of time in my life. As in the poem "Footprints," I discovered that God had carried me.

> In all your ways acknowledge him, and he will make your paths straight. (Prov. 3:6 NIV)

> A man's steps are directed by the Lord. How then can anyone understand his own way? (Prov. 20:24 NIV)

I am coming to see more and more that God uses his Word to guide my footprints on that straight path.

> Your word is a lamp to my feet and a light for my path. (Ps. 119:105 NIV)

Victories in My Life

Jesus Christ is our master who never takes his eyes off us. It is in the *meeting* of the eyes that victory becomes the dominant theme in and through our lives. God can take accidents, street orphans, and any condition and redeem it, work it toward good. My daddy put it another way: "Every setback can be a setup for a comeback."

What about the question "What's on your mind?" When I engage the mental marathon and find the hills rising higher and higher, making it seem more desirable to give in to lustful thoughts, the only true and lasting way to break through that wall, to overcome those temptations, is to say, "Nevertheless, the rewards for running the hills of resistance will far outweigh the deceptive lures of the enemy." Can I run those hills in such a way as to "train to standard"? For me to slack off on the mental hill of resistance is to break training. It is to choose to sin, to basically settle for less. In God's eyes, there is no difference between what goes on in my mind and actually entering into the sexual act (see Matt. 5:27–28). It was easy for me to step up my pace and increase my stride when running with my high school and college coaches watching or, today, others. But when I'm running on a long and lonely stretch of road, can I put my best foot forward and sprint the hills with the knowledge and understanding that the Holy Spirit, my heavenly Coach, is watching and that *that* observation is all in all. He reminds me from time to time that there is a "great cloud of witnesses" (Heb. 12:1) also cheering me on. "Likewise, I say unto you, there is joy in the presence of the angels of God over one sinner that repenteth" (Luke 15:10 KJV).

The long and lonely stretches are just as important to the Father as the easier and visible ones. For me, temptations come in the form of both big hills and little hills. The little hills sometimes carry the challenge of old habits making resistance feel like an uphill run. My Coach tells me not to pay attention to itches and pains along the run; they will pass. And they do. When I ignore them, miles later I realize that I've forgotten all about them because they are no more. Can I do the same with sexual itches? And what about those larger hills? Perhaps a beautiful woman makes a play for me instead of the other way around. Herein lies that mental tug-of-war, with feelings and perceptions pulling on one side and the faith that expects God and his Word to be true pulling on the other side. God does provide a "way of escape" (1 Cor. 10:13). He has enabled me to respond to a suggestive word or move toward me by becoming "confessionally honest," sometimes by telling my story and my struggle. This serves to disarm me or to defuse the energy of attraction. Therefore, it is in the crucible formed between the Word–faith connection and the temptation that the "way of escape" appears. I am learning that God is so absolutely strong that he can afford to appear weak (see 1 Cor. 1:25)—again, "God's strength (being) made perfect in my weakness."

That "nevertheless-of-faith" reminds my mind of the truth that sets (me) free (see John 8:32) as I pray:

> Dear Father, when the "desires of the heart"
> give in to the imaginations of the heart, help me
> to crucify the self, cast down the imaginations
> of the heart, and deaden the deeds of the flesh
> by the nevertheless-of-faith. Take my heart and

form its desires after your will—carved anew with the scapulae of the cross, "the power of God" (1 Cor. 1:18)! Help me retain a "godly sorrow" over my sin-condition which "produces (I'm counting on that word) a repentance that leads to salvation." Make your "strength perfect in my weakness" so that I won't oscillate and wear down but rest on the truth that sets (me) free—to see that Father knows best and his way is always best. Help me to sprint the hill!

Again, I'm being repetitious because we need that kind of training. These trial runs are God-allowed opportunities to exercise the gift of faith so as to be pleasing to the Father (see Heb. 11:6). And when the wind pushes against me as I run to the crest of the hill, that, too, becomes a specialized, God-allowed training ground in the faith. To be an overcomer is a goal to be achieved.

> For everyone born of God overcomes the world. This is the victory that has overcome the world, even our faith. Who is it that overcomes the world? Only he who believes that Jesus is the Son of God. (1 John 5:4–5 NIV)

Yet initial little victories in overcoming certain thoughts or suggestive words can create the illusion that I have arrived, much like the way that succeeding at high school and college athletic trials can make one feel as though he or she has just competed at the Olympics. We know in our heart of hearts that these first trials are just the beginning stages of those yet to come. So it is, as I was to find, in overcoming the hills of temptation.

I have written much on repentance, the battle plan for the mind, and the sacrifice of obedience when facing the challenges, deceptions, and walls that show up in the physical marathons, such as the temptation to step aside, quit, give in. To make a sacrifice in the battle for the mind requires faith—a raw, naked *decision* to crucify the flesh or deny the mind and, subsequently, the body what it wants. This faith exercise trains my spirit to then give direction to my mind and body. Just as I have learned to pay a price when training to run well in a physical marathon and see the rewards, I also have to pay a price to run well in the mental and spiritual races. As disciplined training opens the way for a good contest in running, so does strict training of my mind and spirit make for an ability to resist temptation. For me, this can be done *only* through an exercise of faith, which turns temptations into fields in which to exercise and move from one level of stamina and endurance to another. Part of me has to die when exercising the nevertheless-of-faith in such training. My Coach helps now as he speaks to my mind and heart:

Stand in front of every temptation—thought, word, deed—as though Jesus were standing next to you, looking at that temptation with you, waiting and watching to see your decision. What would you want him to see you do?

The Word speaks of obedience that arises from our faith. The following Scripture from Hebrews also brings me the truth about the enemy's deceptive and short-lived pleasures.

> By faith Moses, when he had grown up, refused to be known as the son of Pharaoh's daughter. He chose to be mistreated along with the people of God rather than to enjoy the pleasures of sin for a *short time.* (emphasis mine; Heb. 11:24 NIV)

Repeatedly, I ask you to recall the Scripture that says, "Without faith it is impossible to please God" (Heb. 11:6). When we run the spiritual race in such a way that we lift up that nevertheless-of-faith battle cry to defeat the desires of the mind and body, exercising the sacrifice of obedience, this pleases God. Soldiers would sometimes ask, "Chaplain, why is that?" My answer was, "'Cause God has everything except one thing. He doesn't have my faith, a trusting relationship with me, unless I give it to him." In fact, God says that he desires inner obedience *more* than outward sacrifice:

> Samuel replied, "Has the Lord as much pleasure in your burnt offerings and sacrifices as in your obedience? Obedience is far better than sacrifice. He is much more interested in your listening to him than in your offering the fat of rams to him." (1 Sam. 15:22 TLB)

And so, dear brothers, I plead with you to give your bodies to God. Let them be a living sacrifice, holy—the kind he can accept. When you think of what he has done for you, is this too much to ask? Don't copy the behavior and customs of this world, but be a new and different person with a fresh newness in all you do and think. *Then* (emphasis mine) you will learn from your own experience how his ways will really satisfy you." (Rom. 12:1–2 TLB) (Verse 2 in the King James Version reads, "be ye transformed by the renewing of your mind.")

Echoing that godly sorrow over our sin that "produces a repentance that leads to salvation" (1 Cor. 7:10), King David wrote:

You aren't interested in offerings burned before you on the altar. It is a broken spirit you want—remorse and penitence. A broken and a contrite heart (the Amplified Bible says "broken down with sorrow for sin and humbly and thoroughly penitent"), O God, you will not ignore. (Ps. 51:16–17 TLB)

Furthermore, God speaks through Hosea:

For I desired mercy, and not sacrifice; and the knowledge of God more than burnt-offerings. (Hosea 6:6 KJV)

My enemy whispers to my mind, saying, *Look what you will give up if you don't pursue this venture.* After the hill is run, then I see what I "gave up" by not giving in to the hill's resistance. My Coach says,

> *You gave up anxiety over consequences from not retaining "level one" in the "fear of the Lord." You gave up anxiety over wondering what you had missed out on by not maintaining "level two" in the "fear of the Lord." In "level three," you gave up anxiety and grief over how you had again wounded God's heart by not using the faith of obedience to, thereby, be pleasing to him. You also gave up the damage to your physical, mental, and spiritual health that more sin would have delivered. And ultimately, you gave up having to stand before Jesus at the judgment with one more thing about which to be ashamed.*

Surely this is a large part of what the apostle Paul described as keeping the goal in mind as we run the race. During grade school, I wrote a well-received paper about my most significant concerns in life. I have saved it all these years in its original form because of its continued importance to me. It is titled "Lasting Things." One statement reads, "One can find true happiness only by consistently living the things that last." On several occasions, I have emphasized to my children that the only thing that lasts is God's Word addressing our life situations. It strikes me as I write this to you, the reader, that I had more understanding in grade school than in my blinded adult, adulterous years.

> Heaven and earth will pass away, but my words will never pass away. (Matt. 24:35 NIV)

God's Word has nailed it down more firmly for me.

> Do not love or cherish the world or the things that are in the world. If anyone loves the world, love for the Father is not in him.

> For all that is in the world, the lust of the flesh (craving for sensual gratification), and the lust of the eyes (greedy longings of the mind) and the pride of life (assurance in one's own resources or in the stability of earthly things)—these do not come from the Father but are from the world (itself).

> And the world passes away and disappears, and with it the forbidden cravings (the passionate desires, the lust) of it; but he who does the will of God and carries out His purposes in his life, abides (remains) forever. (1 John 2:15–17 AMP)

The next Scripture extends the nevertheless-of-faith connection with obedience.

But now is made manifest, and by the Scriptures of the prophets, according to the commandment of the everlasting God, made known to all nations for the obedience of faith" (Rom. 16:26 KJV).

Writing about salvation by God's grace through our faith, apart from anything we can do, the apostle Paul describes an additional part of being "born again"—that is, being enabled to be obedient through our faith in God's help to do so. Otherwise, I fall under the judgment of 1 John 3:8–10. (You will want to let our Coach convict and counsel here.) I need to be about the work of verse 3 in that chapter: "And everyone who has this hope in Him purifies himself, just as he is pure" (KJV).

For we are God's (own) handiwork (His workmanship), recreated in Christ Jesus, (born anew) that we may do those good works which God predestined (planned beforehand) for us, (taking paths which He prepared ahead of time) that we should walk in them—living the good life which He pre-arranged and made ready for us to live. (Eph. 2:10 AMP)

For me, the spiritual dimension of the run meets the greatest challenge when life's circumstances stand diametrically opposed to what God's Word says. The question comes to mind: "Can I take him at his word?" Can I trust him not only for my next breath, next heartbeat, next paycheck, next stride in the present mile, and next day but also for his next "living Word" to speak to me in my current life circumstances? I always can when I overrule the "Dr. Spock" logic and choose not to "lean on my own understanding" (see Prov. 3:5) but to say to those circumstances and feelings, "Nevertheless, this is what God's Word says about the issue at hand. I'm going to stand on it anyway." Then that's when the "gift of faith" (1 Cor. 12:9) begins to help me think, speak, act, decide, and even feel as though God is in control. I become "expectant" about his plans for "mounting up with wings" (Is. 40:31), "hope and a future" (Jer. 29:11), and "godly sorrow producing repentance" (2 Cor. 7:10). This faith-decision builds a momentum in me that helps me to take the hills, both physical and mental, bringing a new motivation and reason for sprinting the hills. Why? Because his Word impregnates my heart, conceives a lively hope in me, making me expectant. Then I see that day come when I can look back over my shoulder and see with my physical and mental eyes what my spiritual eyes of faith had chosen to envision and expect, that is, how God would do his Word in Romans 8:28—*working all things together toward good.* (See Training Regimen #6.) Surely this is what the apostle Paul was teaching when he would say to "walk by faith and not by sight" (2 Cor. 5:7) and "Now faith is the "assurance (substance) of things hoped for and the conviction (evidence) of things not seen" (Heb. 11:1). I find it interesting that this verse begins with the word *now*. "Now faith" can mean "right now faith" *when* God wants us to put it into practice.

This runner firmly believes that we are placed on this earth for the purpose of training primarily on the exercise of faith as preparation for living in the kingdom of heaven. "The Lord said to me, 'I knew you before you were formed within your mother's womb'" (Jer. 1:5a TLB). In one sense, we will be going "back to the future" when we get to heaven. Faith, while the exception here on earth, is the norm in heaven.

As I recall the great gulf between the low point of my sinful condition and the high point of his grace and redeeming will, my Coach says to run in his grace and to remember from where he has brought me—that is, from sins of scarlet to seeing myself at the foot of his cross (washed whiter than snow; Psalm 51:7), my "transgressions removed as far as the East is from the West" (Psalm 103:12). I must resist any pull to cheapen God's grace by using his grace as insurance for sin (see Rom. 5:20–6:15).

The beginning part of any temptation is to the mind what hills are to the body. I have been told that NASA revealed that 80 percent of the energy exerted in a space launch is used up in the liftoff, in breaking the resistance of gravity to overcome inertia. So it is when taking the first step to overcome temptation and run up the hill. When I coach people to run, sometimes I put them on a walk-run program. Guess which step is the hardest to take after the trainee is ready to shift from the walk to the run? That's right, the first step.

But the temptation remains. During my training runs, when the challenge to sprint the hills seems too great because the course is long and I don't seem to have enough wind, I start saying, "Dear Father, I can't sprint this next one. It just isn't in me." My Coach, then, reminds me of the unfathomable, unspeakable, and uncompromising step of faith that Jesus took on the cross when he breathed his last *after* the hill (mission) of Calvary was run (finished). He "went the distance" for me so that I might be forgiven and "transformed by the renewal of (my) mind." *Every* single time that "reminder" comes, I sprint the hill and reach the top amazed and breathless, not just from the physical price but from awe that Isaiah 40:31 came forth again. Sometimes I draw a cross on a piece of paper and place it somewhere as a visible reminder of the hill Jesus ran for me (see again Heb. 12:1–4).

The finish line always looks good after my training runs. I think about the last two words Jesus spoke from the cross. Jesus knew why the Father had "abandoned" him. Surely, following that awful expression of agony and despair as he questioned whether or not the Father had "forsaken" (forgotten) him, he must have begun to see his finish line. He said, "It is finished," and "Into thy hands I commit my Spirit." He had the peace and joy of knowing that he had gone the distance and that the mission was accomplished.

"Dear Father, in Jesus' name, I ask you to forgive me of my sin that caused you to have to look away from your Son on the cross."

> Looking away (from all that will distract) to
> Jesus, Who is the Leader and the Source of our
> faith (giving the first incentive for our belief)

and is also its Finisher, (bringing it to maturity and perfection). He, for the joy (of obtaining the prize) that was set before Him, endured the cross, despising and ignoring the shame, and is now seated at the right hand of the throne of God.

Just think of Him Who endured from sinners such grievous opposition and bitter hostility against Himself—reckon up and consider it all in comparison with your trials—so that you may not grow weary or exhausted, losing heart and relaxing and fainting in your minds. (Heb. 12:2–3 AMP)

These memories strengthen and renew my body to run as a living parable of his grace. They strengthen and renew my mind so I understand that self-worth comes not from what I do but from what has been done for me.

For because He Himself (in His humanity) has suffered in being tempted (tested and tried), He is able (immediately) to run to the cry of (assist, relieve) those who are being tempted and tested and tried (and who therefore are being exposed to suffering). (Heb. 2:18 AMP)

Keep your eyes on Jesus, our leader and instructor. He was willing to die a shameful death on the cross because of the joy he knew would be his afterwards. (Heb. 12:2 TLB; see Training Regimen #8)

The profound statement that most dramatically summarizes life's runs with their respective challenges, wins, and losses is the one from the apostle Paul as he summarized his journey through myriad troubles and victories: "For to me, to live is *Christ*, and to die is *gain*" (Phil. 1:21 KJV). We are not losers either way! The runner who completes a marathon in six or seven hours is just as much a winner as the official winner, for he or she, too, went the distance and "endure(d) unto the end" (Mark 13:13 KJV).

The only open "door" through which I can enter God's kingdom is his grace and my faith in that grace. (You will want to, again, train carefully and consistently on the following interconnected Scriptures: 2 Cor. 5:10; Rom. 1:5; Rom. 4:3–8). The Word of grace "birthquakes" with new life and motives through my spirit and into my mind (soul). And when it is time to transition from this life to the next, my Coach will also guide that "run." He says, "Precious in the sight of the Lord is the death of his saints" (Ps. 116:15 KJV). Why? Because he wants us to come home. "Eye hath not seen, nor ear heard, neither have entered into the heart of man, the things which God hath prepared for them that love him" (1 Cor. 2:9 KJV). In God's eyes, death is a "home run."

Medical and psychological research into the dying process and its transition has made popular something that Scripture has said all along: "separate from the body, present with the

Lord" (see 2 Cor. 5:1–10). Keeping in mind the Scripture that says Satan can take the form of an "angel of light," this research into "out-of-body" experiences needs much spiritual discernment. One of the more celebrated cases involves a medical doctor, George Ritchie, who died of lobar pneumonia during the Korean War. On the way to the morgue, the orderly noticed some sort of motion. He and others resuscitated the doctor, who related many of the common research findings in similar cases: out-of-body awareness of resuscitation efforts, travel through space and time, and seeing people from the past. In Ritchie's case, he encountered a tremendous light source. Moving closer, he found that it was Jesus. This doctor watched scenes from his life as though on a movie screen. He and Jesus watched together. Every now and then Jesus would ask, "George, what have you done with your life?" He couldn't think of much at the time, so they watched more of the scenes until, again, Jesus would ask, "George, what have you done with your life?" Finally, he recalled something and said, "Well, I was an Eagle Scout." Then the doctor describes the accepting humor of Jesus along with the judgment of his life. Jesus told this doctor that he was to go back because his time had not come. He describes difficulty in locating the town, the hospital, and then his room so he could get back into his body. Afterward, he noticed a difference in himself, as people in similar cases also have: he did not have a fear of death as he did before.

Therefore, when I have "run the race and kept the faith," I will seek out loved ones from my past for sure, but my top priority will be my search for the one who "sprinted" the hill of Golgotha so that I could be there. I will want to meet him in person! (See Phil. 2:5–11.)

> He who overcomes (is victorious), I will grant him to sit beside Me on My throne, as I Myself overcame (was victorious) and sat down beside My Father on His throne. (Rev. 3:21 AMP)

As we venture into the months of our gathering years, seeking to train well on our creator's Word, may we "walk the talk" before we "talk the walk" (word change intentional). God's Spirit tells me to "run the write" and then "write the run." It is the only honest (nonhypocritical) way to truly run in his grace.

Solomon, the wisest man to ever live, is credited by most scholars as being the author of Ecclesiastes. In this book, he takes a sober look at life apart from God and posits that "all is vanity." These words cover a wide spectrum and hold the wisdom of someone who has been there and seen much. In his later years, Solomon lets us know that he is writing so that future generations—*and I fully understand that motive in writing*—will not, like him, be carried away from the one true God through relationships in other nations to their gods. God uses the word *abomination* to describe the most severe form of sin, especially in reference to the Antichrist setting his image up in the temple of Jerusalem as a god (see Dan. 11:31ff; Matt. 24:24ff). The word *abomination* means "become nauseated, stomach-wrenching, hated" (see Nelson NKJV Study Bible notes for: Genesis 46: 34, Proverbs 11: 1,

Jeremiah 4: 1, Ezekiel 20: 7, Revelation 17: 4-5). Since, as I have stated, my adultery was a form of idolatry, much of my life probably caused God to look at me and want to throw up! I don't consider myself old as of yet; however, these and many other of God's words cause me to snap to attention and say, "Yes, sir!" The purpose and drive of my life are to become obedient. I want to be able to say one day that this book is a chapter written by a divine hand (Holy Spirit) with pages that have ached for a word that speaks on a theme that is timeless.

The pastor at the church we attend will sometimes raise a sobering question: "If you died today, do you know that you would go to heaven?" I used to reword that question and try to share with fellow soldiers and veterans the answer to "What must I do to make sure I go to heaven?" I must *confess* my sins and then *repent* of them; next, I need to personally *receive* Christ and the price he paid for my sins by letting him live not only in my mind but in my heart of hearts. This book raises the question, can someone so sinful and hypocritical as me be saved? Over the years, I have had to occasionally ask myself which was going to come first, running the write or writing the run. Settling that question is vital because heaven is real and hell is real. We don't need out-of-body experiences to prove either, even though it is added confirmation for medical science to no longer dispute the existence of something beyond this life. Let me present a sobering thought to you. Recall a time that you have experienced a pretty bad burn. Now, think not only of an eternity spent in a lake of fire, outer darkness, and separation from God but also of how changing the word

215

love to *hate* in the above passage (1 Cor. 2:9) could apply not only to heaven but also to hell. That underscores, in a dramatic form, level one in the fear of the Lord!

Yes, it would have been healthier for me to have remembered my Creator better in my earlier years. Yet he has impressed me over the years with his redeeming and healing hand. It reminds me of an old sign I saw once: "Please be patient with me. God isn't finished with me yet." Because of the way his redeeming will is working in my marriage, family, career, retirement, and a small farm, I sometimes feel like I can be on "Coffey grounds" and dance as though no one is watching.

Still, I have not found a way to say to my children many of the things I'm writing in this book. My sorrow for the wounds I caused to their spirits has remained with me through the years. Therefore, one great reason for writing this book, in addition to writing for your eyes and the writing being therapeutic, is to speak also to them of the deeper parts of my journey into repentance. I earnestly pray that both the "run" and the "write" will become an open epistle, read by all as a praise to the glory of God's grace! The apostle Paul summarizes it thus: "This would give me something to be proud of for the Day of Christ, and would mean that I had not run in the race and exhausted myself for nothing" (Phil. 2:16 JB).

I have long known from my seminary days the Greek words denoting the difference in God's time and our time: *chronos* refers to our chronological watch/calendar time; *kairos* refers to God's meaningful, filled-up, immeasurable, unending time. It is the word used in the New Testament in connection with the terms "eternal life," "everlasting life," and "heaven." The closest I have ever seen the two come together is when a minute seems like an hour or vice versa. But now I see God moving his *kairos* directly into my *chronos*. I have come to believe that when I place the name of Jesus over any person or circumstance, the merging of times has begun.

> He hath made everything beautiful in his time.
> (Ecc. 3:11a KJV)

CHAPTER 4

The Far Journey
1994–1999

Thus far, God had shown me that he wanted my feet firmly planted on the road to repentance on the action/behavior level and the thought/imagination level because he sees no difference between those levels (see Sermon on the Mount). In addition, there was another level that he was deadly serious about!

Profound evidence of his sustaining grace came in 1994 during all the downsizing and inactivation within the Army. Following about five weeks of intensive search for a new military home and with only four hours before the 80th Division would declare my military career to be history, a call came from the 79th ARCOM (Army Reserve Command) requesting that I serve to assist military units with stress concerns arising from their being inactivated, concerns through which I had just ventured. Once again, God was using me in that wounded-healer capacity. I found it most like a living parable in that the military patch for this ARCOM depicted the Cross of Lorraine. The 79th ARCOM, because of its outstanding role in France during WWII, is the only Army Reserve Unit in the United States authorized to wear this cross.

In 1995, the senior ARCOM chaplain informed me that, once again, I would probably be history come September of that year because of continued inactivation. I was "over-strength" on the active-duty list and would therefore probably be among the first to be removed from service. Back to the prayer closet I went. In June of that year, I was handed a paper signed by the commander, stating that I had been removed from the "over-strength" category and placed in regular status within the ARCOM. This was made possible through a vacancy created when another chaplain received an active-duty assignment. This action on God's part has been a constant and vivid reminder of that timely and sustaining grace. It also brings to mind how he has coached me about the three levels in the "fear of the Lord (that) is the beginning of wisdom."

Through the past decade, as I signed military and civilian letters, quick looks in three places have reminded me of his grace: one glance at the body of my name underscores the miracle he performed physically; a second glance at the doctoral abbreviation reminds me of the miracle performed mentally; and a third look at the branch and rank insignias brings to mind the miracle performed spiritually. His hand, moving through military channels, has sustained me in level two of "the fear of the Lord": not missing out on his best.

Yet I have to again renew my gritted-teeth thanks concerning career matters. During the October Army Reserve Drill of that year, a sergeant, whom I have only briefly met, came up to me during that weekend drill and said that she had a "word" for me. Since that day, I have come to believe that she has the New Testament gift of a "Word of Knowledge" (see 1 Cor. 12:8) because she has a long history of telling people things that later come to pass. Her "word" to me was that, come the following January, my job and financial picture were going to change and that I would journey far and long into the setting sun—and that my prayers and faith would bring me through the times and trials to higher ground. She had even taken pains to write it down poetically:

You Have Far to Go

Don't tarry here in sorrow,
Don't be filled with woe.
Lift up your head, My gentle friend,
For you have far to go.
You will journey far, my friend,
And you will journey long.
For this your Spirit must not be weak,
But shine forth bright and strong.
The journey won't be easy,
And it may get you down.
But with your faith, your hope, your prayers,
You'll find the higher ground.
The world awaits you now, my friend,
And it is time to go.
There is much that's to be done,
So don't be feeling low.
Don't say I cannot do it,
For you know that you're the one

Who's to spread the word of Gospel,
Into the setting sun.
Take with you my blessings,
My wishes for the best.
And know this in your heart of hearts,
That God will provide the rest.
—SFC Joyce A. Strickland, October 1995

Following that October Reserve Drill, the administrator of the nursing home where I was serving as civilian chaplain called me into her office one day in December to say that the company was terminating its chaplaincy positions because of the budget, effective January 1. One week later, the Army Reserve unit I served received notice that we were to be completely "downsized," inactivated, effective January 13. The next year proved to be long and slippery when it came to finances, a financial marathon with seemingly no end. Again, God, through family members, sent his *rhema* Word, saying that my foot would "not be moved" and that I have "a hope and a future" (see Ps. 121; Jer. 29:11).

The following December (Month of Victory), I received a call from the US Army Reserve Command Headquarters in Atlanta, Georgia. The alert status had shifted from "grazing herd" to "roaring bull;" I was at the top of their list of chaplains who might be willing to be activated in the mobilization to Bosnia. "Here it is," I thought, "the far journey."

One major thing had to be done before I departed for Germany. I met with the children after supper one night as we were all gathered in the living room. I asked for their permission to address three questions to each of them, explaining that the answers were vital to my being able to leave in peace. They all agreed. I look each one in the eye and asked them individually: 1) "Do you believe in God?" 2) "Do you believe God the Father sent Jesus to earth to die for us so that we can be forgiven?" and 3) "Do you believe that God raised Jesus from death so that one day you can also live forever in his kingdom?" Each one answered yes to all three questions. Those questions, followed by those answers, helped me more than anything else to be apart from them given the possibility that we may not see one another again. I looked each one in the eye again and said, "That seals your salvation. Why? Because of two Scriptures:

> For God so loved the world, that he gave his only begotten Son, that whosoever believeth in him should not perish, but have everlasting life. (John 3:16 KJV)

> But what does it say? "The word is near you, in your mouth and in your heart" [a] (that is, the word of faith which we preach): 9 that if you confess with your mouth the Lord Jesus and believe in your heart that God has raised Him from the dead, you will be saved. 10 For with the heart one believes unto righteousness, and with the mouth confession is made unto salvation." (Rom. 10:8–10 NKJV)

After I had flown to Germany and was somewhat settled, just awaiting further orders, Connie mailed me the following:

To those who are sanctified in Christ Jesus, called to be saints, together with all *those who in every place call on the name of our Lord Jesus Christ, both their Lord and ours.* (emphasis hers)

Grace to you and peace from God our Father and the Lord Jesus Christ.

I give thanks to my God always for you because of the grace of God that has been given you in Christ Jesus, for in every way you have been enriched in him, in speech and knowledge of every kind—just as the testimony of Christ has been strengthened among you—so that you are not lacking in any spiritual gift as you wait for the revealing of our Lord Jesus Christ. He will also *strengthen* you to the end, so that you may be *blameless* on the day of our Lord Jesus Christ. God is faithful; by him you were called into the fellowship of his Son, Jesus Christ our Lord. (emphasis hers; 1 Cor. 1:2–9)

Her note to me in the bottom margin read in part, "Here is a message personally given from Paul to you spanning the centuries!" This "Proverbs 31 woman" told me as we parted that she would use our time apart to grow closer to God. Therefore, as I now write this paragraph in Germany, I know by faith that our reunion will not hold the stress resulting from separation and change experienced by the families with whom I worked during Desert Shield and Desert Storm but will be the *adventure* of seeing what God has been growing in and doing with each of us while apart from each other. The void and vacuum caused by her absence will be the training ground God will use to get both of us in better shape—physically, mentally, and spiritually. She is the only human "force" to give me the kind of energy I need in both body and mind. I've asked her permission to print a short article she recently wrote before this Bosnian tour. To me, it mirrors the global vision of a Proverbs 31 woman. It reflects the heart of a woman close to the heart of God, and it also reveals the kind of spirit with whom God has graced me through his redeeming will. I've given it the title "Imagine."

IMAGINE

Can you imagine being just as near to God as you *want* to be? I mean actually *being* filled with Him and having full freedom to relax and enjoy? Imagine your friends are all people who love God perfectly in their speech and with their actions. Their thoughts are pure, and their sole desire is to serve and worship God more and more. Anything not from God is completely rejected.

In fact, you have absolutely nothing to fear because in this place and time *everyone* is filled with love, and all they speak to you and want for you is your good. Here you are free to love everyone without exception. You can love them completely and fully because all that they consist of is goodness and righteousness. Everyone's countenance is relaxed, peaceful, composed, smiling, and radiating warmth. You are free to touch them, laugh with them. No one here has any inclination to ridicule others or to control others or to be better than another. Only words that build up are spoken. Words that speak of a person's worth in terms of *whose* they are— God's child.

In this world, it makes no difference how you really look physically; whether your make-up is the right shade, your hair graying, your teeth exactly even and pearly, your brows tweezed or wrinkles showing. Everyone is declared beautiful, and when they speak, they are heard. Thoughts and feelings are shared, and what a *bond*! There is no grabbing for things, counting out money, and trying to move faster. Activity, whether for purpose or enjoyment, is meaningful and experienced as joy in the doing of it—not as means for other rewards such as a larger house or wardrobe. There is a freedom to let go of these ambitions which the world forces on us. Instead, we embrace the idea of desiring only what our Father wants. We have no self-centered goals, but all energy is directed toward God-given goals.

Can you imagine such a world? No need for defense mechanisms to protect the ego and self-esteem. You are completely safe here to love and to be known, to be loved in a world of people who trust and can be trusted to act *only* out of love; a world where people want to talk and hear about Jesus only, with no concern about offending anyone when speaking of Him.

Her words reflect those of an unknown author who wrote, "Imagine stepping onto a shore and finding it heaven, taking hold of a hand and finding it God's, breathing new air and finding it celestial air, feeling invigorated and finding it immortality, passing from storm and tempest to an unknown calm, waking and finding it home."

It was a joy to use some leave time to fly back from Germany to participate in Brooke's wedding. He asked me to do a toast at the reception, so I raised up my glass and said, "Thank you for blessing us with your union. We know that love is more than just an attraction, more than just emotions, more than just a sacrificial giving unto each other; love is also a decision. My prayer, my toast is that you will always be able to make that decision!"

Just before returning to Germany, it was an honor to say a few words at the golden (fiftieth) wedding anniversary of my parents. One point that stands tall in my mind is that they have modeled the apostle Paul's letter on love—love that "bears all things, endures all things, hopes all things, and believes all things...."

Mindfields

Not only does Bosnia have about 11 million hidden mines; this tour also takes me to minefields of loneliness and temptation. Or should I write *mindfields?* In my struggles, I remember God's Word to provide "a way of escape" (see 2 Peter 1:3–4, 2:9) as his "strength is made perfect in my weakness." Another moment-of-truth prayer prayed there reads as such:

> Dear Father, help me, by an act of the will performed in me by Jesus within me, to exercise the gift of faith into the course of obedience. I need to clearly see the link between casting down the imaginations of my heart and the vision of victory that comes in reaching the top of the hill. Help me sprint those hills to your name's honor and glory in every way.

In addition to sometimes telling about my own struggle as a way of disarming myself, the visitation and counseling policy I am led to adopt for this tour of duty is to conduct team visits, counsel with open doors, and hug only in the presence of others. And I form a good friendship with a Jewish-Christian man who agrees to be my "Nathan," to ask me every now and then, "Chaplain, are you walking the talk," or, in my case, "running the write?'" This, plus level three in the "fear of the Lord," was my mapped-out "way of escape."

> But remember this—the wrong desires that come into your life aren't anything new and different. Many others have faced exactly the same problems before you. And no temptation is irresistible. You can trust God to keep the temptation from becoming so strong that you can't stand up against it for he has promised this and will do what he says. He will show you how to escape temptation's power so that you can bear up patiently against it. (1 Cor. 10:13 TLB)

But the mental tug-of-war between feelings and faith remained. To a beautiful woman who sidled up close to me on this tour and made informal conversation, followed by handing me a piece of paper with her address and phone number, for me to implement the above plan was a "sacrifice of obedience." But I could recall the painful lessons showing me that when I let feelings and circumstances win the tug, I lose; when I let faith win, I win. David said, "I will not offer to the Lord my God sacrifices that have cost me nothing" (2 Sam. 24:24). Women usually see the relationship first; men use their eyes first. My eyes do not want a "way of escape." Only the nevertheless-of-faith can break that attraction to temptation and the clever devices of my deceitful heart. When exercised, the way out leads to a God-given ability to "cast down the imaginations" (2 Cor. 10:5) of my heart like lightning. That's the way Satan was cast out of heaven, like lightning. Jesus performs this like a laser beam for my mind. I practiced recalling his name, "name above all names" (Phil. 2:9), lifted up over my thoughts, making them "captive to (his) obedience" (2 Cor. 10:5). And why would I voluntarily get "out of shape" and break training when it takes such a struggle and long time to get back in shape? It is wise for me to develop the habit of staying in shape year round for running events. In fact, that habit builds a desire in me to consistently train; I fight to protect that time. What applies to that momentum of my physical training applies to the momentum of my mental and spiritual training, as well. I'm repetitious with you for a reason.

During this mobilization, I rest on the prayer prayed on the plane ride over—that God will cause the communication between my wife and me to be *in* spirit *by* his Spirit. His answers to this prayer, along with the *wholistic*-training program on which he has us both engaged, will keep the marriage bond in a state of formation. The bond with God strengthens the marriage bond. It helps me realize the difference between being lonely and being alone. King David's penitential Psalm 51 states in verse 11, "Cast me not away from thy presence; and take not thy Holy Spirit from me." This next verse explains why you and I do not need to pray that previous verse: "And I will pray the Father, and he shall give you another Comforter (Holy Spirit, see vs. 26) that he may abide with you for ever" (John 14:16 KJV). Jesus also said that he would always be with and never leave us (see Matt. 28:20; Heb. 13:5). The vertical bond with God shapes the horizontal bond in marriage, forming a powerful "cross" that cannot be broken. He is the only legitimate third party.

Connie mailed the following Scripture to me with a note saying, "St. Peter writes to you":

His divine power has given you everything you need for life and godliness through your knowledge of Him who called you by His own glory and goodness. Through these He has given you His very great and precious promises, so *that through them you may participate in the divine nature and escape the corruption in the world* caused by evil desires.

For this reason, make every effort to *add to your faith*: 1. goodness (zeal for what God wants) and to goodness, 2. knowledge (necessary for discernment); and to knowledge, 3. self-control; and to self-control, 4. perseverance, 5. Godliness; and to Godliness, 6. brotherly kindness; and to brotherly kindness, 7. love. For if you possess these qualities in increasing measure, they will keep you from being ineffective and unproductive in your knowledge of our Lord, Jesus. But if you do not have them, you are nearsighted and blind, and have forgotten that you have been cleansed from your past sins. Therefore, be all the more eager to make your calling and election sure. For if you do these things, *you will never fall*, and you will receive a rich welcome into the kingdom of our Lord and Savior Jesus Christ. (emphasis hers; 2 Peter 1:5–11 NIV)

She also told me about a worship service she had attended. "I felt very uplifted and went to the altar to thank God and praise him, and I committed our entire family to him, asking that he continue to protect you and provide you ways to escape Satan's devices, who I am sure is prowling like a lion, waiting to devour you. Christ will allow you to always be victorious, not only because of his love for you and our family bond but to allow you to continue being an effective witness in word, thought, and deed and to bless your ministry with fruitfulness. So I and everyone who is on God's side will pray for protection, "Deliver us from evil, and lead us not into any temptation."

You will benefit from studying Ephesians 5:21–27. This passage, describing the "headship" of the husband as being like the headship of Christ for the church, for whom he died, makes the bond connection. For too many centuries, too big a portion of the church has interpreted this headship of the husband to mean that when the husband says to the wife, "Jump," she is to reply, "How high?" On the contrary, headship gives me the responsibility to love my wife so much that I would die for her as well as live for and with her; she submits to that headship. And the husband is also to be the "head" of the wife through sharing the Word with her, which is the same as washing her (see verses 26–27) so as to more completely form her into that Proverbs 31 woman who is so close to the Father (see Proverbs 31:30) that all good for the household flows down from that relationship. My wife was "washing" *me* with the Word from a distance.

As I ran the hills in Germany, his "sustaining" (2 Cor. 9:8–10) grace was always "sufficient" (2 Cor. 12:9–10) and continued to "bless" (John 1:16). He had certainly *done* his Word again (see Jer. 29:11). I had a working (lived out), personal definition of God's grace: God's unearned, undeserved, unconditional, freely given *love* and *forgiveness*. While in Germany, this definition was most beautifully portrayed for me as I recalled stepping out on the front deck of our mountain home back in the States and viewing the distant Allegheny mountain ranges of the Shenandoah. There, in the midst of those ranges, I could see the Independent Baptist church that God used to rescue me by extending a call so I could continue serving as an Army chaplain. It was most symbolic for me as I found myself focused on this vision during cool-downs following the long training runs. I simply raised my arms and said, "Praise your name, Father! Praise your name, Jesus! Praise your name, Holy Spirit!" The Father knew what was needed for his grace to fall so powerfully upon me; Jesus had paid for it by what he accomplished on the cross for me; and the Holy Spirit had worked God's Word to bring it all about. I would recall the tallest mountain peak in those ranges, and with hands lifted and stretched high I still say, "Shema (hear). I want God the Father—the One I identify with the mountains—to hear me." Then I say, "YADAH (premiere word for praise), Jesus (name that covers all). I most certainly do lift up mine eyes unto the hills from whence comes my help." And just as he had said on top of the mountain, "I am with you; I will continue to be with you."

> Be strong and courageous. Do not be terrified; do not be discouraged, for the Lord your God will be with you wherever you go. (Joshua 1:9 NIV)

Psalm 121, as I sing it to the tune of "Chariots of Fire" during training runs, continues to speak as *rhema*. Especially lifting is meditation on these words: "I lift up mine eyes unto the hills, from whence does my help come? It comes from the Lord.... He will not let your foot be moved." My Head Coach was using the physical, mental, and spiritual "hills" to train me to the faith connection, and so he kept my foot ("unmoved") on the land and at home and walking as a chaplain.

Psalm 23, the second psalm I had put to the "Chariots of Fire" tune, also plays in my mind as I run. That psalm assures me that the emotional, interpersonal, spiritual, financial, career-related, and other "marathons" have been and are being lifted. Words from that psalm hit in strong *rhema*-word fashion: "I shall not want," "restores my *soul*" (the New Testament Greek word means "personality"), "yea though I walk through the valley," "the shadow of death," "I fear no evil, for thou art with me." And all of this is done "for his name's sake." God will do these works for me, not for my merit but for the glory of his Word and his name.

> Let the word (spoken by) the Christ, the Messiah, have its home (in your hearts and minds) and dwell in you in (all its) richness, as you … train one another in all insight and intelligence and wisdom (in spiritual things, and sing) psalms and hymns and spiritual songs, making melody to God with (his) grace in your hearts. (Col. 3:16 AMP)

What does God promise when his Word has a home in my heart?

> Jesus answered and said unto him, If a man love me, he will keep my words: and my Father will love him, and we will come unto him, and make our abode with him. (John 14:23 KJV)

One day, during my run, I sang, "Jesus, name above all names, beautiful Savior, glorious Lord, Emmanuel, God is with us, blessed redeemer, living Word." Each of these names for Jesus in the Scriptures is serving me like a giant forklift, removing all the *what if*s and *oh no*s from my mind. My thoughts went something like this: *He is a power above all other powers that could pull my heart and mind in the wrong direction. I need to keep myself centered on the cross ("nothing in my hands I bring; simply to the cross I cling") and what he accomplished there for me!* I was gaining an even deeper inner conviction of who is in control and providing the power for Romans 8:28 to be done. The word *all* in that verse simply states that God is not limited by any circumstances or conditions, only by my lack of faith in his Word.

In study back in my barracks, the Holy Spirit taught and counseled me to see that when the apostle Paul wrote to the churches in Rome and Corinth, saying that God chose and predestined (see Eph. 1:4–5), ordained (see 1 Cor. 9:14) and called us whom he *fore*knew (see Rom. 8:28, 29), this means that God has done for me exactly as his *rhema*-Word foretold because he *knew* I would be as he describes in Psalm 91:14–16. This was not just a matter of the rain falling on "the just and the unjust alike" (Matt. 5:45). God sees his children as "becomers." He knew me in my future; he knew that my spirit, my heart, would respond to his Word. Being in the past, present, and future all at the same time, he could then work those times together toward good (see Training Regimen # 2)! Do you see the depth of what I've just said?

> No one can come to me unless the Father who sent Me draws him; and I will raise him up at the last day. (John 6:44 KJV)

The Holy Spirit coached me to understand: *So the Father chose you before creation, drew you, gave you faith to believe, promises to keep you, keeps you, and now works in you.*

"Then my salvation does not depend on me, because he chose me before I was born, knowing ahead of time that I would respond to him. And when I have conviction of sin, this is you, his Spirit, working with me and a sign that the Father

235

is working with me. If he saved me while I was still evil, he would not 'unsave' me because I continue to sin."

Carry on.

> My sheep hear my voice, and I know them, and they follow me: And I give unto them eternal life; and they shall never perish, neither shall any man pluck them out of my hand. My Father, which gave them me, is greater than all; and no man is able to pluck them out of my Father's hand. (John 10:27–29 KJV)

And he *knew* that I would—through speaking engagements, counseling, and this book—*do* Psalm 118:17, "recount the works of the Lord." Therefore, following the accident, as doctors feared I would die, he gave those words as prophetic statements of things to come. Like the centurion soldier who was confident that Jesus could heal his servant, I need to always say, "Speak the Word only" (Matt. 8:8 KJV). Like the nobleman asking Jesus to heal his son, I need to "take Jesus at His Word" (John 4:50). Like Peter struggling to catch a draught of fish, I need to say, "Nevertheless at thy word I will let down the net" (Luke 5:5b KJV). And like Mary, after hearing the Word from the angel about her pregnancy and despite the rumors and tension that would probably surround that pregnancy, I need to say, "Be it unto me according to thy Word" (Luke 1:38 KJV). For me to say those words to God is for me to welcome the intercourse with his Word, leading to my rebirth. My worth comes, therefore, not from who I am but from *whose* I am and how much I allow my Coach to work his Word through me.

The giant "moment of truth" came in Germany when I prayed "eye to eye" with my heavenly Father during the winter quarter of this tour. I told Him that since I had already prayed for him to take my deceitful heart (Jer. 17:9) and reshape it and since he also looks at me from the heart and knows my heart (1 Sam. 16:7; Heb. 4:12; Rev. 2:23), I was then and there asking him to "nail down" Philippians 2:13, "helping me to will," and 2 Corinthians 7:10, "godly sorrow," into the deepest fabric of my heart. I identified with King David's similar prayer: "But how can I ever know what sins are lurking in my heart? Cleanse me from these hidden faults. And keep me from deliberate wrongs; help me to stop doing them" (Ps. 19:12–13a TLB).

In watching Bathsheba taking a bath on the roof, David surely did not envision death. However, it was that look that moved him to tell his troops to pull back in the heat of battle, away from her husband, so he would be killed, leaving Bathsheba for himself. So, what brought David's heart around from "soap opera sin" to "godly sorrow" over his sins? Listen to God's plan for this to happen:

> So the Lord sent the prophet Nathan to tell David this story: "There were two men in a certain city, one very rich, owning many flocks of sheep and herds of goats; and the other very poor, owning nothing but a little lamb he had

managed to buy. It was his children's pet and he fed it from his own plate and let it drink from his own cup; he cuddled it in his arms like a baby daughter. Recently a guest arrived at the home of the rich man. But instead of killing a lamb from his own flocks for food for the traveler, he took the poor man's lamb and roasted it and served it."

David was furious. "I swear by the living God," he vowed, "any man who would do a thing like that should be put to death; he shall repay four lambs to the poor man for the one he stole and for having no pity.'

Then, Nathan said to David, "You are that rich man!" … "I have sinned against the Lord," David confessed to Nathan. (2 Sam. 12:1–13a TLB)

Until this point there was no convicting Word, no godly sorrow, and no repentance; therefore, only hardness of heart and the judgment of God would follow. The reason David will be remembered as a man after God's own heart is that he quickly and honestly repented; he had found that "godly sorrow." God spoke back: "He that regardeth reproof shall be honoured" (Proverbs 13:18 KJV).

My Coach has me, in my officer's quarters after supper, read and meditate—systematically and often—on Matthew,

Mark, Luke, and John in their accounts of the arrest, trial, and crucifixion. The Word can and does place me there. As the hymn asks, "Were you there?" This cross scene speaks to my past and the pool of pains it left.

Another of King David's bold prayers echoes a still-deeper exposition of my Germany prayer: "Search me, O God, and know my heart; test my thoughts. Point out anything you find in me that makes you sad, and lead me along the path of everlasting life" (Ps. 139:23–24 TLB). I continue to place the name Jesus over my mind with the understanding that all the deceitful "loopholes" in my mind are being "made captive to the obedience of Christ" (2 Cor. 10:5). He is the vinedresser (John 15) who clips away the chaff so that I can grow and change. Sometimes Connie says to me in the late fall of the year that I did not prune the grapevines nearly enough. When I clip them to where it seems there is only a stump, that's when the most growth comes in the spring. This "clipping" is done so that I will be moved and motivated to act in his will through the "fear of the Lord that is the beginning of wisdom." My footnote appended to that prayer is that I will find myself increasingly moved and motivated, not by level one in that "fear" but by levels two and three, in descending order. And further, that where God knows in my future when my strength will fail under temptation, he will "lead me not into temptation" and "deliver me from evil." This is my *shema* (heartfelt, fervent and therefore "heard")—as in 1 John 5:13–15—prayer! This was and is my moment-of-truth prayer for the "mind marathon." What kind of "pruning" would God have in mind?

The Lord is nigh unto all them that call upon him, to all that call upon him in truth. He will fulfill the desire of them that fear him: he also will hear their cry, and will save them. (Psalm 145:18–19 KJV)

I happened to notice that the sheet on which I scribbled notes for the above paragraph following one of my training runs has one of those crosses on the other side that I sometimes draw and place in areas where I can readily see them throughout the course of the day. Those notes for that prayer, residing behind that cross, were and are a living parable. There is no greater force to motivate me to do the Philippians 2:13 Word than his grace, sealed into my heart by the cross. Thanks for taking time to read the footnote.

Some soldiers helped me make a wooden cross for Holy Week while we were on duty in Germany. I received warnings about leaving it up because of the regulation regarding "faith neutrality" (Jewish, Catholic, Protestant, etc.) in the armed forces. Therefore, I put it up in the chapel lawn the night before the Protestant services and took it down the next evening. It felt good to place it, stand back, and let flow into the inner core of my being the amazing grace that towers over me. The cross is a footnote to be added to every paragraph of our lives! Dietrich Bonhoeffer, in his book *The Cost of Discipleship*, wrote, "Only the man who is dead to his own will can follow Christ."

On tour-of-duty in Germany, as backfill for the Bosnian Mobilization called Operation Joint Endeavor, my chaplaincy duties covered five military communities and refugees from eight different nations. After seeking the judge advocate general's advice on how to balance ministry and military community amid the refugees, I preached and counseled the chapel congregation to become "servant minded," centering on Jesus' teaching that true greatness rested in being a servant. They did. Soldiers and families set up an outreach center complete with food, clothing, and shelter. Some Muslims asked, "Why do you do this?" and the soldiers involved would simply point a finger upward and say, "Thank Jesus." As a result, three Muslims converted to the Christian faith, something that is unheard of and that places them in danger of being killed by other Muslims. The loudest sermon had been not preached but lived out for all to see.

One Sunday, seven refugees from seven different nations came up to the microphone at the pulpit and read John 3:16 in their native languages. It was *electrifying*—almost a Pentecost flashback because of the several other tongues speaking the same Word. It was one of those times that I knew God was listening and was pleased. One refugee, an Iraqi soldier, had been a prisoner of war under the Ayatollah Khomeini regime for ten years. His was the most dramatic test of faith of any I have heard.

After chapel service one Sunday, I went to have lunch with one of the military families. They, as usual, had invited some refugees to join them. One of them, the former POW, with the help of a translator, told of his experience, and I asked him to give his testimony for the rest of the congregation to hear how faith can really be tested and tried and ultimately triumph.

I am reproducing here part of his testimony, translated and supervised by two other Christian refugees, Furat and Maria. Read how the Word *lived* in him, giving him strength to endure and overcome the temptations he encountered during this time of persecution.

> In the name of the Father, the Son, the Holy Spirit. Amen. You have heard that it was said, eye for eye, and tooth for tooth. But I tell you, do not resist an evil person. If someone strikes you on the right cheek, turn to him the other also. And if someone wants to sue you and take your tunic, let him have your cloak as well. If someone forces you to go one mile, go with him two miles. Give to the one who asks you, and do not turn away from the one who wants to borrow from you. (Matt. 5:38–46)

> Many, many years ago, it happened in this great world that war took place between Iraq and Iran. In that war, there were many sacrifices, (much) suffering, and painful circumstances. Specifically, the soldiers were the most injured people of that inhumane and brutal war. So you'll hear now (about) a true, painful life for

one of those soldiers, who had a great faith in our Lord that he would protect and save his life. This brave, faithful soldier is Dafer Sabah Behnam. He believed that all what he had passed through was a test from God, and he is proud to tell you this as he is proud of loving our Savior Jesus, for Jesus is the light of right path in this life and the everlasting life."

"Then you will be handed over to be persecuted and put to death, and you will be hated by all nations because of me" (Matt. 24:9–10).

On the sixth of March 1981, he was captured as a prisoner of war, and he believed in Jesus and had spiritual belief in God and his faithfulness to his religion, Christianity. So he (was being coerced) to change his religion to be Muhammadan Muslim, but he firmly answered, "No, no, and a million (times) no." And he said, "I'll not let my Savior down even if I die." For Jesus said, "If anyone would come after me, he must deny himself and take up his cross and follow me. For whoever wants to save his life will lose it, but whoever loses his life for me will find it.

His torment had just started. They did not stop their attempt to force him by many cruel and brutal means, (thinking) that at last he would give up. They fed him three meals a day, (but) his food was full of sand and dirty things and his meal was very little—about 130 grams, which was even not enough for one meal. Moreover, his teeth were pulled with no mercy by pliers, (and he was) taught the Al-Quran by force, chained in an isolated prison for more than three months in 1985, and there in that dark and gloomy prison, he was beaten, punished by whip, and put in deep, cold water. Furthermore, he was punched severely. So what was the cost of that torment? It was his eyes; now he cannot see clearly and there is a scar, but with his pure heart, he can see clearly the great sacrifice of Jesus for all of us. "Do not be afraid of those who kill the body but cannot kill the soul. Rather, be afraid of the one who can destroy both soul and body in hell."

He was also forbidden from praying (in the) name of Jesus, so he kept praying in secret. "And when you pray, do not be like the hypocrites, for they love to pray standing in the synagogues and on the street corners to be seen by men. I tell you the truth, they have received their reward in full."

In his heart, in his soul, he believed that all his suffering during (those) ten years was nothing, because our Savior Jesus suffered and (was) crucified (though) he did not do any wrong,

but indeed to save us from our sins and lead us
to (the) way of salvation.

Did you capture the Word pulsating through this soldier's
spirit? I was proud to be in the same room with someone
who had been this close to Jesus by and through the Word.
He had a "fellowship" with the sufferings of Jesus (see Phil.
3:10). The apostle Paul said, "Salute every saint in Christ
Jesus" (Phil. 4:21a KJV). I sharply salute this soldier of the
cross. He sprinted the hill; he ran the distance!

General George C. Marshall wrote these words about a
soldier: "I look upon the spiritual life of the soldier as even
more important than his physical equipment. The soldier's
heart, the soldier's spirit, the soldier's soul are everything.
Unless the soldier's soul sustains him, he cannot be relied
upon and will fail himself, his commander, and his country in
the end. It is morale … and I mean spiritual morale … which
wins the victory in the ultimate, and that type of morale
can only come out of the religious fervor in the soul. I count
heavily on that type of man and that kind of army."

Training to Standard

During the decade following my accident, I had increasingly
grown to feel that I was truly training to "run in his grace."
Most of that time, I was able to use the weapons my Coach
had provided: the ability to "cast down the imaginations of
(my) heart," "deaden the deeds of the flesh," and "crucify
the self." Especially while on this tour in Germany, I was

thinking that I was doing well in the "battle for the mind." However, my Coach had been telling me that I was moving out on dangerous ground when running in the snow and yielding to my natural pattern of sprinting. He conveyed to me that I should move through that ground with caution and careful footing. Then he made the point. My enemy teamed up with my deceitful heart to rapidly lay the groundwork for a slip or fall on the hills of temptation. I had confidently preached a sermon in which I vulnerably shared my testimony of unfaithfulness. The stage was set for pride to truly go before a fall. But now, as I glance back up at that moment of truth prayer I had prayed about one-third of the way into this tour, I clearly realize why I am about to tell you what happened a little over two-thirds of the way into the tour, the tenth anniversary of that June 1986 accident.

The month of June, fire, is truly that! That month, I learned that legal action was being taken, accusing me of sexual harassment. Four German women who attended services with the military chapel congregation that I serve were bringing these charges against me. They jointly complained about my giving them hugs back in the winter. These hugs were given in open areas and usually in the presence of others, but one of the claims references a kiss.

To a three-star general who later volunteered his services to help me, I explained the kiss as follows: "She and one of the other three invited me to their house for supper one evening. After the meal, I had gotten up to use the bathroom. Upon coming out, I glanced into the kitchen and caught the eye of this one woman, who immediately looked down as if something was wrong. When I stepped into the room, she held up her hand with a cigarette in it. Her body language and expression said that she was waiting for me to scold her. She said, "You caught me." I reached out and hugged her, and as I was stepping back, I gave her a kiss on the mouth. It was the kind the Bosnian refugees would give us on Sundays in greetings at the chapel."

Two days after hearing about the charges, I was summoned to the desk of the commander, where I listened to him read information saying that I was to be removed to another duty location until an investigating officer had completed his work.

As I packed everything up, I inwardly cried that special trimmings that had been donated to help prepare my quarters for my wife's visit in June had to be boxed up and returned, unseen. When I got to my new station and began unpacking, I found myself just walking from room to room with no idea of what I was doing, simply trying to make sense out of anything. I recall a spiritual growth and healing conference I attended in my younger years during which one of the leaders came up to me following a prayer meeting to say with conviction and intensity, "You will be tested." God says, "The refining pot *is* for silver and the furnace for gold, but the LORD tests the hearts" (Prov. 17:3 NKJV).

As I continued to walk around for some time, at one point the words *Psalm 37* came to mind almost as though a light bulb had been turned on in a dark room. I thought, "What does this mean?" A minute later, I said to myself, "Maybe I'm supposed to read it." So, I got my Bible, lay down on the mattress, and began to slowly pore over the verses. Then, when I got to verses 5 through 7 and the last two in the chapter (39–40), I felt as though I was being told, *Sit up. Listen. You're being spoken to.* Jesus, the "Word made flesh," was speaking." I provide these verses for you below, as they are in the King James Version, emphasizing key words that the Holy Spirit later expanded on and brought to me in *rhema* fashion. The italicized words are the basis for the rest of this story.

Over the next two days and nights, I was numb as I awaited my wife's plane from the States and kept repeating to myself, "This is really happening"; I had to convince myself that it was not just a bad dream. People who knew of her arrival time prayed over those two days for God to prepare her heart— prayers that went up without my asking and were answered. The three weeks from her arrival to her departure were filled with eye-to-eye talk, tears, and tourism, the last of which was difficult to get into because of the dark cloud hanging over me. Connie not only showed me her understanding of my past weakness and God's redemption of it, she also lived up to her name, Constance, which means "faithfully enduring." At the beginning of her visit, I shared with her the Psalm 37 Scripture that I now share with you.

> 5 *Commit* thy way unto the Lord; *trust* also in him; and he shall bring *it* to pass.

6 And he shall *bring* forth thy *righteousness* as the light, and thy *judgment* as the *noonday.*

7 *Rest* in the Lord, and *wait* patiently for him: *fret not* thyself because of him who prospereth in his way, because of the man who bringeth *wicked devices* to pass....

39 But the salvation of the righteous is of the Lord: he is their strength in the time of trouble.

40 And the Lord shall help them, and *deliver* them: he shall deliver them from the wicked, and save them, *because* they *trust* in him.

During that first week of June, I was summoned to the MP station, where a special agent questioned me for three hours. Afterward, he said that all the interviews were completed and that he found "no malice or intent toward harassment" on my part. He said that all the paperwork would be forwarded to the legal department, which will determine whether there is "conduct unbecoming an officer." He then went on to state that if there was anything in the case that might result in a letter of reprimand, it would be that kiss. The Chief of Chaplains office in Washington, DC, and United States Army Reserves Europe (USAREUR) told me that I was required to inform my endorsing agent—the one who had endorsed the Independent Baptist call for me to continue in the Army Chaplaincy—of this action.

Two key questions that the special agent asked during my interview were, "Why do you think that these four German women jointly raised this charge?" and "What would you do differently now?" I had been led to give deep thought to both those questions by a warrant officer who had, during the week prior to the interview, just moved into the building in which I had been the sole tenant since the beginning of the tour. He had undergone a similar experience in his career.

To the first question, I pointed out three reasons that had been brought to my attention by others right after the charges were made. One was that German women usually are more affronted by hugs than American women. I didn't put much stock in that answer; neither did the agent.

Second, since the four knew one another and talked frequently, perhaps the momentum had built during their interactions. I put a little bit more weight on that reason.

And third, someone suggested that, since I had been so transparent in sharing my testimony, which related my unfaithfulness to my first wife, "there may be some who hear that and expect (me) to continue in the old way." My contribution to this possibility was that they all had issues that were related in some way to mine: one of the two married women struggled with unfaithfulness and the other struggled with thoughts of leaving. One felt defensive after being accused by the women's Bible study leader of possibly having a "spirit of lust," and the other was bitter about a sexual harassment suit concerning her daughter that had not been settled to her satisfaction. The two unmarried women suffered from problems of low self-worth, evident in the fact that they compared their lives with those of others in the congregation. My point was that all of their hurt could have created a need to project the hurt away from themselves. These answers, however, deflected the blame, or root cause, away from me.

To the second question, about what I would do differently now, I said that when my wife came over, she shared a Scripture with me that hit like a bullet. It was 1 Thessalonians 5:22, which says that we are not to give any "appearance of evil." The military uses the expression "train to standard." From that Scripture, I said, I clearly saw that I had broken training for God's standard; therefore, my mind would be reconditioned to the more natural action of shaking hands instead of hugging—I had made a list of nineteen women and six men whom I had hugged on the tour. I also told him that I would be very reserved in sharing my testimony as I had done in a sermon back in January. And last, I would shift my tendency to give comfort when in counsel to simply addressing the presented need.

Something that came to me later was the idea that all of the above could have facilitated a subconscious setup; that is, one of the four women would regularly wear revealing clothing and sit with her legs crossed in an immodest manner. And, at the time of the alleged harassment, I had not sensed any resentment from any of them. Nonetheless, if I had truly been healed of my lustful heart, I would have run from any temptation so as not to "allow the appearance of evil," placing the spotlight on the leopard's spots. My testimony gave the impression that I wanted to see how close I could get without being burnt. I was soon to learn how hot the fire could become.

> Adulterers and adulteresses! Do you not know
> that friendship with the world is enmity with
> God? Whoever therefore wants to be a friend
> of the world makes himself an enemy of God.
> (James 4:4 NKJV)

My quarters, following my wife's departure, serve as both a prison and a refuge. Day and night, I spent hours poring over the Word, especially Psalm 37. I studied it in the King James Version with all the theological notes in the Scofield Bible and in the Amplified Bible with its comparably rich translations of the original Hebrew and Greek texts. I asked my Coach to bring the Word to me *exactly* the way the Father wants me to receive it, word upholding word. I now share with you what unfolded.

The first word that hit me, of course, was the word *commit* in verse 5. The KJV note says, "Roll thy way upon the Lord." My wife reminded me of the Scripture that says his burden is light when we cast ours on him (see Matt. 11:28–30). This is exactly the understanding I needed right then and there because my mind had a million cares and concerns rolling around. So I systematically began placing the name Jesus over each and every thought (feeling, memory, and anxiety) as they showed up. Reinforcements came from the Word continuously.

The King James Version citations took me back to Psalm 37:

> Though he fall, he shall not be utterly cast down: for the Lord upholdeth him with his hand. (Ps. 37:24 KJV)

The Amplified Bible referenced the following:

> Casting the whole of your care—all your anxieties, all your worries, all your concerns, once and for all—on Him; for He cares for you affectionately, and cares about you watchfully. (1 Peter 5:7 AMP)

Through one of my sisters, he relayed a word to me that refers to a form of pride in worrying or fretting. Worrying and fretting expose my thoughts as saying that things are, or have to be, in my control. Matthew 6:25–34 focuses my mind on the stupidity of not trusting the God who looks after the smallest of creatures. The following centers me more on what it takes to journey out of the pit of anxiety into trust in the Father's care:

> Do not fret or have any anxiety about anything, but in every circumstance and in everything by prayer and petition (definite requests) with

thanksgiving continue to make your wants known to God. And God's peace (be yours, that tranquil state of a soul assured of its salvation through Christ, and so fearing nothing from God and content with its earthly lot of whatever sort that is, that peace) which transcends all understanding, shall garrison and mount guard over your hearts and minds in Christ Jesus. (Phil. 4:6–7 AMP)

But Jesus said to the woman, Your faith has saved you; go (enter) into peace—in freedom from all the distresses that are experienced as the result of sin. (Luke 7:50 AMP)

The word *garrison* in the above Scripture from St. Paul reminds me of the mission we had as I served in an Army garrison. The word means to "surround, provide, and protect." Was God preparing to do this for my mind and heart? I began to see the link between "peace *with* God" and "peace *of* God." The former comes to me through the righteousness that Jesus achieved for me and my faith in his work; the latter comes through continuously making the sacrifice of praise along with unceasing prayers and constant meditation and leaning on his Word. Note that the above Philippians passage states "prayer … *with* thanksgiving." My closing prayer to the above Scriptural journey was, "Dear Father, help me to let go and let God."

I also desperately needed the words in Psalm 37:7. *Rest* and *wait* are amplified to mean, "Be still … and patiently stay yourself upon Him" and, from the KJV note about the original Hebrew, "be silent to the Lord." Then a verse came to mind: "Thou wilt keep him in perfect peace, whose mind is stayed on thee: because he trusteth in thee" (Is. 26:3). Would keeping my mind stayed on the Word be the same as keeping it stayed on him? I thought about John 1:1–14. As the days grew into weeks, I repeatedly wrestled between thinking "This could happen" or "That could happen"—leaving my stomach feeling as though the bottom had just dropped out of it—and the decision to rest on the Word I had been given. I was right there with Peter trying to walk on the water, stepping out on faith, and then sinking with fear as I tried to "lean on (my) own understanding."

Several times, I made the journey up to the headquarters building, thinking that if I talked with the commander, it might do some good. But each time I got to the entrance door, I stopped, remembering the Scripture about trust and "being silent to the Lord." And each time I exercised the decision to be silent in this way, I found some peace of mind. Then, the Word *trust* in verses 5 and 40 took on broader proportions. The KJV note to verse 40 refers me to Psalm 2:12 with a note saying, "to take refuge, to lean on, to roll on, to stay upon." Once again, I recalled the Word given to me following my accident by Rev. Larry Christenson, a renowned leader in the faith and author of *The Renewed Mind*: "Trust in the Lord with all thine heart; and lean not unto thine own understanding" (Prov. 3:5). If there was any leaning to be done, it needed to be toward God, not the commander or anyone else. The KJV footnote to that proverb refers to the above psalm. Scriptures were beginning to support Scriptures like fabric being sown together by a master seamstress. God meant what he said: "but by *every* (emphasis mine) Word that proceedeth out of the mouth of God." As I was increasingly enabled to "patiently wait" on God and trust that the Father not only knows best but does best, I was then led to pray the following prayer: "Dear Father, since you and the Word are the same, I pray that you help me trust your Word so that it can do what it has been 'sent out' to do. Therefore, I am going to trust you and 'be silent to' your Word."

Then the word *it* catches my eye in Psalm 37:5, "bring it to pass." What was "it"? Verse 6 provides the answer: "my righteousness." Then I have to say, "But, Father, I am not righteous." My Coach leads me through the concordance to the following Scriptures concerning righteousness, giving me a firm understanding that the righteousness God was talking about is "imputed" righteousness that God executes in response to faith and trust in him:

> For what saith the scripture? Abraham believed God, and it was counted (reckoned, or imputed, i.e., put to the account of) unto him for righteousness.... But to him that worketh not, but believeth on him that justifieth the ungodly, his faith is counted (imputed) for righteousness. Even as David also describeth the blessedness of the man, unto whom God imputeth

righteousness without works.... and being fully persuaded that, what he had promised, he was able also to perform. And therefore it was imputed to him for righteousness.   Now it was not written for his sake alone, that it was imputed (reckoned) to him; but for us also, to whom it shall be imputed, if we believe on him that raised up Jesus our Lord from the dead. (See Rom. 4:1–8, 21–24 KJV.)

But if Christ lives in you, (then although your natural) body is dead by reason of sin and guilt, the spirit is alive because of (the) righteousness (that He imputes to you). (Rom. 8:10 AMP)

This righteousness from God comes through faith in Jesus Christ to all who believe. There is no difference, for all have sinned and fall short of the glory of God. (Rom. 3:22–23 NIV; see also Phil. 3:9)

I said, "Thank you, Father. I certainly need that understanding!" I had been asking how I could recognize and know that the Psalm 37 Word was addressing me and my cause, and the answer came in 1 Corinthians 2:9–14 as "spiritually discerned." I had already learned that this means discernment brought directly through the Word by the Holy Spirit. He is the only one who knows precisely which block of Scripture to place upon another to build and furnish the Father's house of grace. As I move through this house, the bathroom cleanses me of the filth and debris gathered, the kitchen feeds me, the living room nurtures and comforts me, and the bedroom refreshes me and gives me rest. So it is with the Word. Through faith in Jesus, I am also a "son of Abraham," having "imputed righteousness" (see Luke 19:9).

Next, my Coach took me on a journey through the words *judgment, fret not, wicked devices,* and *deliver.* He would bring about my "judgment as the noonday." The footnote to these words cites the following Scripture:

> I will bear the indignation of the Lord, because I have sinned against Him, until He pleads my cause and executes judgment for me. He will bring me forth to the light, and I shall behold His righteous deliverance. (Micah 7:9 AMP)

The Amplified Bible stated verse 6 of Psalm 37 as "your justice and right as (the shining sun of) the noonday." I began to gain inner conviction that Jesus, my high priest (see Hebrews 4:14–15, 7:25; 1 John 2:1–2), was going to plead my case in response to my trust. One day, I even asked the Holy Spirit to pray for Jesus to plead my case to the Father so I could be sure that the prayer was right on target and in the Father's will. The verbs in Psalm 37:5–6 (*bring forth* and *make*) conveyed to me that God was simply going to make it happen. He said, "In returning to Me and resting in Me you shall be saved; in quietness and in (trusting) confidence shall be your strength" (Is. 30:15b AMP). The time of waiting will be the time of his "indignation" because I have broken his standard by allowing the "appearance of evil" (1 Thess. 5:22).

From what was God going to deliver me? My deliverance would be from those who "bring wicked devices to pass." The context for Psalm 37, Jeremiah 20:7–13, and Micah 7:9 spells out deliverance from specific wicked devices. I said, "Yes, but these are not wicked or bad people."

My wife and I took a one-day cruise on the Rhine River. At one point, the boat docked for a while along the shore, and I sat by her with my elbows on my knees, looking from one side to the other. I happened to notice as I glanced toward the water that it looked as though the boat was moving, but a look to shore at some very stable landmarks revealed we were not. I looked at my wife and said, "Maybe this is what's happening in this case. Everybody is telling it the way they 'see' it," to which God later replies, "But they're going about it in the wrong way." With the help of my "Nathan" and my Coach as I pore over the Scriptures, I find more evidence that God is going to rescue and deliver me. I see what he means through the following Word concerning "wicked devices":

> Dear brothers, if a Christian is overcome by some sin, you who are godly should gently and humbly help him back onto the right path, remembering that next time it might be one of you who is in the wrong. Share each other's troubles and problems, and so obey our Lord's command. (Gal. 6:1–2 TLB)

How is it that when you have something against another Christian, you "go to law" and ask a heathen court to decide the matter instead of taking it to other Christians to decide which of you is right? Don't you know that someday we Christians are going to judge and govern the world? So why can't you decide even these little things among yourselves? Don't you realize that we Christians will judge and reward the very angels in heaven? So you should be able to decide your problems down here on earth easily enough. Why then go to outside judges who are not even Christians? I am trying to make you ashamed. Isn't there anyone in all the church who is wise enough to decide these arguments? But, instead, one Christian sues another and accuses his Christian brother in front of unbelievers. (1 Cor. 6:1–6 TLB)

If your brother sins against you, go and show him his fault, just between the two of you. If he listens to you, you have won your brother over. But if he will not listen, take one or two others along, so that "every matter may be established by the testimony of two or three witnesses." If he refuses to listen to them, tell it to the church; and if he refuses to listen even to the church, treat him as you would a pagan or a tax collector. (Matt. 18:15–17 NIV)

Next, my Coach has me settle into the words, "Fret not." I was informed that if the charges were upheld, I could lose my commission or even be court-martialed. The warrant officer also advised me that often the system will make one "sweat it out." For the entire month of June, I wrestled between those thoughts that caused my stomach to sink and the decision to rest, stay myself, and wait patiently on God's Word. I would wake up in the middle of the night and not be able to go back to sleep because of my worrying.

> When I was in distress, I sought the Lord; at night I stretched out untiring hands and my soul refused to be comforted.... You kept my eyes from closing; I was too troubled to speak. (Ps. 77:2, 4 NIV)

The only way I could calm down enough to sleep was to get up and dive headlong into the Word until it, again, sunk into my spirit, into my mind, and finally into my body to rest. I asked God to keep speaking his Word to me as I slept. If Satan were to awaken me again, I would simply remind him and myself that God was working on things while I slept.

> Out of the depths I have cried to You, O
> LORD;
> LORD, hear my voice!
> Let Your ears be attentive
> To the voice of my supplications.

If You, LORD, should mark iniquities,
O LORD, who could stand?
But *there is* forgiveness with You,
That You may be feared.

I wait for the LORD, my soul waits,
And in His word I do hope.
My soul *waits* for the LORD
More than those who watch for the
morning—
Yes, more than those who watch for the
morning. (Ps. 130:1–6 NKJV)

My belt tightened by three notches as I ate to live, not vice versa. The Word has said that fret "only leads to harm." I had to make a faith-decision and choose to think, speak, act, feel, and decide according to the Word given. This required informing my right brain to function accordingly. Body and mind both needed to feel or register what my spirit knew. Choosing to attend praise services where hands were clapping to the music helped some in that decision, to do what I do not feel like doing because I was "fretting." I took my own medicine and gave some of that tearful and gritted-teeth thanks: "Dear Father, thank you for allowing these events to be just as they are. Thank you for what you can do with them." This is part of God's answer to my prayer for him to help me make that *decision* of faith. The deeper truth lay in the fact that this faith-decision had to be one like a little child makes in trusting his or her parents to fix what is hurting, not knowing how they will do it, just that they will. This faith would not employ any "possibility thinking," "power of positive thinking," visualization techniques, or special rituals or mental steps I could go through. It would not be just a feeling that God is going to do something; it would simply be a trusting relationship, expecting the Father to send his Word forth to do what he has promised, "in his way" (Is. 55:8) and "in his time" (Ecc. 3:11). In the words of Zechariah 4:6b, "Not by might, nor by power, but by my spirit, saith the Lord of hosts." This deeper truth is actually a relief to me. His Word saluted that decision:

> For he (God) himself has said, I will not in any way fail you nor give you up nor leave you without support. (I will) not, (I will) not, (I will) not in any degree leave you helpless, nor forsake nor let (you) down, (relax my hold on you).—Assuredly not! (Heb. 13:5b AMP).

> In God I will praise his word, in God I have put my trust; I will not fear what flesh can do unto me. (Ps. 56:4 KJV)

> You have seen me tossing and turning through the night. You have collected all my tears and preserved them in your bottle! You have recorded every one in your book.... This one thing I know: God is for me! I am trusting God—oh, praise his promises! I am not afraid of anything mere man can do to me! Yes, praise his promises. I will surely do what I have promised, Lord, and

thank you for your help. For you have saved me from death and my feet from slipping, so that I can walk before the Lord in the land of the living. (Ps. 56:9b–13 TLB; see Heb. 13:5b–6; Ps. 118:6)

About the middle of this "month of fire," I charted a new running course up a steep hill behind the military base. The trees there were tall and majestic. It was raining, and at the top of the hill I lifted up my arms in a most anguished and painful sacrifice of praise (tearful thanks) for *all*. My tears, then, began to give nature's raindrops some competition. It was a much-needed release.

The Wall

By the end of the second week, my Coach began to show me what the "month of fire" was really about. It burned in two directions at once, creating a back draft that almost smothered me with fear. As mentioned in Chapter One, I had sketched out notes for a devotional book, with each month having a theme. I had not, until this experience, realized the utter depth with which God had charged this month's theme. This was the month to actually "crucify the self" (Gal. 2:20 KJV). Was this the "still-deeper level" on the road to repentance that I had sensed God was "deadly serious" about? He wanted not only repentance for thoughts and actions but also for the "appearance of evil."

In one direction, the fire burned with a fear of the unknown as I engaged in the marathon of waiting. The other direction burned with the following Scriptures:

> There is no use trying to bring you back to the Lord again if you have once understood the Good News and tasted for yourself the good things of heaven and shared in the Holy Spirit, and know how good the Word of God is, and felt the mighty powers of the world to come, and then have turned against God. You cannot bring yourself to repent again if you have nailed the Son of God to the cross again by rejecting him, holding him up to mocking and to public shame. (Heb. 6:4–6 TLB)

> If anyone sins deliberately by rejecting the Savior after knowing the truth of forgiveness, this sin is not covered by Christ's death; there is no way to get rid of it. There will be nothing to look forward to but the terrible punishment of God's awful anger which will consume all his enemies. A man who refused to obey the laws given by Moses was killed without mercy if there were two or three witnesses to his sin. Think how much more terrible the punishment will be for those who have trampled underfoot the Son of God and treated his cleaning blood as though it were common and unhallowed, and insulted

and outraged the Holy Spirit who brings God's
mercy to his people. (Heb. 10:26–29 TLB)

The word that sinks deep into my mind from this last text,
desperately demanding a response, is *deliberate*. The King
James Version uses the word *willfully* and cites the following
text as an exposition of its meaning:

> For if, after they have escaped the pollutions of
> the world through the knowledge of the Lord
> and Savior Jesus Christ, they are again entangled
> in them and overcome, the latter end is worse
> for them than the beginning. For it would have
> been better for them not to have known the way
> of righteousness, than having known it, to turn
> from the holy commandment delivered to them.
> (2 Peter 2:20–21 NKJV)

I just hit the wall in the June (Month of Fire) marathon; this
wall "tremored" with quakes and aftershocks. My mind and
body did not want to go on. I was more frightened by the
above Scriptures than I was of the charges. Like Hezekiah
on his death bed, my "face is to the wall" (2 Kings 20:3).

One day, as I sat numbly in the chair that had become my
"altar," the only thing that came to mind was an old children's
song: "Jesus loves me, this I know … because the Bible tells me
so." My mind was saying that the above Scriptures condemned
me to a hopeless condition. I wondered if I had trampled the
new covenant, which holds so much more power than the

old covenant, and thereby deserved double punishment with no hope of remission? These words and the Sermon on the Mount (Matt. 7) were confronting me with "having a form of godliness, but denying the power thereof" (2 Tim. 3:5). Paul adds, "Moreover it is required in stewards, that a man be found faithful" (1 Cor. 4:2). I said to myself, *Here my wife has been in the States these many months getting in shape to be with me in body, mind, and spirit as God's gift to me; and here I am in Germany hugging other women. A leopard really can't change its spots. Am I a "wolf in sheep's clothing"* (Matt. 7:15)? To this disposition came the words: "Why art thou cast down, O my soul? And why art thou disquieted in me? Hope thou in God: for I shall yet praise him for the help of his countenance" (Ps. 42:5 KJV).

The next day, before I ran, I repeatedly—almost as though I thought he was hard of hearing—asked God to give me a clear and certain understanding about those hard-hitting Scriptures as they related to me and to the Psalm 37 Word of deliverance. I was asking for a moment of truth during that run, as he so often gives. Just minutes prior to starting the run, the words "Thy Word is truth … and you shall know the truth and the truth shall make you free" came to my remembrance. During the run, he directed me to turn my thoughts again, sharply, to Romans 7. (I invite you to slowly read this entire chapter from your own Bible. Anyone who reads it will identify with every word, especially verses 7–25.) I realized later, as I sat down for a good, long read, that since the words *deliberate* and *willful* did not apply to me, I could count on the following words in my case: "And by this we know that we are of the truth, and shall assure our hearts before Him. For if our heart condemns us, God is greater than our heart, and knows all things. Beloved, if our heart does not condemn us, we have confidence toward God" (1 John 3:19–21 NKJV).

The above Scripture revealed the truth to me that says I was not "deliberately or willfully" sinful, for that would cheapen God's grace like those who, mentioned earlier, the apostle Paul addressed in Rome and who said that if grace always abounded to cover their sins, then why should they not just go out and sin all the more? I grew up on a dairy farm. How would it do for me to watch a cow give all her milk, as directed, into a bucket and then for me to just casually walk over and kick it over, cheapening it? I am thankful for a growing hatred (Amos 5:15) of that very idea.

But instead, not only had I been saved from the guilt and penalty of sin, I was in the process of being set free from the habit and dominion of sin (see Rom. 6:14; Phil. 2:12–13; Rom. 8:2). Furthermore, Jesus is the "author and finisher of (my) faith" (Heb. 12:2) to obedience, and one day I will be set free from the very presence of sin (see footnote, Scofield Reference Bible, p. 1192). If I just believe that my sins have been forgiven and that I will remain "justified" with God only if I never sin again, then I fail to understand that God's presence, the Holy Spirit, will always remain with me (see John 14:16). John wrote, "We know that whosoever is born of God sinneth not" (1 John 5:18 KJV), but the original text means "does not *practice* sin." The Amplified Bible translation reads, "We know (absolutely) that anyone born of God does not (deliberately and knowingly) practice committing sin, but the One Who was begotten of God carefully watches over and protects him—Christ's divine presence within him preserves him against the evil—and the wicked one does not lay hold (get a grip) on him or touch (him)" (1 John 5:18 AMP).

My "wall" passages refer to someone who rejects Jesus as the way of salvation. Taken in the context of the whole of Scripture, my sinful condition is not the same as that rejection! But I needed confirmation. God says, "Without counsel purposes are disappointed: but in the multitude of counsellors they are established" (Prov. 15:22 KJV). Renowned Bible teacher Kenneth Hagin wrote me with the counsel that "the sin unto death" is committed by someone who is "mature in the Word and operating in the gifts of the Spirit. Then, when that person deliberately turns their back on God and decides to go back into a life of sin and service to the devil, they can reach a point when the Holy Spirit will no longer deal with them— they have already made their life's choice." He further pointed out that the Hebrews passages were Paul's words to Hebrew Christians who were under the threat of excommunication by other Jews if they did not reject or deny Christ.

God was directing me to carefully search out his Word so as to bring me still deeper on that road to repentance and unfold a more profound understanding of "the fear of the Lord." Proverbs 24:6 says, "In an abundance of counselors there is victory and safety." Accordingly, two calls to the Billy

Graham counseling staff, asking for their confirmation on the above, brought that confirmation as they drew my attention to the following Scriptures:

> All whom My Father has given (entrusted) to Me will come to Me; and him who comes to Me I will most certainly not cast out—I will never, no never reject one of them who comes to Me. (John 6:37 AMP)

> The sheep that are My own hear and are listening to My voice, and I know them and they follow Me, And I give them eternal life, and they shall never lose it or perish throughout the ages—to all eternity they shall never by any means be destroyed. And no one is able to snatch them out of My hand. (John 10:27–8 AMP)

One of their counselors gave me permission to use an illustration that I found to be very helpful. What happens when you take a triangle and start rolling it over and over? Pretty soon, the edges get worn off, resulting in no friction with the ground. When we sin deliberately and willingly, this is what happens to our conscience, leaving no room for "godly sorrow over our sins." If I feel that friction and the bump or thump on the road, then I have not fallen into the "wall." My Coach reminded me of my training regimen (to cast down, deaden, crucify) and then led me to a Scripture: "For if you live according to (the dictates of) the flesh you will surely die. But if through the power of the (Holy) Spirit you are habitually putting to death—making extinct, deadening—the (evil deeds prompted by the body, you shall (really and genuinely) live forever" (Rom. 8:13 AMP).

A third "counselor," an Independent Baptist pastor steeped in the Word, made these reflections on my "wall" Scriptures: After citing instances in which David, Moses, Samson, Abraham, Noah, and Jacob willfully sinned with "acts" of sin—not a "practiced lifestyle of sin"—he summarized by saying, "In this passage we are *not* dealing with acts of sin by which we are repentant and seek God's cleansing and forgiveness. This is willful, continual sin. This is willfully choosing a life of sin and not turning to God."

The part of this counselor's advice that still grabbed my heart with conviction is the part addressing a "lifestyle" of sin. So I wrote the following letter to the Billy Graham Guidance Department and to David Wilkerson, author of the famous book *The Cross and the Switchblade,* and received the subsequent replies from both:

> Dear Dr. Graham,
>
> I understand Paul's words in Romans 7 to outline the impossibility of keeping the old covenant law due to our fallen humanity and that the cross and 1 John 1:9 address that fall. I understand the hard-hitting Word in Hebrews 6:4–6 as addressing those Jews who had come to accept/believe the new covenant but then

rejected it. However, Hebrews 10:26–31 has become a spiritual "wall" for me! When I look at this passage, my heart condemns me for my weakness and hypocrisy. I have "had a form of Godliness but denying the power thereof," served as a "wolf in sheep's clothing," compromised my testimony, and became a "byword"—shame to His Name! As Hebrews 13:17 states, I will have to give an account of my unfaithful servanthood. The more I search the Scriptures, the way I see it, the best I can hope for is 1 Corinthians 3:14–15, "saved; yet so as by fire," the alternative being Hebrews 10:27: "but only a fearful expectation of judgment and of raging fire that will consume the enemies of God."

My sin seems more of a "lifestyle" of sin in the sense of having a mind full of lust and, therefore, idolatry. So how do I find the balance or whole truth as I weigh out the above Scriptures? As they stand alone, I stand condemned. Does the parable of the wages equally paid to the servant who came in at the last hour apply to me? My "prodigal walk" has been too long to be considered as coming in at any other hour. My posture is that of the publican who could only beat his chest as he fell down before Jesus to say, "Have mercy on me, a sinner" and that of the penitent thief on the cross.

Over the past decade, God has been convicting me that I need to have three levels in the "fear of the Lord (that) is the beginning of wisdom." Level one: fear of the consequences of my sin; level two: fear of missing out on God's best; level three: fear of wounding God's heart any more with my sins. Even though I've prayed for God to help me have "godly sorrow (over my sin) that produces a repentance that leads to salvation" (2 Cor. 7:10) and for Him to "help (me) want to obey Him, and then to help (me) do what He wants" (Phil. 2:13), I worry that my *fear of the Lord* rests more on level one than the other two.

The Word tells me that "there is strength in many counselors." That's the reason for my seeking out faithful servants of the Word. When I called the Billy Graham counseling staff, the counselor concluded by saying, "You need to stop reading those Hebrew passages." Yet, the Holy Spirit coaches me that I need to remember God saying to live by "every Word." Your modern-day "John-the-Baptist like" leadership and authority through the Word are what guide me to write this heavy question to your care and counsel. I greatly need your help both for my salvation security and for a book I'm writing about all this, to one day hold the truth from His Word!

Following words of assurance about Christ's provision for forgiveness, repentance, and overcoming, Graham's reply was as follows:

> It is clear that the writer does not expect the people to whom he is writing to miss salvation; see verse 9. In addition, verse 6 makes it clear that he is not talking about people who think they have rejected Christ and *want* to repent and find restoration. The people he is talking about are people who truly reject the gospel and then no longer have any interest in repentance and restoration.
>
> This passage should not be seen as sweeping away the availability of forgiveness for those who desire it. That would cast doubt upon the completeness of God's mercy. The way back to God after any kind of sinning is through confession, repentance and forsaking sin. God will not turn away a repentant sinner. Note Isaiah 1:18, John 6:37, and 1 John 2:1–2.
>
> The basis for the interpretation of Hebrews 10:26 is the word "knowledge." If a person rejects the truth of Christ's death for sin, there is no other sacrifice for sin available and no other way to come to God; read Acts 4:12.

The book of Hebrews was written to persecuted people who were wondering if they were right in following Jesus rather than establishing their righteousness by fulfilling the ordinances of the law. They were considering the return to the temporal institutions and ordinances of the Old Testament, which had been fulfilled in Jesus Christ. With this knowledge, therefore, the return to the works of the law could be regarded as an open rejection of the blood of the covenant which was shed for one and all in the perfect sacrifice for sin, namely, Jesus Christ.

Hebrews, chapter 10, emphasizes the finality of Christ's sacrifice by contrasting it with the lack of finality of the Old Testament law and sacrifices. Christ's redemption needs no repetition and no supplementation. Therefore, the rejection of Christ's sacrifice on the cross is final and unforgivable, and the only sin that God cannot forgive. We trust this is helpful to you.

Wilkerson wrote in response,

While there is life, there is hope. You are not yet at the judgment seat of Christ, and we believe that if you did fall into the category of no repentance, you would not be concerned about it. No matter how many times you have fallen, or how deep the pit is that you have fallen into, the love of Christ is deeper still. The devil is a liar and seeks to keep you away from the Lord with this tormenting lie. I quote from Adam Clarke's Commentary on Hebrews 10:26–31:

> This is the meaning of the apostle, and the case is that of a deliberate apostate— one who has utterly rejected Jesus Christ and his atonement, and renounced the whole Gospel system. It has nothing to do with backsliders in our common use of that term. A man may be overtaken in a fault, or he may deliberately go into sin, and yet neither renounce the Gospel, nor deny the Lord that bought him. His case is dreary and dangerous, but it is not hopeless; no case is hopeless but that of the deliberate apostate, who rejects the whole Gospel system, after having been saved by grace, or convinced of the truth of the Gospel. To him there remaineth no more sacrifice for sin; for there was but ONE, Jesus, and this he has utterly rejected. (From Adam Clarke's Commentary, electronic database, Copyright ©1996 by Biblesoft)

Wilkerson continued, referring to Scriptures (Micah 7:19; Ez. 36:25–27; Jer. 32:40) to address my "hills." I especially liked the following from Psalm 37, which God had been sinking deep into my heart: "The Lord ... forsaketh not his saints; they are preserved forever" (Ps. 37:28). He closed with a word about having a "contrite heart" and said that God is preparing me for something greater in which he can use even those things that Satan intended to destroy me.

Still a fifth counselor, Arno Froese, the head of a global outreach effort centered squarely on the Word, Midnight Call Ministries, also wrote a very clear and caring response to my letter of spiritual dilemma. His response, which follows, and my letter were printed in the Midnight Call International magazine in 2002:

> Hebrews 6:4–6 documents that it is impossible to be saved twice. Hebrews 10:26–30 tells that sinning deliberately and purposefully will lead to the judgment of God. This "sin" is not identified, but it is obviously the sin of ignoring or even rejecting the already accomplished work of Jesus on Calvary's Cross. This does not speak of sins such as identified in 1 John 1:7–10. Note that it says in verse 9: "… and to cleanse us from all unrighteousness." Hebrews 10 speaks of the deliberate rejection of the work of salvation. What will happen? The Bible does indicate that Heaven is like a house wherein are vessels unto honor and vessels unto dishonor (see 2 Tim. 2:19–22).

The fact that you believe in Jesus and wish to serve Him does not place you in the category of those who openly and deliberately reject the sacrifice of Jesus. You need not despair, because if you sin "willfully" and "deliberately," then you'd have no intention to confess. The devil continues to lead you into a seemingly hopeless dead-end situation, but remember, he is the father of lies and is defeated the moment you practice (1 John 1:8–10).

In another letter exchange with this fifth recognized spiritual leader, I wrote, "I have long viewed you as a modern day "Moses figure" when it comes to clear exposition of the Scriptures! After my four-page letter to you, describing my sin battle and its death grip—making it hard for me to wrestle away from "my sins being ever before me," as David expressed—my coach said: "Forgetting those things which are behind and reaching forward to those things which are ahead" (Phil. 3:13), thereby simply trusting 1 John 1:9 to be enough."

Froese wrote in response, "The great apostle Paul recognized that he fell short of the glory of God, but as a new creature in Christ, he recognized that it is the absolute work of God—it is a miracle, perfect and eternal. When you stand before the judgment seat of Christ, He cannot say, 'Depart from me for I never knew you' because He does know you. The judgment seat of Christ determines your reward, not salvation or damnation."

Catherine Marshall, wife to Peter Marshall—outstanding chaplain to the US Senate— writes in *A Man Called Peter* that her husband "paused and seemed lost in thought as he stirred his third cup of tea. 'I think I may have to go through the agony of hearing all my sins recited in the presence of God. But I believe it will be like this—Jesus will come over and lay His hand across my shoulders and say to God, 'Yes, all these things are true, but I'm here to cover up for Peter. He is sorry for all his sins, and by a transaction made between us, I am now solely responsible for them.'" (See Heb. 7:25; 1 John 2:1; 1 Cor. 1:8.) I, timidly, beg to disagree with the chaplain on the point of "hearing all my sins recited in the presence of God." Why? If God forgives my sins by forgetting, erasing, healing, covering, removing them as far as East is from West, and makes even the scarlet white as snow …, why would they be brought back up? Let the reader discern.

> "Blessed is he whose transgression is forgiven, whose sin is covered. Blessed is the man to whom the Lord does not impute iniquity, and in whose spirit there is no deceit" (Ps. 32:1–2 KJV).

The long journey through the Word at this point tells me that there is an important difference between "sin" and "sins." The former is my old nature; the latter are revelations of that nature. Because Jesus gives me a new nature through what he accomplished for me on the cross and my faith in that work, I can say that my heart, through forgiveness and grace (his unmerited favor), does not condemn me (see 1

John 3:20–21), and repentance can still be performed (see Ez. 18:21–32). King David's sin was willful and deliberate; yet, God saw David with a "heart after God's own heart." Since I have not hardened my heart as described in Hebrews 3:7–4:3, to the point of no return, the "wall" Scriptures do not condemn me like they do those people who will be surprised by the judgment in Matthew 7:21–23. When I begin my prayer with honest confession and then receive, by faith, God's mercy and forgiveness, I am then wearing the "breastplate of Jesus' righteousness" (*imputed* to me). In the words of King David's Psalm 51, God has created in me a clean heart (verse 10). Therefore, the promise made in 1 John 3:22—"And whatsoever we ask, we receive of him, because we keep his commandments, and do those things that are pleasing in his sight"—is firm and good to go in my case. It does not mean that I have become sinless, but I am, nevertheless, training to sin less. "Let your heart therefore be perfect with the Lord our God" (1 Kings 8:61a KJV). The footnote in the Scofield Reference Bible (p. 399) states that the word *perfect* in that verse "implies whole-heartedness for God, single-mindedness, sincerity"—not sinless perfection. I am to constantly engage the battle and "work" of believing in Christ that enables me to "put on" (see Col. 3:8–14) that new nature. The difference between "sin" and "sins" is clearly pointed out in the following:

> If we say we have no sin—refusing to admit that we are sinners—we delude and lead ourselves astray, and the Truth (which the Gospel presents) is not in us—does not dwell in our hearts. If we

(freely) admit that we have sinned and confess our sins, He is faithful and just (true to His own nature and promises) and will forgive our sins (dismiss our lawlessness) and continuously cleanse us from all unrighteousness—everything not in conformity to His will in purpose, thought and action. (1 John 1:8–9 AMP)

Further, I can count on the following Scripture because his Word is truly "abiding" in me more than ever: "If ye abide in me, and my words abide in you, ye shall ask what ye will, and it shall be done unto you" (John 15:7 KJV).

This joins the promise of 1 John 3:22. Both say "whatever you ask." And these words firmly bond with the following:

And this is the confidence—the assurance, the (privilege of) boldness—which we have in Him: (we are sure) that if we ask anything (make any request) according to His will (in agreement with His own plan) He listens to and hears us. And if (since) we (positively) know that He listens to us in whatever we ask, we also know (with settled and absolute knowledge) that we have (granted us as our present possessions) the requests made of Him. (1 John 5:14–15 AMP)

Deliverance is a "whatever." In summary, these three Scriptures told me that I had God's own word on it that my heart was okay with him, that his Word remained in me, and that I was praying his will because I was praying his Word. My Coach was, again, stacking up the Word as building blocks for the Father's house of grace, furnished by his Son. An "old" (from the early years of this decade of trials) *rhema* Word came to me again:

> Because he has set his love upon Me, therefore will I deliver him; I will set him on high, because he knows and understands My name (has a personal knowledge of My mercy, love and kindness; trusts and relies on Me, knowing I will never forsake him, no never). He shall call upon Me, and I will answer him; I will be with him in trouble, I will deliver him and honor him. With long life will I satisfy him, and show him my salvation. (Ps. 91:14–16 AMP)

The King James and Amplified versions cite, in exposition, the following:

> And they who know Your name (who have experience and acquaintance with Your mercy) will lean on and confidently put their trust in You; for You, Lord, have not forsaken those who seek (inquire of and for You) (on the authority of God's Word and the right of their necessity). (Ps. 9:10 AMP)

And call upon me in the day of trouble: I will deliver thee, and thou shalt glorify me. (Ps. 50:15 KJV)

And this verse addresses the "month of fire": "When thou walkest through the fire, thou shalt not be burned; neither shall the flame kindle upon thee" (Is. 43:2b KJV).

To "set (my) love" on God (see above, Ps. 91:14) means that I do not want to hurt his heart with my weak, sinful nature. Should I decide to go my own way, turn from the faith (the way out of my bondage to sin as described in Galatians 5:13–25), and reject Christ's work formed in me through his Word and by his Spirit living in me (the new nature), then my end is as described by those words from Hebrews and 2 Peter, which placed me before that overbearing "spiritual wall." It would amount to the Judas kiss of death. The Word's saying that we are to "work out (our) own salvation with fear and trembling" (Phil. 2:12b KJV) is taking on a new dimension. "Fear and trembling" is amplified to read, "(self distrust, that is, with serious caution, tenderness of conscience, watchfulness against temptation; timidly shrinking from whatever might offend God and discredit the name of Christ)" (AMP).

About one week after hitting that wall, I phoned my wife. During our conversation, she told me that she had accidentally cut down one of the pine trees she had planted back in the spring. She had planted three hundred to replace the ones we had sold as Christmas trees and for landscaping through the years. I thought, after asking her to order some back in the winter, that she would get some of the boys to plant them, but she meticulously planted each tree herself.

A few weeks after our phone conversation, I daydreamed about how she must have felt after accidentally cutting down that little tree. Then I began to imagine myself there, trimming around the trees and accidentally cutting down one that she had planted. I could see that I would feel terrible, especially after all the hard work she had put into it while I was away. As an extension of that daydream, God's Spirit had me begin thinking about how the Father must feel when recalling all the work and suffering his Son went through in order to pay the price for my salvation and forgiveness and then seeing me slip up and undercut it all. For me to do that undercutting "deliberately" or "willfully" is what the author of Hebrews describes as to "trample under foot the Son of God" and "insult … the Holy Spirit (who imparts) grace.…" I prayed, "Dear Father, remove me as far as the East is from the West to make sure I never come anywhere close to doing that ere the day of grace be ended!'" (See Training Regimen # 9.)

Psalm 37 becomes, again, "active," "alive," "sent out," "watched over," and "performed" (see Heb. 4:12; Is. 55:11; Jer. 1:12). The following two weeks were filled with prayers and directive words from Scripture that added momentum to my trust in God to *do* his Word. I needed evidence that I was not trying to turn faith into a work in order to persuade God to help me. Then his Word again came to the rescue: "This is the work of God, that ye believe (faith) on him whom he hath sent" (John 6:29 KJV). "The effectual fervent prayer of a righteous man availeth much" (James 5:16b KJV)—confirming that, since God has chosen to "impute" (reckon) to me "righteousness" through my trust in him, I can know that the prayers he leads me to pray will be "right prayers that bring right results." My Coach was leading me to pray the Word right back to the Father. All the prayers were asked in the name of Jesus and preceded by confession and requests for mercy, forgiveness, and deliverance to clear the way for them to be heard. Some of them were as follows:

> Continue to help me trust you, to be confident in your Word so that you can continue to "impute" righteousness to me from Jesus so that the Word is free to go out and perform what you send it out to do regarding these charges.

> Build your Word so deeply within me that nothing else from level one in the "fear of the Lord" will ever again be needed to move or motivate me to be firmly in your will. Deliver me from being my own worst enemy. When I, through the fear of the Lord, come to the "beginning of wisdom," help me keep that wisdom tightly bound within me so as to never again have to be motivated by those first two levels in "the fear of the Lord." Help me to let your wisdom (Word) be sufficient.

> He spoke through Proverbs 14:26–27 (KJV): "In the fear of the Lord there is strong confidence,

and His children will have a place of refuge. The fear of the Lord is a fountain of life, to turn one away from the snares of death."

I continued to try hard to go deeper into an honest conversation:

Deliver me from the evil one and forgive me for giving him the ammunition he needed to enable "wicked devices" to be brought forth. Deliver me from the consequences that could arise from what has been set in motion, even as you did for Mary Magdalene.

Plant the cross so deeply within my heart (1 Cor. 1:18) that it shapes and molds it to fit your will and Word, building the Shema to a pinnacle where I will really love you by keeping your commands (John 14:15), never again to be a shame to your name! I will love you more and more because you first loved me (1 John 4:19). This daily exercise will form my obedient heart, as I "forget not all your benefits" (Ps. 103:2). Let me, therefore, see that day when you can look at me and say that I have a heart after your own heart!

He answered, in my time of study, the last two prayers:

> Is not My Word like fire (that consumes all that cannot endure the test)? says the Lord, and like a hammer that breaks in pieces the rock (of most stubborn resistance)? (Jer. 23:29 AMP)

I replied as follows:

> I open my whole being to you. Help me in the "crucifixion of my self" (old nature) by letting me will my heart to you in that death of the self. I place that old heart on your operating table and ask you to perform "open-heart" surgery with your sharper-than-a-two-edge-sword Word, thereby transforming me through a transplant of Jesus' heart for mine.

> Make your Word increasingly "abide and live" (John 15:7) in my heart. Cleanse my heart thoroughly through honest confession and your mercy and forgiveness, making it pure and uncondemning (1 John 3:19–22) so that I can, as these two Scriptures promise, "ask whatever (I) will and (see that) it shall be done for (me)."

Yes, sir, this prayer hit the nail right on the head, didn't it?

In response to these last two prayers about my heart, I was led to this Scripture: "And I will give you a new heart—I will give you new and right desires—and put a new spirit within you. I will take out your stony hearts of sin and give you new hearts of love. And I will put my Spirit within you so that you will obey my laws and do whatever I command" (Ez. 36:26–27 TLB).

And as he said to Israel about a new covenant with them, "I will imprint My laws upon their minds, even upon their innermost thought and understanding, and engrave them upon their hearts" (Heb. 8:10b AMP). I continued praying.

> Holy Spirit, I ask you to pray for my deliverance, prayers that only you know need to be prayed for the Father's Word to go out on this case. Bypass my fears and self-centered requests and pray what will truly connect my mind and heart with his. I ask you to do what the Word promises in Romans 8:26–27 (TLB): "And in the same way—by our faith—the Holy Spirit helps us with our daily problems and in our praying. For we don't even know what we should pray for, nor how to pray as we should; but the Holy Spirit prays for us with such feeling that it cannot be expressed in words. And the Father who knows all hearts knows, of course, what the Spirit is saying as he pleads for us in harmony with God's own will."

> As you see that day coming for the announcement of deliverance from these charges, prepare me in the Word–faith connection so as to honor your Word and name. Lead me to have an expectant

hope and a confident trust in you. Thank you, Father, even before my eyes see it. Praise your name that it will be "not by might, nor by power, but by my spirit, saith the Lord of hosts." (Zech. 4:6b KJV)

You may wonder how I have remembered the words to all those prayers. The secret is that after each one has been prayed, I write it down because I know the day will come for me to "recount" (Ps. 118:17) so that you and others can see that these were right prayers that brought right results. Written down, they, first of all, bring greater inner conviction as the Word confirms them. In fact, for the most part, they are the Word being prayed right back to the Father. I also came to rest on the Scripture that says, "For thou hast magnified thy word above all thy name" (Ps. 138:2b KJV). I continue to recruit others who I know can pray the Word, the prayer of faith. If the apostle Paul asked for prayer support under severe stress, certainly it would be wise for me to do the same (see 2 Cor. 1:8–11; Rom. 15:30–31a).

Three more steps toward inner conviction came in my training runs during the month of fire. The runs provided the stage for my Coach to settle the Word much more securely into my mind and spirit. Those moments of truth were so meaningful to me that I wrote them down in the journal I started keeping on this tour for Connie. One entry in that journal follows:

In today's run, I asked God to build a "confident trust" in his Word and the understanding he has given me about his deliverance from these charges. First, he clearly said to my spirit and mind, in that order, "I have given you My Word. Nothing can be more 'sure' than that. It is even written down." [Later, a review of Hebrews 11:1 in the Amplified Bible underscored this for me. The original text for the word *assurance* is amplified to read, "the confirmation, the title-deed." I have seen the written (Psalm 37) "title-deed."]

In a second step, he said that since I have an inner conviction that these charges have been allowed as his way to answer my prayer from back in the winter quarter—the one in which I asked him to *take my deceitful heart and close up any loopholes still there*, as only he knew what it would take to motivate me to get deeper into his will on level three in the "fear of the Lord"—I can rest in the knowledge that he considers *that* "conviction" to be faith and that it will, therefore, be "done unto (me) according to (my) faith." I said, "Thank you for knowing what my mind needed."

Third, I asked during the run if he had still another boost to my confidence. He began to "garrison" (surround, protect, provide) my heart and mind as he continued to cause Word to uphold Word (bind by twisting together). He led me into the mental singing of his Isaiah 40:31 Word. The thoughts that came to me are enclosed in parentheses in the following: They that *wait* (that's what the Psalm 37 Word is saying) upon the Lord ... (to wait on his Word is to wait on him) mount up with wings like eagles (that would be deliverance as the "noonday sun"). Next, as I sang,: "Jesus, name above all names" (he is in control of *all* these other circumstantial "names"), "beautiful savior, glorious Lord" (he knows how to save and deliver as Savior and how to train me into the faith of obedience as my Lord), "Emmanuel, God is with us" (he remains "with me" as he told me once when I was high on a mountain that he would), blessed redeemer (nothing that he can't work with and bring something good out of), "living Word" (as in Heb. 4:12 and Is. 55:11). Psalm 121 and Psalm 23, which I had set to tune of the "Chariots of Fire" theme song, came next. Psalm 121 includes the phrases, "unto the hills" (so often this is where he brings me his Word, moments of truth), "help comes from the Lord" (help is what his Psalm 37 Word promises), "not let your foot be moved" (from Germany, from chaplaincy, from "hope and a future"), "keep ... from all evil" (also, as stated in Psalm 37), "from this time forth" (Your Word is good for yesterday, today, and tomorrow). Then Psalm 23 includes "my shepherd ... not want" (he, *being* the Word, directs it to me as needed), "down in green pastures ... still waters" (one day I will be homeward bound), "restores my soul for his name's sake" (yes, he will do this deliverance according to his Word of grace and for his name's sake), "yea, though I walk through the valley of the shadow of death, I will fear no evil" (his deliverance is promised in Psalm 37), "rod and staff comfort me" (his Word is his power over all; even to the Goliaths out there, "it" will go forth like a rock from a great slingshot to the mark), "cup overflows" (his grace has been poured out 'superabundantly'), and "dwell in the Lord's House" (as in 1 Cor. 11:32).

At that point in the run, I was close to the steep path through the woods above the military base where I had the previous week lifted up my arms and cried. Today, as I get to that point, I simply pray, "Dear Father, help me have the kind of faith in your Word that pleases you. Thanks for reminding me that when circumstances and feelings say one thing, I can say, "Nevertheless, God's Word says that if God is for me, who can be against me? He will rescue me and deliver me, not let my foot be moved, and guide me through the shadow of death. It is not necessary to repeat shameful things from the past. In quietness and in confidence shall be my strength, as I trust in you and not me."

After another training run, I record an additional boost to my trust level:

> I can recall saying to people that sometimes the faith that waits can be the hardest faith. I'm living those words now. Today, God's Spirit, my Coach, tells me to ask him to pray the Lord's Prayer for me regarding this case, that I might view it from the "glasses" of those petitions. Here's what unfolds as we run and pray:
>
>> "Our Father" (he's the Father of all in this case), "hallowed ... name" (Dear Father, deliver me through your grace so that I will be moved through level three in the "fear of the Lord" to never again be a shame to your name). "Thy

kingdom come" (bring it to pass—your deliverance—as you said to me in your Word). "Thy will be done" (your Word is your will; thank you for giving it to me. I believe you will, therefore, do Romans 8:28 and Philippians 2:13 with all forces in this case. I trust you at your Word.) "Give … daily bread" (thank you that the bread of your Word is coming to me daily. It feeds me.) "Forgive us as we forgive …" (thank you for leading me to forgive my accusers for 'bringing wicked devices to pass.') "Lead us not into temptation" (rescue me in my future where you know my weakness will fail your Word, your will). "Deliver us from evil" (thank you for your promise to do this through Psalm 37:5–8 and 39–40 and Micah 7:9). "Thine is the kingdom" (order of what will be), "the power" (your Word is your power), "and the glory" (all to be done to raise your Word over all and for your name's sake, as in Psalm 138:2). "Amen" (yes, sir, it is truth; it is done!).

From yet another run, my Coach led me to dwell on the hymn "Standing on the Promises." He then helped me envision the connection between that hymn and Peter trying to walk on the water to Jesus. As I ran and meditated, it dawned on me that standing on the promises of God's Word is like Peter's walking by faith on the water and sinking when he shifted to his own understanding or perception of things. That is what had been happening in me. But each time I *decide* to stand on what the Word has said, "It" keeps me from sinking into depression and despair; I break through the "wall." About halfway through the run, the story of the Prodigal Son comes to mind. For some reason, I am focused on the ring the father placed on his son's finger when he returned home, the robe he wrapped around him, and the shoes he placed on his feet. Then it dawned on me what this means in my case. The ring stood for being a royal member of the household in good standing; the robe meant that all in the household were available to him; and the shoes proclaimed that he was no longer a slave to his former condition. These three symbols announced the "(imputed) justice of my cause … like the noonday sun." My Coach told me that my confession and repentance, the Father's grace, and the promised Word mean that, like the prodigal son, I am "homeward bound." My Coach says, "I (can) know whom I have believed and (be) persuaded that he is able to keep that which I have committed unto him against that day" (2 Tim. 1:12 KJV).

One more confirmation that God was with me, which I'll enjoy telling you about, centered on my physical training test. I was told during the last week in June that I had to have mine done by June 28. The month of fire was still underway. I got up that morning at 0510 in preparation for the 0630 test. I was thinking, "I've broken training three weeks of June by not running regularly." This was, in part, due to spending time with my wife and the struggle with despair. I recall thinking the day before that my belt had come up still another notch. As I jogged up the long hill to the physical training site, my Coach said to me, "Wait upon the Lord" by keeping your mind on his Word of deliverance. Just like he can and would renew my strength in that "race," I knew he could do the same in this P.T. test. I said, "Okay" and decided to think, speak, act, feel, and decide, accordingly. The first event was push-ups: sixty-two would have maxed it, but I did seventy-seven. I felt better. Next were sit-ups (my weakness since the accident): sixty-seven was the maximum score and I managed seventy-three. Then came the two-mile run. As I moved into it, my Coach reminded me to "keep the stride." I quickly knew that meant to stand on the Word. So I maintained a good and long stride, letting the physical training run be a parable of the "June run." Next, he said, "Keep the pace." Quickly, again, I discovered that my pace automatically picked up with my stride. I knew that Jesus was the pace running within me—"God's strength (being) made perfect in my weakness." Then he said, "Keep the faith." I placed my face sternly into the wind, knowing that he means I should run with the "nevertheless-of-faith" when there seems to be no breath, will, stamina, or endurance. It is then that I felt his pleasure, as in Hebrews 11:6. Ahead I saw the finish line ("the mailbox"). I didn't feel the pavement or hear anything. I just knew that he was with me. As I crossed the finish line, I did hear "12 minutes, 47 seconds," maxing for someone in his midtwenties. As I did my warm-down, the evaluator came up and asked my age. When I said, "Fifty in two months," he said, "You're the best in the Army." I shook his hand and then raised mine and said, "Thank You, Father! Thank you, Jesus! Thank you, Holy Spirit!" This was the second opportunity for me to score a top mark of 300 on a physical training test since the accident; the first was at Fort Indiantown Gap, with a two-mile running time of eleven minutes and thirty-seven seconds, earning me the Physical Excellence Badge. Just months prior to the accident, I had run the same distance at Fort Jackson with a time of ten minutes and twenty-six seconds. I have, again, "run in his grace."

God's Answer

My wait stretched well into July, which was noted in my devotional book as the "month of endurance." And so it was, as I continued to wait for the Army's word that would reflect God's Word. I didn't know from day to day whether or not God would require me to wait until August (the month of hope) to hear his Word as "final provision." A fellow chaplain reminded me of a basic Scripture pertaining to these themes: "but he that shall endure unto the end, the same shall be saved" (Mark 13:13 KJV). I began praying for the kind of confidence in God's Word that would be like the apostle Paul's words, "in all these things we are more than conquerors" (Rom. 8:37). I want to see with the "eyes of faith" that God's promised deliverance is *more* than done, a "present possession," even as I wait. His Word came back to me: "Let be and be still, and know—recognize and understand—that I am God" (Ps. 46:10a AMP). When I break through a "wall" in any kind of marathon (body, mind, spirit), I know, from that point, that I will cross the finish line. I don't know how soon, just that I will make it. Once I'm through the wall, I'm in another world, not understanding how but just trusting (knowing) that I will get there. Therefore, it is a matter of taking one deliberate step (day) after another, dwelling only on the step (day) at hand. The steps, the days have got to occur. I'll see the "mailbox" in his time.

In one of my calls back home, my wife informed me that the rest of the household was worrying about not hearing from me. After outlining the situation, I concluded my letter to them as follows:

> I'm sorry for not writing; I haven't known what to say. I didn't want everybody having to go through the unknown with me. (It was the seventh week into this marathon of waiting.) The last thing I heard was that the commander sent up a recommendation for a letter of reprimand to the next level of command. But Army Europe—5th Corps (higher command) needed to approve it.

> The only peace I've had is in prayer, praise, and Scripture. A Word and a promise to which I believe God has led me in all this is Psalm 37:5–8, 39, 40 and Micah 7:9. The word *righteous* in these verses is defined by Romans 10:1–10; Romans 3:22–23, 4:1–8 and 21–24, 8:10; and Philippians 3:9 as God's "imputed" or "attributed" righteousness. The words *wicked*

devices are defined by Matthew 18:15–17; 1 Corinthians 6:1–8; and Galatians 6:1–2 as the manner in which the charges were brought forth; and the word *deliver* is confirmed by 1 Corinthians 1:18 as "by his grace"; Psalm 91:14–15 as I "trust" in him; and Hebrews 4:16 "in his time."

Would you join with me and pray that God would work his Philippians 2:13 Word through the 5th Corps—that he would "help (them) to will (decide) and to do His good pleasure"?

As the waiting marathon continued, I knew that the prayers I had prayed in the early years of this decade after the accident, the ones in which I asked for God to "transform me by the renewal of my mind" for true repentance brought about through "godly sorrow over my sin," were reaching their destination point because people were seeing that I was a different person. God was putting me through his coaching so that I could be better trained to his standards. Throughout this time of waiting, I held to the conviction that God had allowed the charges as his way of answering my prayer as he hammered that nail down deep and tied up any loopholes still in my heart (see Phil. 2:13 KJV). For convenience's sake, let me repeat what this verse says, "For it is God which worketh in you both to will and to do of his good pleasure."

Until the rapture occurs, every greeting to a woman who is not my wife, my daughter, or my mother needs to be a handshake. Each time I exercise that restraint, it will reflect the binding covenant between my heavenly Father and me. My arch of concern will still be to communicate care. That cannot be faked. People instinctively know whether a word or motion conveys care or carries a sexual overtone. I believe God can help me use a handshake to perform the former. A handshake can carry more meaning than a hug when God is behind it. Hugs, for me, break training. How? They do not constitute deadening the deeds of the flesh or crucifying the flesh (self). Once again, from across the ocean, my wife sent a Scripture from the apostle Paul that spanned the centuries:

> For you, brethren, were (indeed) called to freedom; only (do not let your) freedom be an incentive to your flesh and an opportunity or excuse (for selfishness), but through love you should serve one another. (Gal. 5:13 AMP)

So, the training on the road to repentance will continue and deepen. I will always carry the "shrapnel" from that Scripture that hit, the one my wife shared with me saying not to allow the "appearance of evil" (see 1 Thess. 5:20). The Holy Spirit reminds me that faith is an exercise. Just like God helps when I run but does not reach down with his hands and pick up my feet for me, I must *do* the steps of faith. James's words, widely quoted as "Faith without works is dead," originally read, "Faith without corresponding action is dead" (see James 2:17, 20, 26). My Coach spoke:

There is wonderful joy ahead, even though the
going is rough for a while down here. These
trials are only to test your faith, to see whether
or not it is strong and pure. It is being tested as
fire tests gold and purifies it—and your faith
is far more precious to God than mere gold. (1
Peter 1:6b–7a TLB)

The "battle plan for the mind," which involves 1) confession,
2) God's forgiveness, and 3) placement of the name Jesus over
each and every thought to become "captive to (his) obedience"
(see 2 Cor. 10:5), has picked up pace dramatically. Verse 6 of
this last Scripture again reminds me that in God's "army," he,
too, requires that I engage in "readiness training" and "train
to standard." That verse instructs me to "(be) in readiness
to punish every (insubordinate for his) disobedience, when
(my) own submission and obedience … (is) fully secured and
complete" (AMP). James succinctly sums it up: "So do away
with all the impurities and bad habits that are still left in
you—accept and submit to the word which has been planted
in you and can save your souls" (James 1:21 JB). This Scripture
demands that my thoughts line up under this stricter standard
and march to his orders. I need to daily pick wrong thoughts
out of my mind like weeds pulled from a garden. From my
garden, I've learned to rake over and pull weeds when they are
little and easy to handle; this saves me from such a struggle
dealing with them when they are big and have already sapped
up the goodness from the ground. My Coach said to apply
the same understanding to the weeds of temptation and bring
both body and mind under submission through vigorous

training, deciding through faith to be obedient to his Word. In today's language, I am to "just do it." "But be doers of the word and not hearers only, deceiving yourselves ... but a doer of the work, this one will be blessed in what he does" (James 1:22–25 KJV). "But the word is very near you, in your mouth and in your heart, that you may do it" (Deut. 30:14 KJV). "Now therefore perform the doing of it; that as there was a readiness to will, so there may be a performance also out of that which ye have" (2 Cor. 8:11 KJV). My prayer is, "Direct my steps by your Word, and let no iniquity have dominion over me" (Ps. 119:133 KJV; see also Eph. 4:23, Acts 20:32).

And this faith-decision to obey is to be and remain an expression of thanks and praise for his grace. I was being placed on his training program on a significantly different level, thereby moving me into his answer to that prayer that was repeatedly lifted up during the winter quarter. My heavenly Father knew that, had that moment-of-truth prayer and these charges not taken place, I was in danger of one day falling from grace because of what could proceed from those loopholes in my heart (right brain's feelings, memories, desires). I had already painfully learned that what gets my mind gets me (see James 1:13–15). Now, God was making it crystal clear that I need to run from any setting that would allow my eyes to catch the form of a beautiful woman, triggering the temptation to lust or launch thoughts out into the "imaginations of the heart." I need to, in every setting, instinctively "cast down, deaden, crucify." I need the wisdom of level three—the sign of the cross—to flash across my mind like a bolt of lightning over every temptation as I fall on my knees and tell Jesus: "Thank

You for fighting and winning this battle for me on the cross, and I'm trusting you to make it a practiced exercise (making the *sacrifice* of obedience) in my everyday life." There is a price to pay when sprinting the hill.

> Let your eyes look straight ahead, and your eyelids look right before you. (Prov. 4:25 NKJV)

> For if we searchingly examined ourselves— detecting our shortcomings and recognizing our own condition—we should not be judged and penalty decreed (by the divine judgment). (1 Cor. 11:31 AMP)

The Romans 7:21–24 "law" that "works within" me does not want to die but rebels when I proceed to "punish each insubordinate thought." Temptation is powerful; but I need to salute and do an about-face.

> For we naturally love to do evil things that are just the opposite from the things that the Holy Spirit tells us to do; and the good things we want to do when the Spirit has his way with us are just the opposite of our natural desires. These two forces within us are constantly fighting each other to win control over us, and our wishes are never free from their pressures. (Gal. 5:17 TLB)

He has placed me, through the guidance of my Coach, on his training program. He knew these actions, through the months of fire and endurance, would help train me to standard, as the Word resides in me as wisdom, leading me, when tempted, to frequently ask, "What would Jesus do?" Wisdom would be the force that enables me to continue with the practice of 2 Corinthians 10:5 (captive thoughts) so as to continually be at the exercise of Philippians 2:13 (willing and doing).

> Let not your heart envy sinners, but continue in the reverent and worshipful fear of the Lord all the day long. For surely there is a latter end (a future and a reward); and your hope and expectation shall not be cut off. Hear, my son, and be wise, and direct your mind in the way (of the Lord). (Prov. 23:17–19 AMP)

> If you will turn (repent) and give heed to my reproof, behold, I (Wisdom), will pour out my spirit upon you, I will make My words known to you. But whoso hearkens to me (Wisdom), shall dwell securely in confident trust, and shall be quiet without fear or dread of evil. (Prov. 1:23, 33 AMP)

Solomon, the preacher of vanities in the Book of Ecclesiastes, summed it up as follows:

> Let us hear the conclusion of the whole matter: Fear God, and keep his commandments: for

this is the whole duty of man. For God shall bring every work into judgment, with every secret thing, whether it be good, or whether it be evil. (Ecc. 12:13–14 KJV)

His Word also informs me that what I, through honest confession and repentance, bring to light on earth for his forgiveness will not have to be judged when I stand before him (see Heb. 10:17–18; 1 Cor. 3:13–15, 4:5, 11:31; 2 Cor. 5:10, 21; 1 John 1:9) and that the angels in heaven will clap their hands when they see me being repentant down here. I need to long for those ovations (see Luke 15:10.) Thus far, I could "know that I know."

My wife had given me a paragraph on faith, penned by British author M. Louise Haskins and spoken by King George VI of England in his 1939 Christmas message to the British Empire, to help with the "unknown" factor:

I said to the man who stood at the gate of the year, "Give me a light, that I may tread safely into the unknown," and he replied, "Go out into the darkness and put your hand into the hand of God. That shall be to you better than light and safer than a known way."

What I have written thus far, I have written as a step of faith, as "evidence" of my "conviction." Each step, each day of this "marathon" is taken in light of Philippians 2:12. That verse instructs me to "work out my salvation with fear and trembling." And that I'm doing! Repeatedly I ask, often sensing a trembling in my knees, for the Coach to help me be sure that I am rightly discerning and understanding his Word. I meditated upon "crucifixion of self," as in Galatians 2:19–20. I was led to write out in big letters where I could readily see it: OBE-<u>DIE</u>-NCE. My Coach gave me a prerace locker-room pep talk:

> But I say, walk and live habitually in the (Holy) Spirit—responsive to and controlled and guided by the Spirit; then you will certainly not gratify the cravings and desires of the flesh—of human nature without God. If we live by the (Holy) Spirit, let us also walk by the Spirit. If by the (Holy) Spirit we have our life (in God), let us go forward walking in line, our conduct controlled by the Spirit. (Gal. 5:16, 25 AMP)

God began coaching me through this "run," by saying, "Trust … and he would bring it to pass." He concluded the Psalm 37 message with, "He would deliver me because I trusted in him." In faith, I recall him saying it will be as the "noonday sun."

At this juncture, the marathon of "waiting" had entered the last week of the "month of endurance." It appeared that it was not God's will to grant my petition that I not have to wait for the month of hope (August) to have resolution. There seemed, however, to be circumstantial evidence of God's will in the matter of these charges; the way the interview with the investigating officer went and the counsel I had received from others who had either been through something very similar or witnessed a number of cases indicated that the time factor suggested that the case might just fade away. I prayed again, "Dear Father, I know you don't want me to lean on my own understanding, but I thank you for both your Word and the understanding." He had said to me years earlier that his Proverbs 3:5 Word about trusting him and not leaning on my understanding did not mean that I should not have any understanding.

However, it does mean that I should continuously go back to the Word. My favorite Scripture at the time, of course, was Psalm 37:5–8, 39–40. Just like that first day at my new duty station and billets, I decided, again, to read slowly and prayerfully through the *entire* psalm, not just the verses that had become alive and active for me to that point. This time, when I reached verses 23 and 24, it was again time to sit up and listen. The light bulb had once more turned on in my mind as it had in my original reading.

> The steps of a (good) man are directed and established of the Lord, when He delights in his way (and He busies Himself with his every step). Though he fall, he shall not be utterly cast down, for the Lord grasps his hand in support and upholds him. (Ps. 37:23–24 AMP)

For years, during my training runs and the mental "singing" of Psalm 121, I would lift up my arms in praise when the words "he will not let your foot be moved" came into my focus. The King James Version of Psalm 37:23 says, "The steps of a good man are ordered by the Lord." I have to say again, "But Father, I'm not good, just like the apostle Paul wrote, 'For I know that nothing good dwells within me'" (see Rom. 7:18). He reminds me that any "righteousness" or "goodness" is there only because he has "imputed" it because I trust him. He has allowed me to take the fall from my original assignment, yet he is not going to let me "be utterly cast down." He is still doing Romans 8:28 and Philippians 2:13. While these Scriptures mark time, three other verses from my favorite psalm jump out at me. My Coach leads me to read the words "wicked devices" in place of the words *wicked* and *evildoers* in the following Scripture:

> For (wicked devices) shall be cut off; but those who wait and hope and look for the Lord, (in the end) shall inherit the earth. For yet a little while and the (wicked devices) will be no more; though you look with care where (they) used to be, (they) will not be found. For the arms of the (wicked devices) shall be broken. (Ps. 37:9, 10, 17 AMP)

Could this be a prophecy of what God is going to do—just let it die out? In the military, when someone calls out, "Attention to orders," all come to attention, eyes forward and ready to salute. This was God's attention to orders. He was asking me to give my undivided attention, keep my eyes forward, and be ready to salute his Word. Therefore, I boldly asked God to commission his angels (warring, guarding, and ministering) to work and assist his Word in moving all who have anything to do with the final decision on the charges.

Following is a summary of the Word given to me. I was to "commit" (pray through) each care of my load to him. This word lives up to the original Hebrew translation of "to roll"; it becomes more and more an active verb as the marathon continued. As I wait for the time of God's "indignation" to end and for Jesus to "plead (the justice of) my cause," I can count on God's deliverance in two ways: one, from not being in "right standing" with him; and two, from "wicked devices." Both Psalm 37 and Micah 7:9 speak from the context of being delivered from such devices. Even the investigating officer, following his three-hour questioning of me, had, to my surprise, stated that the manner in which the charges had been brought forth was not right according to God's instructions. I had brought this all down on myself by giving Satan the ammunition he was seeking, but the manner in which the charges were brought was part of Satan's continued attempt to utterly cast me down.

On one occasion, during the conclusion of a training run, I was running through the woods above the military base up the top of the steep hill mentioned earlier. A strong image of a giant snake, standing straight up and trying to chase me out of the woods, formed in my mind. This was symbolic of evil coming against me. My sisters and brother-in-law had warned that Satan might have one last strike once God's deliverance was pronounced. In that regard, one of my sisters said that she was standing on the following Scripture:

> But no weapon that is formed against you shall prosper, and every tongue that shall rise against you in judgment you shall show to be in the wrong. This (peace, righteousness, security, triumph over opposition) is the heritage of the servants of the Lord (those in whom the ideal Servant of the Lord is reproduced). This is the righteousness or the vindication which they obtain from Me—this is that which I impart to them as their justification—says the Lord. (Is. 54:17 AMP)

When I spend real time with and maintain real focus on the Word, I always come to that point of inner peace and balance, almost like a little child who can ask a parent about something and then forget it as he or she goes out to play. I have not reached that level, but I get glimpses of it.

Because of advice from my counselor (Holy Spirit) and the counsel of family members, I see that I need to stop just rehearsing the Word and my conviction and start verbally and actively thanking God for his deliverance. This results in a deliberate shift in activities, one that would demonstrate to God and to myself and others that I actually do have the "title-deed" in my hands. One of my sisters pointed out that the word *meditate* means "to mutter." Worry is a form of muttering but the wrong type of meditation. I need to do a direct, diametrical shift away from worry to the muttering of the Word. It is time, past time, for me to shift from a gritted-teeth or tearful posture in the sacrifice of praise to a joyful/ expectant faith-propelled "thank-you" for God's answer. So I was speaking out the Word these days, and it was rising up within me to lift and direct not only my human spirit but my mind and body, also. It is like those times when "singing the Word" out loud as I run (see Rom. 10:10). This faith-activity with the Word was hiding me in God's secret place:

> He who dwells in the secret place of the Most High shall remain stable and fixed under the shadow of the Almighty (Whose power no foe can withstand). I will say of the Lord, He is my refuge and my fortress, my God, on Him I lean and rely, and in Him I (confidently) trust! For (then) He will deliver you from the snare of the fowler and from the deadly pestilence. (Then) he will cover you with His pinions, and under His wings shall you trust and find refuge; His truth and His faithfulness are a shield and a buckler. (Then) You shall not be afraid of the terror of the night, nor of the arrow (the evil plots and slanders of the wicked) that flies by day. (Ps. 91:1–5 AMP)

The consequent and "wholistic" health Word follows:

A calm and undisturbed mind and heart are
the life and health of the body (Prov. 14:30a
AMP).

A new surge of confident trust resulted as well:

The Lord is my rock, my fortress, and my
deliverer; my God, my keen and firm strength
in Whom I will trust and take refuge, my shield,
and the horn of my salvation, my high tower.
(Psalm 18:2 AMP)

You shall establish yourself on righteousness—
right, in conformity with God's will and order;
you shall be far even from the thought of
oppression or destruction, for you shall not fear;
and from terror, for it shall not come near you.
(Is. 54:14 AMP)

For God did not give us a spirit of timidity—
cowardice, of craven and cringing and fawning
fear—but (He has given us a spirit) of power and
of love and of calm and well-balanced mind and
discipline and self-control. (2 Tim. 1:7 AMP)

Will Daylight Come?

August, the "month of hope," includes the day that the
military announces God's answer. On August 6, I wrote the
following in the journal I was keeping for my wife:

"This is the day which the Lord hath made; we will rejoice and be glad in it" (Ps. 118:24 KJV). "Sing praise to the Lord, you saints of His, and give thanks at the remembrance of His holy name. For His anger is but for a moment, His favor is for life; weeping may endure for a night, but joy comes in the morning" (Ps. 30:4–5 KJV). God's answer, through military channels, holds both discipline and grace. I am summoned to the Commander's office where he issues a Letter of Reprimand. It addresses the hugs as "inappropriate" and unbecoming an officer and a chaplain. It goes on to say that the Major General and the Lieutenant General who decided the case were undecided as to whether the letter will become part of my military record. Concluding remarks state that this reprimand is an "administrative measure" and "not punishment under the Uniform Code of Military Justice." I can clearly see that God has, in actual fact, done Philippians 2:13 through those two- and three-star generals in the 5th Corps.

I keep my promise and go to the top of that hill where I conclude my training runs. There, for the better part of an hour, I give God deepest thanks for his grace, once again poured out for me. He did his Word! He disciplined me, proving his love for me (see Proverbs 3:12);

yet, he showered his grace, ushering in joyful tears and joyful thanks. But, do you recall from the movie *Chariots of Fire* the scene in which Harold Abrams, after finally winning, fell into a depression because he couldn't take winning? I'm sitting here feeling the same about God's grace.

And sitting here with no way to tell you all this but to write it down. I'll have to wait until 12:00 tomorrow so as to catch you before you go to work and tell you what God has done. I have now the Final Provision. It has been done as it has been written."

> The Lord has chastened me severely, but he has not given me over to death. (Ps. 118:18 KJV)

> How enviable the man whom God corrects! Oh, do not despise the chastening of the Lord when you sin. For though he wounds, he binds and heals again. He will deliver you again and again, so that no evil can touch you. (Job 5:17–19 TLB)

One hour before leaving to begin outprocessing from Germany, a call came saying that I could not leave until I had signed my Officer Efficiency Report (OER). A courier brought it for me to sign. All three raters had given favorable comments about the work done. Then I read the final attack, as my sisters had warned. The final comment from the senior rater read, "Do not promote; should be separated from the Army." I discovered that an agreement had been reached between the US commander who originally requested the letter of reprimand and the Germany 5th Corps, who disagreed with the commander and wanted the letter to provide for something stronger than an "administrative measure." The agreement was that I would receive an "unfavorable OER." This last "weapon formed against me" could, I found out, cause me to be retired early. So, back into the prayer closet we all went. Psalm 142 became my battle plea, especially verses 6–7:

> Attend unto my cry; for I am brought very low:
> deliver me from my persecutors; for they are
> stronger than I. Bring my soul out of prison
> that I may praise thy name: the righteous shall
> compass me about; for thou shalt deal bountifully
> with me. (Ps. 142:6–7 KJV)

When we arrived at Fort Benning, I told some of the other chaplains, "The ground looks better and the air smells fresher." I felt like that soldier who, several years earlier, had gotten off the plane, stooped down, and kissed the ground. The very next day, word came that a two-star general in the States had taken my case under advisement and recommended, through channels, that legal steps be taken to remove both the Letter of Reprimand and the OER from my Army personnel records. As a result, they never showed up in my military record jacket and, a year later, could not be found in the official military personnel file. This is Psalm 37:9, 10, 17 in action. They—the "wicked devices"—would be "broken," "cut off," and "not be found." Outside legal sources said that since there was "no judgment," nothing further can be done against me. I quickly and quietly recalled Psalm 37:6, in which God said that he would "bring forth (my) *judgment* as the noonday sun!" Then every word of Isaiah 54:17, such as "no weapon formed against me shall prosper," becomes "active and alive," "sent out," "watched over and performed," as are his many other words to me.

> He forgave us all our sins, having canceled the written code, with its regulations, that was against us and that stood opposed to us; he took it away, nailing it to the cross. And having disarmed the powers and authorities, he made a public spectacle of them, triumphing over them by the cross. (Colossians 2:14 NIV; see also vs. 13 and 15)

Another moment of truth prayer from this unfaithful servant went as follows:

> Dear Father, I know you don't want just my arms lifted up in praise and thanks. You want me to be able to thank you with my obedience (Matt. 7:21–23). I'm sorry for my sin placing me in "house arrest" instead of faithfully completing the last part of the mission—serving your people

to help bring them closer to you. I'm sorry for the waste I've been and caused. I'm sorry for causing you to have to be so "long-suffering" (Num. 14:18; Rom. 2:4; 2 Pet. 3:9) with me on the road to repentance! Help me to exercise the faith and sacrifice of obedience, in all things, as my "thank you" to you. By your Spirit, help me to recall the wisdom of your Word, letting Jesus' eyes and hands move through mine for all thoughts, words, actions, feelings, and decisions! May it one day be said, "He must have really loved God; look how he learned to obey him."

My Coach replied to me, *It's time to shift from the obedience of thanks to the thanks of obedience.* He was telling me that the time had arrived to activate level three in the "fear of the Lord"—revealing the "love of obedience." His Word came back to me:

> Jesus answered, If a person (really) loves Me, he will keep My Word—obey My teaching; and My Father will love him, and We will come to him and make Our home (abode, special dwelling place) with him. (John 14:23 AMP)

> He replied, "Yes, but even more blessed are all who hear the Word of God and put it into practice." (Luke 11:28 TLB)

"Behold, to obey is better than sacrifice." (1 Sam. 15:22 KJV)

RIGHT PRAYERS BRING RIGHT RESULTS

PRAYING THE WORD

A Scriptural Journey on the Road to Repentance

Thank you, Father, that today I can stop having a "form of Godliness and denying the power thereof" (2 Tim. 3:5) and that I can be "transformed by the renewing of (my) mind" (Rom. 12:2) because I am going to

Cast down the imaginations of (my) heart— making all of (my) thoughts captive to the obedience of Jesus. (2 Cor. 10:5)

Deaden the deeds of (my) flesh. (Rom. 8:13)

Crucify (my) self. (Gal. 2:20, 2 Cor. 5:15)

so that

I can do all things through Christ who strengthens me. (Phil. 4:13)

Become more than a conqueror through Christ who loved me and gave himself up for me. (Rom. 8:37)

317

Have "God's strength made perfect in my weakness." (2 Cor. 12:9)

so that

One day I can say, "It is no longer 'I' who live but Christ Who lives within me." (Gal. 2:20)

Why?

Because he is the Word and the Word is him. The Word now lives in me; therefore, so does he.

And

There hath no temptation taken but such as is common to man: but God is faithful, who will not suffer you to be tempted above that ye are able; but will with the temptation also make a way to escape, that ye may be able to bear it. (1 Cor. 10:13 KJV)

The following psalm, shared by my wife, has become my personal "Declaration of Independence":

Bend down and hear my prayer, O Lord, and answer me, for I am deep in trouble.... Be merciful, O Lord, for I am looking up to you in constant hope.... O Lord, you are so good and kind, so ready to forgive; so full of mercy for all who ask your aid. Listen closely to my prayer, O God. Hear my urgent cry. I will call to you whenever trouble strikes, and you will help me.... May every fiber of my being unite in reverence to your name. With all my heart I will praise you. I will give glory to your name forever, for you love me so much! You are constantly so kind! You have rescued me from deepest hell. (Ps. 86:1, 3, 5, 6–7, 11b–13 TLB)

As in Daniel's account of the furnace (Dan. 3:19–29), God had removed me from the fire, unscathed. I had fallen, but my foot has not been removed (Ps. 121:3); I had not been "utterly cast down" (Ps. 37:24). Romans 8:1 and 2 Corinthians 5:17 announce God's "Declaration of Independence"—that is, to be "found *in* Christ" was and is to have the Word pulsating in my heart. The war has been won; only the daily skirmishes surrounding the "crucifixion of the self" through the power of the Word living in me remain. The mountain (problem) has been "spoken" to and is removed (see Mark 11:22–24; Is. 54:10).

My "national anthem" in the faith is and will remain "Amazing Grace," with "Standing on the Promises" serving as my "constitution." I stand tall and at attention before the cross and sharply salute my number one Commander-in-Chief as I pledge allegiance to the "Lamb of God who takes away the sin of the world." Through his Word and by his Spirit, he has redeemed both time and circumstance, as he answered my moment-of-truth prayer from those winter months, leading me through the months of fire and endurance into the one of hope—all things good, done, "in his time." Once again, I give joyful thanks over what used to get gritted-teeth and tearful thanks.

Thank you, reader, for "going the distance" with me through this last marathon. I hear you asking me, "Why such a long chapter and so much attention to this Germany experience?" God, again, brought down the hammer of his law so as to plant my feet more firmly on the road to repentance. He is deadly serious about *every* level of repentance: actions, thoughts, and appearances! Why? Because he is a holy God who says to me, "Be ye therefore perfect, even as your Father which is in heaven is perfect" (Matt. 5:48 KJV). John 3:16, I told the soldiers, was not enough; even the demons, says Scripture, "believe and tremble" (James 2:19). John 3:16 addresses salvation and needs, like those ropes, to be "bound by twisting together" with those Words stating that repentance is necessary for the remission of sins, the power of the cross, and godly sorrow for salvation. The Scripture stating the connection (see Mark 1: 4, Luke 3: 3, Acts 26: 18) of repentance with remission/forgiveness of my sin is, by itself, just enough rope to theologically hang myself. These words from God, standing together, hold the power to move us from head belief to heart obedience as we "work out (exercise) our salvation with fear and trembling"!

So, from where does the strength come? I "lift up mine eyes unto the hills, from whence cometh my help. My help cometh from the Lord" (Ps. 121:1–2a KJV). While on tour in Germany, a fellow chaplain told a story about a hiking trip he and his wife took in the mountains of Switzerland. His wife had an excessive fear of heights and would ask as they rose along the steep trail, "Will it get better?" It got worse. Finally, they were at a point of no return. They had to go on. A steep diamond-face drop rested behind them as they walked an increasingly narrow strip up the mountain. It got so tense for the wife that she clutched her husband's shirt from behind, sometimes digging into the skin, and would not let go as they climbed. Every now and then, her husband would say to her, "Just do as I do." And, doing that, they both made it. After hearing that story, with a vivid mental picture of it resting in my mind, I began to realize the wisdom of holding on tightly to Jesus (the Word) and being fearful of ever letting go. This story provides a picture of the difference between conversion and salvation. The former is a change of mind; the latter is something one actually receives. The wife knew she had received salvation from a deadly mountain when her feet settled on sure ground. A wise question now forms for me to continually ask as I go through life from now on: "What would Jesus do (WWJD) in this setting or that circumstance?" I need to strive and train to do as he would do. The prayer I had prayed for Jesus to help me make it on the water all the way to his hand was another good and wise prayer. I need to never let that hand go. Read what Jesus says concerning himself and the need to hold a guiding hand: "Jesus replied, 'The Son can do nothing by himself. He does only what he sees the Father doing, and in the same way'" (John 5:19 TLB).

The Word tells me that it (the Word) will burn away at the judgment everything in my life that does not stand up to its standard—"saved; yet so as by fire" (1 Cor. 3:14–15; see also John 12:48). I will stand before Jesus ashamed of right things done with wrong motives; I believe I will not be judged for those things confessed and forgiven. "Dear Father, take your Word and burn away here everything not up to your standard so that it will not have to be burned there!" Can the exercise of obedience be something I carry out as for "a cause"? (See 1 Sam. 17:29.)

Now my Coach takes me deeper and higher at once. *See all your thoughts, words, deeds—each one of them ready to be thought, spoken, acted—as though you were standing before Jesus at the judgment. How would you want them to be evaluated? Think, speak, and act accordingly. What do you want to hear him say to you: "Depart from me you worker of iniquity," "Depart from me for I never knew you," or "Well done, thou good and faithful servant. Enter into the joys thereof"? Or do you prefer, "Enter in but suffer loss"?*

In summary, salvation judgment means you are covered by the cross; rewards judgment means you are motivated by the cross; and overcoming judgment means you are empowered by the cross.

To be an overcomer (see Rom. 8:13) is a goal for which I need to strive, mightily! This exercise builds confidence, much in the same way that when I know I am in shape, I have more confidence to run. A footnote to Revelation 2:17 (NKJV) reads, "Overcomers are promised supernatural sustenance in the resurrected state to enable them to function effectively as corulers in Christ's kingdom." And overcomers will be rewarded as "in the Greek athletic games … to the victor in a contest, or gladiators at the Roman games."

I raised another question to the director of Midnight Call Ministries International. "Does the promise of great rewards in heaven for overcomers apply not only to tribulations and trials that come upon me, but also to temptations and sin patterns plaguing most of my life?" He said: "Personal trials and temptations are part of being a Christian" and pointed me to 1 Pet. 1:6–7: "Wherein ye greatly rejoice, though now for a season, if need be, ye are in heaviness through manifold temptations: That the trial of your faith, being much more precious than of gold that perisheth, though it be tried with fire, might be found unto praise and honour and glory at the appearing of Jesus Christ."

> He who overcomes shall be clothed in white garments, and I will not blot out his name from the Book of Life; but I will confess his name before my Father and before his angels. (Rev. 3:5 KJV)

> He that overcometh shall inherit all things; and I will be his God, and he shall be my son. (Rev. 21:7 KJV; see also Rev. 2:11, 17, 26; Rev. 3:12; 1 John 5:4–5; Rev. 22:14; Rev. 3:7–13)

My Coach and I talked this over. "I don't see myself ever having a good testimony again," I said. "I have torn it to shreds!"

My Word has exposed you to the light.

"Yes, it put the spotlight on the ugliness of my sin."

The Word has also purified and washed you.

> The lamp of the body is the eye. Therefore, when your eye is good, your whole body also is full of light. But when your eye is bad, your body also is full of darkness. Therefore, take heed that the light which is in you is not darkness. (Luke 11:34–35 NKJV)

"So, there will be a testimony for people to see? I know I have a two-edged testimony of: 1. Being a wounded-healer example of what not to do; and 2. How God has superabundantly showered me with His Grace! But, will I ever be or have a good testimony for others to see?"

> If you are filled with light within, with no dark corners, then your face will be radiant too, as though a floodlight is beamed upon you. (Luke 11:36 TLB)

> Therefore if any person is (engrafted) in Christ, the Messiah, he is (a new creature altogether,)

a new creation; the old (previous moral and spiritual condition) has passed away. Behold, the fresh and new has come! (2 Cor. 5:17 AMP)

Let us draw near with a true heart in full assurance of faith, having our hearts sprinkled from an evil conscience, and our bodies washed with pure water. (Heb. 10:22 KJV)

Upon retirement from the Army, I was asked to say some parting words to an International Convention of Chaplains (Army, Navy, Air Force) at Ft. Dix, New Jersey. My Coach suggested that I make it short and sweet. After viewing the large body of fellow chaplains, I said, "When I look over my life and realize that if I got what I deserve I'd be taken out and shot, I then look back over it and see the superabundant grace God has poured down on me—allowing me to continue to serve. (pause) There's where the power comes for true repentance." They gave a standing ovation, and I knew they were applauding what God had done.

The next morning, the assistant chief of chaplains for the Armed Forces saw me in the parking lot, ran over to me, hugged me, and said, "Chaplain, there was one sermon preached last night, and you preached it!" Later, the chaplain for the United States Army Reserve Command wrote, giving me high marks for service. I wrote him back, saying, "Sir, for me to hear words of grace read such as *good work, spiritual help*, and *faithful service*—sent from my military Bishop—was a crowning confirmation. The reason I couldn't look you in the eye and speak with you when getting off the plane from Germany is that you were the number one military person I was most ashamed to face given my failure to faithfully complete the last part of the mission. Your communiqué was like God's tap on the shoulder saying, *You're training well; you're running the right course.*"

The personnel at Ft. Dix gave me a farewell/retirement dinner. One of the gifts was a ring with a cross at its center. My wife gave me one to wear around my neck, along with a tie she found with crosses and footprints on it. A niece painted me a picture of a cross with Jesus' head looking down upon the planet, which was covered in blood. The cross image seared into the heart erases the need of one for the eyes. It moves me like nothing else to no longer be a shame to his name. Now, at the writing of these words, my Coach says, *I want you to wear the golden scepter of the cross/forgiveness as a crown.*

Train well and consistently on his Word. Psalm 119:81 (which I call the Word Psalm) says in part, "I put my hope in your Word"; verse 130 says the entrance of the Word provides light and understanding, verse 160 explains that God's words are true, and verse 133 is my perennial prayer adopted from King David: "Order my steps in thy word: and let not any iniquity have dominion over me." Psalm 138:2 tells us that he has magnified, for our benefit, "his Word even above his name." Job said, "I have esteemed the words of his mouth more than my necessary food" (Job 23:12 KJV). I've seen God "order my steps" on all the pavements: body, mind, and spirit! At the top of the hill on our farm, I placed a US flag and three crosses; I stand tall, at attention, and sharply salute each.

As this book has noted, I need to endlessly train on his Word and to elevate it above all. So, dear reader, as you engage in your physical, mental, or spiritual marathon, run with knowledge and confidence of the following: To keep the stride is to connect with the Word that God the Father "sends out" to us. To keep the pace is to connect with God the Son—the "Word made flesh," Jesus, our champion—establishing in us the stamina needed. To keep the faith is to connect with God the Holy Spirit, who links up the cables so that the power flows from the Word to our hearts. As the "author and finisher" of our faith, he makes this connection by strengthening our faith as he brings the Word to the forefront of our minds and spirit. "So then faith cometh by hearing, and hearing by the Word of God" (Rom. 10:17 KJV). To run in his grace is to experience and know the *shalom* (balance/peace) needed to endure the run.

Close your eyes for a moment and imagine or visualize yourself stepping out into a stride grounded on God's Word addressing you in *rhema* fashion: if your circumstances are chaotic, pray Romans 8:28; if your life is disobedient, pray Philippians 2:13; if you have broken relationships, pray Ephesians 1:16–19, 3:14–19. Next, see yourself comforted and strengthened by the discovery that Jesus is the pace setter, doing the impossible work surrounding your life situation. Our Coach, the Holy Spirit, is the power source now ready for the complete flow of the Word; see yourself stepping out, not quitting, but with the nevertheless-of-faith connection. Would this not be the reason Jesus said, "And whatsoever ye shall ask in my name, that will I do, that the Father may be glorified in the Son" (John 14:13 KJV)? Scripture tells us that prayers made in the name of Jesus that are in the Father's will are heard, and are therefore, in God's eyes, already answered (1 John 5:13–14). Keep firmly in mind that to pray his own Word right back to him is to pray in his will! Can you see the surge of power, strength, and renewal as it originates in the Word that is "sent out" (Is. 55:11)? Can you see it move with deliberate force through Jesus, the "name above all names" as you make the faith connection? Can you take up this gauntlet and exercise on the Word?

> For the Word that God speaks is alive and full of power—making it active, operative, energizing and effective; it is sharper than any two-edged sword, penetrating to the dividing line of the breath of life (soul) and (the immortal) spirit, and of joints and marrow (that is, of the deepest parts of our nature) exposing and sifting and analyzing and judging the very thoughts and purposes of the heart. (Heb. 4:12 AMP)

A magnificent eulogy for any of us would indicate that we were, in some respect, a vehicle or servant of his Word. For the greatest honor—not attribute or characteristic, but greater than being a president or king—that any of us can ever have is to be a vessel for his Word, an instrument of his peace.

And we also thank God continually because, when you received the word of God, which you heard from us, you accepted it not as the word of men, but as it actually is, the word of God, which is at work in you who believe. (1 Thess. 2:13 NIV)

Those who are wise (who impart wisdom) will shine like the brightness of the heavens, and those who lead many to righteousness, like the stars for ever and ever. (Dan. 12:3 NIV)

However, I consider my life worth nothing to me, if only I may finish the race and complete the task the Lord Jesus has given me—the task of testifying to the gospel of God's grace. (Acts 20:24 NIV)

And the Word behind all his *rhema*-words to me is the one he gave to the woman praying about my medical condition while working in her garden as I lay knocking on death's door. It was a most prophetic Word!

I shall not die, but live, and declare the works and recount the illustrious acts of the Lord. (Ps. 118:17 AMP)

From time to time, following speaking engagements or other events in which I have the opportunity to exercise the above Word to "recount," people ask me, "Are you still running?"

and "How many more years will you continue to run?" Then, after I have told them yes and shared something of what my life is like now, I like to say that my running hero is Johnny Kelly, a legend in his own time who won the Boston Marathon in 1935 and, again, in 1945. He would possibly have won it a third time if he hadn't tapped the lead runner as he ran past him on the last hill before the finish line. This tap angered and energized the other runner to the point that he passed Kelly and won; hence, the name "Heartbreak Hill." Kelly ran it for the sixtieth time at the age of eighty-four in 1992—the same year I first ran it, my feet on the same pavement as his. His favorite song is "Young at Heart." To me, that is in keeping with the verse, "For as he thinketh in his heart, so is he" (Prov. 23:7 KJV). I sometimes tell folks that my goal is to run at least until I am eighty-seven. The year before this book was made ready for the publisher, I ran the 2011 Boston Marathon at the age of sixty-four and qualified for age sixty-five. That's forty-eight marathons total, forty-four of them after the accident—the doctors just shake their heads. Twenty-seven were the Grandfather Mountain Marathon, listed along with Pikes Peak as the toughest in the country. Of eleven Marine Corps and five Shamrock marathons, five were qualifying runs for Boston; my feet on the Boston pavement were a portrait of God's healing grace! After I run one, I usually find myself introspectively asking, *Am I still running in his grace?* Increasingly, I see that when I exercise the "wisdom of obedience" by thinking on the things in God's Word—letting them give shape to my words and actions—I see far greater rewards than I get from giving in to the suggestions of the enemy, where I simply end up saying to God how foolish I have been! I find it like a parable that, during my retirement years, instead of trying to run me off the road, folks go out of their way to give me much more room than I need when I'm running. That picture tells me that they see a different person. In the more recent years of our marriage, I made a plaque for Connie with the words, "Grow old along with me; the best is yet to be!" This plaque, too, was prophetic.

In apologizing to my children for not reading verses of the Bible to them before bedtime when they were little, I told them, "If I had done that, it would have planted the value and importance of reading something from the Bible every day into your minds. It is good and right to read the Bible every day, just like eating meals. This idea can still grow roots in your minds, though, by asking God to help you *want* to know him better." And, as you know, God will do that by taking them into and through his Word. He and the Word are one and the same! An illustration I have used with soldiers through the years about this is of high school sweethearts who are beginning to court each other more seriously just before the girlfriend's family moves to another state. She writes several love letters to her boyfriend and then calls to see what he thinks of them. When she asks him, he pauses and then says, "Well, I haven't gotten to them yet, but I'm going to." Several weeks pass, and she calls again, asking, "Did you like them? What about the part …?" Again, he stutters to say that he hasn't read them but has every intention of doing so. Does God feel the way that girl must feel when we fail to read his love letter to us? He has poured out his heart to us about all that matters. If I'm not on the road of repentance, then I won't talk to him and say, "Come quickly, Lord Jesus" (see Rev. 22:20). But if I am on that road, I will long for his coming to take me home.

My Coach says that honest and ongoing talk with my wife is wise and strengthens our bond; so it is with my heavenly Father. When I pray, that's me talking to God; when I read his Word, that's him talking to me. My wife is a great cook. She can fix one of those country meals that just keeps on going, taking several tables to hold it all. Let's say that our "Brady Bunch" of seven children and eleven grandchildren is going to be home for one of those meals. And here we are—just look at that spread! But no one's hungry, so no one eats. That's how it is with God's Word; he has prepared one great meal for us! Along with the writers of wisdom literature of the Old Testament, the prophet Jeremiah said, "Thy words were found, and I did eat them" (Jer. 15:16). French philosopher Simone Weil wrote, "The danger is not lest the soul should doubt whether there is any bread, but lest by a lie, it should persuade itself that it is not hungry." Can I pray for God to help me be hungrier for his Word? Yes, because he says I am blessed when I "hunger and thirst after righteousness" (Matt. 5:6); so this prayer is in his will and, therefore, heard and answered (1 John 5:14–15). My prayer has increasingly become that God would help my children practice his presence by placing them on his M&M's—that is, to *memorize* and *meditate* on his Word so it becomes hidden in their hearts (see Ps. 119:11). This is of the utmost importance!

> For skillful and godly Wisdom shall enter into your heart, and knowledge shall be pleasant to you; discretion shall watch over you, understanding shall keep you; to deliver you from the way of evil. (Prov. 2:10–12a AMP)

> But his delight and desire are in the law of the Lord, and on His law—the precepts, the instructions, the teachings of God—he habitually meditates (ponders and studies) by day and by night. (Ps. 1:2 AMP)

This "readiness training" for God's "alert roster" comes by none other than *daily* reading, meditating, and praying through the Word. And the Word from the cross has become my ark through troubled waters, providing a "way of escape" from temptation and helping me to become a "doer" and not just a "hearer"—making faith-decisions to be obedient (see, again, 2 Cor. 7:10). The Word that formed us and saved us now coaches, counsels, and comforts us. I no longer just read my Bible; my Bible reads me! (See Heb. 4:12.) I want God's word working in me like a thread weaving a fine fabric for flowers and fruits!

When Jesus said we are to have faith like a "grain of mustard seed," he, according to science, really said something profound. A seed that was placed under a radioactive isotope and then planted produced negative results; the ear of corn that grew from it became deformed. A mustard seed was placed under a radioactive isotope for seventy-two hours and was still a regular mustard seed. The seed holds life, so a hybrid will not survive. Efforts to make a mustard seed into a hybrid failed. Jesus was telling us that faith, like that seed, should not be camouflaged or grafted into false doctrine, such as new age religion or others that teach us to love and serve ourselves as inner gods with the ability to educate humanity into salvation. Quite to the contrary, the critical word needed for this earth is the one of sin conviction and the fear of the Lord, outlined in the Bible (see Prov. 2:1–5.) Again, if I look at an electrical receptacle and wonder if it holds any power, that's one thing; if I put an electrical plug in it, that's another story. Faith is the plug; the Word is the receptacle.

As I come to the run's symbolic end and reach the "mailbox" to read his letter written upon our hearts, will I not see the crucible of the cross leading me home? Fanny Crosby, the writer of over eight thousand hymns who was born blind, writes in the hymn "Near the Cross," "Bring its scenes before me, help me walk from day to day with its shadow o'er me." D. L. Moody asked her, "What is the one thing you would wish for in life?" Without hesitation, her reply was, "That I would always be blind so to see the things of God." My natural sight had actually made me blind to the deeper things of God. "So are the paths of all that forget God; and the hypocrite's hope shall perish" (Job 8:13 KJV). The cross stands sentinel to my past, my future, and my present all at once; the cross look is life and death for me!

> That I may know Him and the power of
> His resurrection, and the fellowship of His

sufferings, being conformed to His death, if, by any means, I may attain to the resurrection from the dead. (Phil. 3:10–11 NKJV)

Have you ever exchanged letters with someone or talked on the phone without having ever seen them? Perhaps you found yourself in love with this person you had never seen. Reading God's letter to me makes me want to see him. The intimacy of being known is like the security of a warm blanket around your shoulders while sitting in the living room on a cold night. His Word also "reads" me. I am not only one-eighth *Jewish*—enough blood to have qualified me for execution during the Holocaust and for the right to settle in Israel—but have long believed, as stated earlier, that I am also part Cherokee, although I can't prove it. Anyway, one of the Cherokee sayings used when they feel as though they really are beginning to know someone and hold them in their hearts is, "I *see* you." I want to be able to say that to God (see Jeremiah 29: 13-14)!

To my children, I wrote this:

> As the years and the miles add up, God is increasingly coaching me to just seek his face— not looking for what he can do or perform for me—just to want his presence. As you know, God has already done wonders for me through his mighty grace! A Scripture event that grabs my attention is the one where Moses, after receiving the Ten Commandments from God's

hand, simply asked to see him. So, God let him hide in the cleft of the rocks while he passed by—shielding Moses' face with his hand so that Moses would be protected from the awesome power of his presence; for no one can see God and live. So I have been asking folks to place me deep into their prayer closets for this new direction. I am ashamed that it has taken my whole life to get to this goal; nevertheless, better late than never! My Coach says, *When my Word comes to you as* rhema, *you have seen my face!*

Homecoming—what will it be like? When I arrived at the airport from Germany and that moment came when I saw my wife on tiptoe with arms ready to hug, that was the posture of expectant joy over the bond of love we had longed to celebrate in his grace. Now it was time to "live it out." We read God's love letter (his Word), and we talk to him in prayer. The day will come when it is time to celebrate. The bride (Church) awaits her groom (Jesus) and says, "The voice of my beloved! behold, he cometh.… My beloved is mine, and I am his" (Song of Solomon 2:8, 16 KJV). The truly great and good news is from the Word, and the final chapter says that through Jesus, "we win!" As a famous hymn states, "How firm a foundation … is laid for your faith in His excellent Word. What more can he say than to you he has said, to you who for refuge to Jesus have fled." This book, guided by my Coach, will do what God said he would do while I lay in the hospital with the angel of death close by: "For he shall not die, but live to recount the works of the Lord" (Ps. 118:17). So I say to you,

> Come and hear, all of you who reverence the Lord, and I will tell you what He did for me: For I cried to him for help, with praises ready on my tongue. He would not have listened if I had not confessed my sins. But he listened! He heard my prayer! He paid attention to it! Blessed be God who didn't turn away when I was praying, and didn't refuse me His kindness and love. (Ps. 66:16–20 TLB)

Any of us could write a book about what we see God doing in our lives (see 1 John 5:10), and that book would build up the lives of others *if* our testimonies give the glory to God and do not center on ourselves and the "fire" *we* had to endure. That focus on self makes our testimony smell too much like smoke. Our writings would chronicle our journey through time, reminding us of the great gulf between where we have been and where God has brought us. Such a legacy of our faith will convey our deepest convictions of *things not seen and assurance of things hoped for.*

> My heart is overflowing with a good theme;
> I recite my composition concerning the King;
> My tongue *is* the pen of a ready writer. (Ps. 45:1 NKJV)

And the Lord answered me, and said, Write the vision, and make it plain upon tables, that he may run that readeth it. (Hab. 2:2 KJV)

because

He sends his command to the earth; his word runs swiftly. (Ps. 147:15 NIV)

and

Then said the Lord to me, You have seen well, for I am alert and active, watching over My word to perform it. (Jer. 1:12 AMP)

The overarching prayer for this book has been and remains that God will use it as a "pointer" for the reader's heart to journey closer to God's heart. I pray that one day my children will read this book and see that I am writing to them, also. Perhaps, in the words of the apostle Paul, they will read it and then say, "No, you are all the letter we need, a letter written on our heart; any man can see it for what it is and read it for himself. And as for you, it is plain that you are a letter that has come from Christ, given to us to deliver: a letter written not with ink but with the Spirit of the living God, written not on stone tablets but on the pages of the human heart" (2 Cor. 3:2–3 NEB; see also 2 Cor. 4:6).

One day, a book called the Book of Life will be opened. This book will contain our names and the whole history of our lives as we trained on his Word in readiness for his kingdom (see Mal. 3:16–17; Rev. 20:12, 21:27). And I do not want that book to be closed on me with my name not recorded. History becomes "his-story." The only chapter in that book that will allow me to enter the kingdom is the one describing God's grace poured out on me in a superabundant manner and how I allowed it to "mentor, mold, and motivate" me to grow into his will and purpose. Just like the honor I felt in having my feet on the same pavement that held those of world-class athletes during the Boston Marathon, I will be overwhelmed to walk the streets of gold that are under the feet of world-class saints. In heaven, we will, perhaps, hear what I like to call the annals of the kingdom. And the greatest chapter in those records will be the story and the glory of his grace—"To the praise of the glory of his grace, wherein he hath made us accepted in the beloved" (Eph. 1:6 KJV). An unknown author framed it poetically:

GOD'S ALBUM

We may write our names in albums;
We may trace them in the sand;
We may chisel them in marble,
With a firm and skillful hand.
But the pages soon are sullied,
And inscriptions fade away.
Every monument will crumble,
And our earthly hopes decay.
But, dear friends, there is an album,
Full of leaves of snowy white,

Where no name is ever tarnished,
But forever pure and bright.
In the book of life, God's album,
May our names be penned with care,
And whosoe'er hath written,
Write it forever there.
As it has been written, so shall it be done!

Looking over this past quarter of a century, I see the cross weaving God's grace and redeeming will like thread through all. The cross is truly "the power of God" (see Rom. 1:16; 1 Cor. 1:18, 23–25). You have seen the great gulf between what I deserve and where his grace has placed me. I could stand on the words of deliverance and healing from him because of his great grace lavishly poured down on me! This, too, was for "his name's sake" (Ps. 23:3; 1 Sam. 12:22; Ps. 106:8; 1 John 2:12).

As the years have come and gone, when I deserved nothing but *condemnation*, God, in his grace, has chosen to have the Army, from time to time, award me *commendations*. The play on words is purposeful. For example, the chief of chaplains for the Armed Forces nominated me to receive the National Bible Association's highly prestigious Witherspoon Chaplain Award for most creative use of Scripture; the award is given in annual rotation to a chaplain—one year to one in the Army, one year to one in the Navy, and another year to one in the Air Force. When presented to me in New York City at the 1998 National Bible Week inaugural luncheon, the award cited "outstanding service rendered in the promotion of Bible reading, study and appreciation." As the cloak was placed around me for this presentation, it felt like the Father's arms were welcoming home the prodigal. Two months later, in 1999, I was nominated for and received the National Chaplain of the Month Award from the Veterans Affairs Medical Center National Headquarters for "creativity in using the Scriptures in preaching and research for ministry and healing among patients and staff." "For those who honor Me I will honor" (1 Sam. 2:30b KJV). In my retirement years, adding up his grace superabundantly poured over me is what makes me rich and content!

Why did God do all these things for me?

"But I obtained mercy for the reason that in me, as the foremost (of sinners), Jesus Christ might show forth and display all His perfect long-suffering and patience for an example to (encourage) those who would thereafter believe on Him for (the gaining of) eternal life" (1 Tim. 1:16 AMP).

In parting, I'd like to request that you do an exercise. Would you ask God to give you a mental picture of the cross as he would want you to see it? When it is formed in your mind's eye, let its shadow fall over the following Words as you read them:

> Because he hath set his love upon me, therefore will I deliver him: I will set him on high, because he hath known my name. He shall call upon me, and I will answer him: I will be with him

in trouble; I will deliver him, and honour him.
With long life will I satisfy him, and shew him
my salvation. (Ps. 91:14–16 KJV)

Faith, hope, and love—each one a decision. For this runner, faith stood up against the odds for the body marathon, hope rose up for the mind marathon, and love made up for the spirit marathon, breaking through the "walls." Seeing these decisions, God was pleased! Keep the stride, keep the pace, keep the faith, and run in his grace!

I shall not die, but live, and declare the works
of the LORD. (Ps. 118:17 KJV)

—A fellow runner

As this book is now being made ready for publication, today, for me, is another day of training on God's Word; and, so will be tomorrow, the day after, and all days remaining until into the gathering time. Like St. Paul, I need to see that "I have not yet attained; but I press on to the mark, the high calling of Christ, Jesus" (see Phil. 3:12–14). The addendum to this book contains ten spiritual training regimens that could prove, for the reader (trainee), to be a jump-start for deeper training on his Word. It will illustrate the importance of seeing each word from God in context of the whole (see Matt. 4:4) Word of God when talking of repentance, salvation, redemption, and so on.

As mentioned earlier, the Army, from time to time, will announce that "Year of Training" is its theme for that year. In God's army, *every* year is the Year of Training. He also wants us to "train to standard." The US Army motto, "Be all you can be," is paralleled by God's standard and "Army" motto: "Be ye therefore perfect, even as your Father which is in heaven is perfect" (Matt. 5:48 KJV). "A disciple is not above his teacher, but everyone who is perfectly trained will be like his teacher" (Luke 6:40 KJV). Practice makes perfect. Can I practice his Word? Following is a potent "shot in the arm" to journey into better whole-person training.

Building Spiritual Strength

1. Pray—asking the Father— to lead you through (program your mind) with his *logos*-Word in such a way that his Holy Spirit can address (bring up on the screen of your mind) his *rhema*-Word to you and your life concerns. It is also important to remember that text taken out of context is only pretext. God's Holy Spirit, our number one Coach in life, is the only one who can consistently raise up a Word that lives in the context of *every* Word from God. Ask him to show you the "truth (that) set(s) you free."

2. Use a good Bible concordance; look up any words that address topics or issues of current concern. Read all the biblical references listed about that word. Meditate on and memorize the one(s) that jump out at you or speak to you personally, letting those words be the center or point of focus as you meditate—pore over them as though reading a letter from your first girlfriend or boyfriend. Herein we find ourselves not just knowing *about* Jesus but knowing *him*! This, in computer language, saves the words in your memory bank. Viktor Frankl, in his book *Man's Search for Meaning*, tells how he and his fellow prisoners in the Nazi concentration camps were deprived of any reading material. But enough of them had memorized portions

of Scripture that they could almost completely reconstruct the Holy Bible. He says this reliance on the Word was what got them through such an experience. He named it "Logo-therapy."

3. Make an entry in your journal at the end of each day; write what you come to understand and learn from the above.

4. Share those moments of truth gathered from your prayer and meditation with someone you love and trust.

5. Decide, as a step of faith, to believe and trust God to act (see Rom. 8:28) on your requests that are confirmed by his Word. This faith-decision nails down the Word, tightly connecting your body, mind, and spirit. God will feed your human spirit by that Word—moving your mind to direct your body (see Prov. 18:14). Then, sprint the next hill by standing on Romans 8:29–30. This Word will direct us to move away from focusing on the self, being a "pew potato," to serve God. He wants us to serve him by exercising our faith into action on behalf of others. If we do no service for Jesus, our faith becomes weak and we have to start training all over again. D. T. Niles wrote, "Christianity is one beggar telling another beggar where the bread is." Be the wounded healer that God,

the Holy Spirit, is forming and training you to be (see 1 Peter 3:15–16). This formation and training is handled by the greatest wounded healer, Jesus, living in you through the Word. Or as Jesus said, "I tell you the truth, whatever you did for one of the least of these brothers of mine, you did for me" (Matt. 25:40 NIV).

The Word does it all! Thank you, Jesus, for being the Word the Father sent out at creation saying, "Let there be …" and there was. Thank you, Jesus, for being the "Word (that) became flesh and dwelt among us." Thank you, Holy Spirit, our Coach, for being the power and presence of the Father and the Son with us now—delivering the Word in a most timely way!

> The unfolding of your words gives light;
> it gives understanding to the simple" (Ps. 119:130 NIV)

> And we also (especially) thank God continually for this, that when you received the message of God (which you heard) from us, you welcomed it not as the word of (mere) men but as what it truly is, the Word of God, which is effectually at work in you who believe—exercising its (superhuman) power in those who

adhere to and trust in and rely on it. (1 Thess. 2:13 AMP)

Let the word (spoken by) the Christ, the Messiah, have its home (in your hearts and minds) and dwell in you in (all its) richness. (Col. 3:16 AMP)

Jesus answered, "It is written: 'Man does not live on bread alone, but on every word that comes from the mouth of God.'" (Matt. 4:4 NIV; see also John 6:30–60)

For ever, O Lord, thy word is settled in heaven. (Ps. 119:89 KJV)

Train yourselves toward godliness (piety)—keeping yourself spiritually fit. For physical training is of some value—useful for a little; but godliness (spiritual training) is useful and of value in everything and in every way, for it holds promise for the present life and also for the life which is to come. This saying is reliable and worthy of complete acceptance by everybody. (1 Tim. 4:7b–8 AMP)

As it has been written, so shall it be done!

Amen (It is truth; it is done)

TRAINING REGIMENS

Training Regimen #1

COURSE: Prayer and Repentance

TRAINEE: I see that, for the writer of this book and by the predominance of his discussion, prayer became a most important exercise in staying spiritually fit.

COACH: One regimen of fitness to help produce a repentant mind centers in a profound manner on the prayer Jesus taught his disciples to pray as a model prayer. For example, ask yourself, "Can I pray—

Our—while I am self-centered;

Father—and not show that I daily look to him that way;

Who art in heaven—if I pursue only earthly things;

Hallowed be thy name—if I am not "set apart" for him;

Thy kingdom come—and not trade my control for his control;

Thy will be done—and continue to give in to my will, not his;

On earth as it is in heaven—and not be a willing instrument of his peace here and now;

Give us this day our daily bread—and not feed others in need;

Forgive us our trespasses as we forgive those who trespass against us—and continue to nurture bitterness and resentment;

Lead us not into temptation—if I seek out settings as open targets for temptation;

Deliver us from evil—while not using the sword of the Word;

Thine is the kingdom—and not continually be his servant;

Thine is the power—and fear people and circumstances more;

Thine is the glory—if I act primarily for self-recognition;

Forever and ever—and worry about the footsteps ahead;

Amen—and not really mean it."

TRAINEE: I've tried this and that to change my thinking, but it simply doesn't work. I identify with St. Paul in the struggle to stop doing what I actually do not want to do (see Rom. 7).

COACH: Yet, God's Word is persistent and encouraging:

WORD: "Therefore then, since we are surrounded by so great a cloud of witnesses (who have borne testimony of the Truth), let us strip off and throw aside every encumbrance—unnecessary weight—and that sin which so readily (deftly and cleverly) clings to and entangles us, and let us run with patient endurance and steady and active persistence the appointed course of the race that is set before us....

"Looking away (from all that will distract) to Jesus, Who is the Leader and the Source of our faith (giving the first incentive for our belief) and is also its Finisher, (bringing it to maturity and perfection). He, for the joy (of obtaining the prize) that was set before Him, endured the cross, despising and ignoring the shame, and is now seated at the right hand of the throne of God.

"Just think of Him Who endured from sinners such grievous opposition and bitter hostility against Himself—reckon up and consider it all in comparison with your trials—so that you may not grow weary or exhausted, losing heart and relaxing and fainting in your minds.

"You have not yet struggled and fought agonizingly against sin, nor have you yet resisted and withstood to the point of pouring out your (own) blood." (Heb. 12:1–4 AMP)

"So, since Christ suffered in the flesh (for us, for you), arm yourselves with the same thought and purpose (patiently to suffer rather than fail to please God). For whoever has suffered in the flesh (having the mind of Christ) has done with (intentional) sin—has stopped pleasing himself and the world, and pleases God, so that he can no longer spend the rest of his natural life living by (his) human appetites and desires, but (he lives) for what God wills. For the time that is past already suffices for doing what the Gentiles like to do, living (as you have done) in shameless, insolent wantonness, in lustful desires...." (1 Peter 4:1–3a AMP)

TRAINEE: How, then, can I have "the mind of Christ"?

COACH: When you have God's Word hidden and settled in your mind and heart, you have the "mind of Christ."

Training Regimen # 2
(How to draw close to God)

COURSE: Climbing to a Higher Level

TRAINEE: Just how do we move into that third dimension of "the fear of the Lord?"

COACH: The Word tells you how:

WORD: "Seek first his kingdom and his righteousness, and all these things will be given to you as well." (Matt. 6:33 NIV)

"Delight yourself in the Lord and he will give you the desires of your heart." (Ps. 37:4 NIV)

TRAINEE: How do we delight in and seek him first?

COACH: By loving him for just *who* he is. He is your heavenly Father. Think for a moment: do parents want their children to love them just because of what they can give them, or do they want their children to love them simply because of *who* they are? So it is with God.

TRAINEE: How does that happen?

COACH: It happens as you take in his Word. Recall the first chapter of John's gospel. He states that the Word, Jesus (see Rev. 19:13), was, in the beginning, sent out (see Gen. 1 and Is. 55:10–11). Then he says that the Word *was* God. You could stop right there and know that to delight in God's Word is to receive him into your heart and mind. But John continues, saying, "and the Word was *with* God."

TRAINEE: What does that mean?

COACH: The creation narrative tells that God said, "Let there be …" and there was. He also said, "Let us make man in our own image."

TRAINEE: To whom was he talking?

COACH: The answer to this comes in John, chapter one, where he states that "the Word became flesh and dwelt among us." You know this to be Jesus, born in Bethlehem, dying on a cross, and rising from the dead.

WORD: "He is the image of the invisible God, the firstborn over all creation. For by Him all things were created that are in heaven and that are on earth, visible and invisible, whether thrones or dominions or principalities or powers. All things were created through Him and for Him. And He is before all things, and in Him all things consist." (Col. 1:15–17 NKJV)

"But in these last days he has spoken to us by his Son, whom he appointed heir of all things, and through whom he made the universe. The Son is the radiance of God's glory and the exact representation of his being, sustaining all things by his powerful word." (Heb. 1:2–3a NIV)

"By the word of the Lord the heavens were made, and all the host of them by the breath of his mouth." (Ps. 33:6 KJV)

TRAINEE: Putting all the above together, what do we have?

COACH: You have a consistent and persistent message that God's Word *is* God and that Jesus was preexistent at the very point of creation in the form of the Word (see John 17:5). That Word is still with you in written form. To take it in, read and meditate God's Word is to receive him (Jesus).

WORD: "You are already clean because of the word I have spoken to you. Remain in me, and I will remain in you." (John 15:3–4a NIV)

COACH: God wants you to desire and delight in his Word because to do so is to desire and to delight in Him! His own words say this:

WORD: "My son, keep my words and store up my commands within you. Keep my commands and you will live; guard my teachings as the apple of your eye." (Prov. 7:1–2 NIV)

"O taste and see that the Lord is good: blessed is the man that trusteth in him." (Ps. 34:8 KJV)

"When your words came, I ate them; they were my joy and my heart's delight." (Jer. 15:16a NIV)

"How sweet are your words to my taste, sweeter than honey to my mouth!" (Ps. 119:113 NIV)

COACH: When you eat something good, it benefits your whole system.

WORD: "But his delight and desire are in the law of the Lord, and on His law—the precepts, the instructions, the teachings of God—he habitually meditates (ponders and studies) by day and by night." (Ps. 1:2 AMP)

TRAINEE: Is this the reason God was so pleased with Solomon's choice of wisdom for God's gift to him—out of all the things he could have selected—so pleased that he gave him everything else?

COACH: To choose wisdom is to choose God's Word, and to choose his Word is to choose Jesus.

WORD: "He was clothed with garments dipped in blood, and his title was 'The Word of God.'" (Rev. 19:13 TLB)

"So we have these three witnesses: the voice of the Holy Spirit in our hearts, the voice from heaven at Christ's baptism, and the voice before he died. And they all say the same thing: that Jesus Christ is the Son of God." (1 John 5:7–8 TLB)

TRAINEE: God promises to be close to me with his Word?

WORD: "When thou goest, it shall lead thee; when thou sleepest, it shall keep thee; and when thou awakest, it shall talk with thee." (Prov. 6:22 KJV)

COACH: No wonder Paul told the early Church:

WORD: "I can do all things through Christ which strengtheneth me." (Phil. 4:13 KJV)

          "God's strength is made perfect in my weakness." (2 Cor. 12:9 KJV)

          "We are more than conquerors through him that loved us." (Rom. 8:37 KJV

          "It is no longer I who live but Jesus within me." (Gal. 2:20 NIV)

COACH: The Father knows the Word you need; the Son is the strength and life of that Word in you; and I, the Spirit, deliver that Word to you in a most timely way.

Training Regimen # 3

COURSE: God's Plan of Salvation

COACH: Good medicine checks first for vital signs; what are the spiritual vital signs of salvation? First, see that you are to be judged: 2 Corinthians 5:9–10. Second, see that you are viewed and evaluated by the judge through the cover of Jesus' blood: Romans 4:3–8—much like your fist representing the reality of your sin but, with a handkerchief draped over it, it's still there but covered from sight. Third, see that you receive this coverage through a step of faith, choosing to believe it is real and true: Romans 3:27–31. Fourth, see that you are not to cleverly "cheapen" that coverage by some manipulative use of that faith: Romans 3:5–8; 6:1–2. Fifth, see that you are to exercise faith also as an act of obedience, belief that acts on that belief: Romans 1:5. Sixth, see that you are to practice daily placing your faith in what has been worked out for you; this is your part: Philippians 2:12. Seventh, see that when you backslide or "break training," your Coach has a re-entry plan to bring you back into training: Philippians 2:13.

WORD: "'Return, faithless people; I will cure you of backsliding.' 'Yes, we will come to you, for you are the Lord our God.'" (Jer. 3:22 NIV)

"He hath shewed thee, O man, what is good; and what doth the Lord require of thee, but to do justly, and to love mercy, and to walk humbly with thy God?" (Micah 6:8 KJV)

TRAINEE: If I think I've "got it made," that's when I break training (not running in his grace).

COACH: Read and heed Paul's words on this:

WORD: "I don't mean to say I'm perfect. I haven't learned all I should even yet, but I keep working toward that day when I will finally be all that Christ saved me for and wants me to be.

"No, dear brothers, I am still not all I should be but I am bringing all my energies to bear on this one thing: Forgetting the past and looking forward to what lies ahead, I strain to reach the end of the race and receive the prize for which God is calling us up to heaven because of what Christ Jesus did for us.

"I hope all of you who are mature Christians will see eye to eye with me on these things, and if you disagree on some point, I believe that God will make it plain to you—if you fully obey the truth you have." (Phil. 3:12–16 TLB)

COACH: Again, the Word provides a "way of escape" (1 Cor. 10:13) from your backsliding:

WORD: "His divine power has given us everything we need for life and godliness through our knowledge of him who called us by his own glory and goodness. Through these he has given us his very great and precious promises, so that through them you may participate in the divine nature and escape the corruption in the world caused by evil desires." (2 Peter 1:3–4 NIV)

"So also the Lord can rescue you and me from the temptations that surround us." (2 Peter 2:9 TLB)

TRAINEE: Many times I hear on television and radio the message that says that all you have to do is accept Christ as your personal Savior or just believe in order to be saved. These are some favorite Scriptures often quoted:

- "For God so loved the world, that He gave His only begotten Son, that whosoever believeth in Him shall not perish, but have everlasting life" (John 3:16 KJV).

- "But what does it say? 'The word is near you; it is in your mouth and in your heart,' that is, the word of faith we are proclaiming: That if you confess with your mouth, 'Jesus is Lord,' and believe in your heart that God raised him from the dead, you will be saved" (Rom. 10:8–9 NIV).

COACH: But let's look at another Scripture. Speaking about the last judgment, Jesus said:

Not every one that saith unto me, Lord, Lord, shall enter into the kingdom of heaven; but he that doeth the will of my Father which is in heaven. Many will say to me in that day, Lord, Lord, have we not prophesied in thy name? and in thy name have cast out devils? and in thy name done many wonderful works? And then will I profess unto them, I never knew you: depart from me, ye that work iniquity. (Matt. 7:21–23 KJV)

Did they believe? Yes, they called Him "Lord." But were they saved? No. Why? Because, they— like you—have a sin problem. Jesus put it plainly when speaking to his own people in Galilee: "But unless you repent, you too will all perish" (Luke 13:3 NIV).

In the parable of the sheep and the goats, the goats believed, but were they saved? No. Why? Because their faith was not active in love. They had not "done it unto the least of these" and, therefore, had "not done it unto (Jesus)." When the people of the early church asked Peter what they should do to be saved, he answered: "Repent—change your views, and purpose to accept the will of God in your inner selves instead of rejecting it" (Acts 2:38 AMP). Have a fellowship with Christ's sufferings as you reach out to those in need (see Matt. 25:31–46). If Jesus, the Word, lives in your heart, you will not have to hear Him say, "Depart from me, for I never knew you." Peter told the church to, "repent … and turn to God, so that your sins may be wiped out, that times of refreshing may come from the Lord" (Acts 3:19 NIV; see also Acts 17:30, Mark 2:17).

TRAINEE: From where does the power come?

COACH: When God says, "The fear of the Lord is the beginning of wisdom," this does not just mean a fear of the consequences or the "pickle" you get in when stepping out of his will or even the fear of missing out on his best. It is the fear of wounding his heart any more because of your sin. It is the posture of King David, writing Psalm 51 while reflecting on his adultery with Bathsheba, the murder of her husband, and the avalanche of harm it did. David became sorry for what he had done against God's heart, will, and Word. So David writes, "For I know my transgressions, and my sin is always before me. Against you, you only, have I sinned and done what is evil in your sight" (Ps. 51:3–4 NIV). The apostle Paul nailed it down with these words: "For godly sorrow worketh repentance to salvation not to be repented of: but the sorrow of the world worketh death" (2 Cor. 7:10 KJV). Other translations read that godly sorrow "produces" a repentance.

TRAINEE: What does godly sorrow look like?

COACH: Can you stand before the cross of Jesus and see him taking in to his body and mind all that Satan could do through the Roman soldiers and bystanders and even hear him cry out in pain in his spirit as he felt the wrath of the Father, "Father, why have you forsaken me?" God the Father will not look upon sin. "God made him who had no sin to be sin for us, so that in him we might become the righteousness of God" (2 Cor. 5:21 NIV). In that agony of body, mind, and spirit on the cross, can you look there and see that you were on his mind as he hung there? Would you then step back and not be moved to repent? See the power in these words: "For the message of the cross is foolishness to those who are perishing, but to us who are being saved it is the power of God" (1 Cor. 1:18 NIV). All Israel will be saved when they see the one they have pierced (see Zech. 12:10; Jn. 19:37; Rev. 1:7). The New Covenant will be written on their hearts. The same is true for you as you see the piercing your sins (past, present and future), have done. Godly sorrow over these sins will, then, transform you by the renewing of your mind, giving you the mind of Christ.

TRAINEE: So when Jesus says that "many are called but few chosen" and that we should enter by the "narrow door," what does this mean?

COACH: If you somehow try to show the Father that you deserve the kingdom because you have performed greatly or by pointing to your awards for service, then you are too big to fit through the "narrow door." Notice the outline of markings on Christ as he hung on the cross. His wounds form the shape of a door. No one comes to the Father except through Jesus and the "power of the cross" (see John 14:6). Mt. Sinai found its completion in Mt. Calvary.

Training Regimen #4

COURSE: Peace from the Power and Practice of Praise

WORD: "Be happy (in your faith) and rejoice and be glad-hearted continually—always. Be unceasing in prayer—praying perseveringly; Thank (God) in *every*thing (emphasis mine)—no matter what the circumstances may be, be thankful and give thanks; for this is the will of God for you (who are) in Christ Jesus (the Revealer and Mediator of that will)." (1 Thess. 5:16–18 AMP)

"At all times and for everything giving thanks in the name of our Lord Jesus Christ, to God the Father." (Eph. 5:20 AMP)

"Through Him therefore let us constantly and at all times offer up to God a sacrifice of praise, which is the fruit of lips that thankfully acknowledge and confess and glorify His name." (Heb. 13:15 AMP)

COACH: Giving God thanks in *all* things builds trust, thereby freeing God's hand to work in *all* things. The above three Scriptures, therefore, "marry up" with the following two Scriptures.

WORD: "(Not in your own strength) for it is God Who is all the while effectually at work in you—energizing and creating in you the power and desire—both to will and to work for His good pleasure and satisfaction and delight." (Phil. 2:13 AMP)

"And we know that in all things God works for the good of those who love him, who have been called according to his purpose." (Rom. 8:28 NIV)

COACH: God's twofold response to the sacrifice of praise is as follows:

1. "The peace of God that passes all understanding"—like the "eye of a hurricane." The Hebrew word for peace, *shalom*, does not refer to peace

in the *absence* of war or stress but peace in the *midst* of it.

"And the peace of God, which passeth all understanding, shall keep your hearts and minds through Christ Jesus" (Phil. 4:7 KJV).

2. Miracle—where he rolls up his sleeves, so to speak, and works with those things you and I cannot do anything about.

WORD: "For though we live in the world, we do not wage war as the world does. The weapons we fight with are not the weapons of the world. On the contrary, they have divine power to demolish strongholds." (2 Cor. 10:3–4 NIV)

Training Regimen #5

COURSE: God's Perfect Will and His Redeeming Will

TRAINEE: What is the difference between these two "wills"?

COACH: God's perfect will was for Adam and Eve to have never sinned in the garden of Eden. In spite of his will, they used their free will to go against his. God found another route to bring you back into his peace and presence. This new way is his redeeming will, involving his Son and a cross.

Although God's perfect will was for the people of Israel to march out of Egypt and into the Promised Land, free will choices led the Israelites away from God's timely best. Their choices cost them a forty-year journey through the wilderness for a trip that should have taken about three weeks by camel. Nevertheless, God's redeeming will led them into the Promised Land. God can do the same with marriage and family.

TRAINEE: Does this mean that his redeeming will, when worked through marriage and family, is somehow to be considered a second-class will?

COACH: No! If it were, then what God did through his Son and the cross would have to be similarly rated. There is no church body in all of Christendom prepared to do so. God can take the broken pieces of your marriages and families and find a way to redeem them, too. His will is his will, period!

WORD: "In him we have redemption through his blood, the forgiveness of sins, in accordance with the riches of God's grace that he lavished on us with all wisdom and understanding." (Eph. 1:7–8 NIV)

Training Regimen #6

COURSE: God's Help

TRAINEE: How does God work his Word in Romans 8:28?

COACH: A translation of the Greek text reads:

WORD: "For God is in all things working toward good for those who love Him and are called according to His purpose."

COACH: The KJV best reflects this original text:

WORD: "And we know that all things work together for good to them that love God, to them who are the called according to his purpose." (Rom. 8:28 KJV)

TRAINEE: "How does God actually *do* this?"

COACH: How would you react if a famous cook asked you to sample some lard, baking soda, oil, raw eggs, or flour, each one by itself? The thought of

369

sampling an ingredient has little, if any, appeal. But what happens when that cook begins to mix a number of these and other ingredients *together* into delicious, flaky, somewhat moist-looking biscuits or a cake? The totally unique factor of God's "working all things together toward good" is that he can even take the ingredients supplied by Satan (the evil planted in your lives by Satan and by your deceptive hearts) and *work* them toward good. God has done this through the redeeming will performed by his Son.

Yet there is an important Word of caution here. Let the following Scriptural correlation bear on your mind. That is, Romans 8:28 includes the words "for those who love Him." Those words go hand and glove with the following:

WORD: "Jesus answered, If a person (really) loves Me, he will keep My word—obey My teaching" (John 14:23a AMP). And "For it is not merely hearing the Law (read) that makes one righteous before God, but it is the doers of the Law who will be held guiltless and acquitted and justified." (Rom. 2:13 AMP)

TRAINEE: So, for me, a wise and right prayer says, "Dear Father, help me obey the great commandment— the Shema—more and more." God wants me to show him that I love him by obeying him.

And does "casting down imaginations of the heart," "deadening the deeds of the flesh" and "crucifying the self" constitute the love of obedience?

COACH: Yes! And the conclusion to that verse says, "to them who are the called according to his purpose" (Rom. 8:28b KJV). God has a purpose in showering his grace down on you and for exercising his redeeming will through your life. He looks at your heart to see what impact the cross of his Son has made, leading you into obedience.

TRAINEE: My prayer is that he would help me line up more and more with his perfect will; therefore, again I pray Philippians 2:13 so as to have healthier material with which he can work and less garbage from me. I want to be used and called "according to His purpose(s)" as a most willing participant, wanting what he wants!

WORD: "For the eyes of the Lord search back and forth across the whole earth, looking for people whose hearts are perfect toward him, so that he can show his great power in helping them." (2 Chron. 16:9a TLB)

Training Regimen #7

COURSE: The Word and Prayer

TRAINEE: So, how can I *know* whether or not my prayer (talking/listening relationship with God) on a given concern is in God's will, that I've heard God's *rhema*?

First "Know"

COACH: If that conviction is there, it is "the assurance of things hoped for, the conviction of things not seen" (Heb. 11:1). (The KJV reads, "substance of things hoped for, the evidence of things not seen." Something substantial gives great assurance, like having a title deed in hand. Evidence goes with conviction, whether in legal matters or spiritual concerns.) Such conviction rises from your use of the faith gift. It is very much like what one Middle Ages monk, Brother Lawrence, called "practicing the presence" of Jesus.

TRAINEE: I need something to back up my conviction, to know God is really talking to me when I pray.

Second "Know"

COACH: Second, does God's Word confirm and address your conviction? Does the Word echo your prayer?

372

If so, you have the strongest confirmation possible. When you pray God's own Word right back to Him, then you *know* you are praying in his will! The Word assures and gives substance to the prayer. That Word feeds your spirit. Inspired by the Word, your spirit will launch and renew the activity of your body and mind, including feelings.

Third "Know"

COACH: Do you have godly, wise counsel of others who are steeped in the faith? "For by wise counsel you can wage your war, and in an abundance of counselors there is victory and safety" (Prov. 24:6 AMP). Do they witness to your convictions and confirmation from the Scriptures? If so, you have still further confirmation.

Fourth "Know"

COACH: Do you have an inner peace, much like that eye of the hurricane—calm, balanced, and stable while everything around you is chaotic? Can you turn over and go to sleep? If so, that's another confirmation.

Fifth "Know"

COACH: Is there circumstantial evidence? Do thoughts, conversations, actions, feelings, decisions, plans, and so on point toward what you believe is "meant to be"? This may occur following some prayers; with others, it may not exist. Should it not, rest firmly on the confirmation of God's Word. That Word will lift up faith. God's Words are events! A "tug-of-war" may ensue where faith in the Word overrules whatever feelings and circumstances may be trying to dictate— "(walking) by faith and not by sight." When I let feelings or circumstances win, I lose; when I let faith win, I win! Recall the story of Peter trying to walk on the water (Matt. 14:22–32), standing at first on the *rhema* (personal) Word of Jesus saying to "come forth" but then trying to stand on his feelings as they dwelt on the wind and the waves.

TRAINEE: I like the story of Gideon as he questioned God about his promise to deliver Israel from the Midians with a small clan under Gideon's leadership:

WORD: "Then Gideon said to God, 'If you are really going to use me to save Israel as you promised, prove it to me in this way: I'll put some wool on the threshing floor tonight, and if, in the morning, the fleece is wet and the ground is dry, I will know you are going to help me!'

And it happened just that way! When he got up the next morning he pressed the fleece together and wrung out a whole bowlful of water!

Then Gideon said to the Lord, 'Please don't be angry with me, but let me make one more test: this time let the fleece remain dry while the ground around is wet!

So the Lord did as he asked; that night the fleece stayed dry, but the ground was covered with dew!" (Judges 6:36–40 TLB)

TRAINEE: As you say, God might not show me an outward sign of his will; however, I am learning that he often honors an "emotional fleece." For me, this centers on Psalm 37:4 in that I sometimes say to God, "Dear Father, if this really is what you are going to work out in my life, then build the desire of my heart for it; if not, then let that desire die out."

COACH: To nervously put out that fleece can sometimes amount to nothing more than a lack of faith on your part.

Sixth "Know"

COACH: Sixth, is there unconfessed sin? This blocks God's hearing (1 John 5:13–15; Is. 59:1–3,

12–15) of your prayers. Confession and God's forgiveness clear the way. "He that covereth his sins shall not prosper: but whoso confesseth and forsaketh them shall have mercy" (Prov. 28:13 KJV).

TRAINEE: "Dear Father, I have sinned against you; I confess *all* my sins (thoughts, words, deeds), including the secret thoughts and desires that I cannot fully understand but that are all known unto you. I do earnestly repent and am heartily sorry for these, my many offenses. Now, in the name of Jesus, I ask you to forgive (cover, erase, forget, heal) me and have mercy on me. To cleanse, strengthen, heal, guide, bless, and protect me. And deliver me from the consequences of not having the "fear of the Lord" on all three levels. By the power of your Spirit living in me, I place the name of Jesus above every thought in my mind. I ask that the Holy Spirit (my Coach) pray for me those prayers needed but not formed in my mind. And, like the disciples who, when they saw the intensity of his prayers, asked Jesus to teach them to pray, I ask that you teach me to pray more and more in your will, to become a true, tried, and tested prayer warrior, one from whom you want to hear. Amen (Yes, sir! That's my understanding; it is done)."

COACH: Look for the final/actual provision, which is the ultimate confirmation of God's will in the matter. In the military, you do not go anywhere until you have orders in hand. Your number one commander-in-chief does deliver those orders from his Word as a final provision.

Pray continually, "without ceasing." Seven days without prayer will make "one weak." Be like the woman who knocked on the door for a loaf of bread until, said Jesus, the householder opened up to her. Jesus said to pray like that. Do not regard God as hard of hearing, but be persistent. To "pray-through" means nothing short of not giving up, to go the distance. Sandwich each day with prayer and the Word!

WORD: "For whoever would come near to God must (necessarily) believe that God exists and that He is the Rewarder of those who earnestly and diligently seek Him (out)." (Heb. 11:6b AMP)

"You will seek me and find me when you seek me with all your heart. I will be found by you, declares the Lord." (Jer. 29:13–14a NIV; see Deut. 4:29; Prov. 8:17)

COACH: Following the above steps, be persistent in giving God thanks for his answer, even before your eyes see it. "See it" with the "eyes of faith." And, by the way, you will find Mark 11:23 and Romans 10:9–10 to be true to its Word, also. What you say with your mouth, following a prayer-faith connection, comes to pass. Practice reminding yourself of how well the Father can answer your prayer (Eph. 3:20).

Training Regimen #8

COURSE: The Day-by-Day Journey

TRAINEE: I'm impressed, but how do I go about putting this all together?

COACH: Have you ever watched a child with building blocks, trying to stack one upon another? Just the slightest shift in stacking those blocks can make the whole structure off balance, causing them to all tumble down. So it is with the building blocks of God's Word. For example, the first block I handed you was centered on my work to "convict of Truth":

WORD: "O Lord, You have searched me (thoroughly) and have known me.... Search me (thoroughly),

O God, and know my heart! Try me, and know my thoughts!" (Ps. 139:1, 23 AMP)

"I, the Lord, search the mind, I try the heart, even to give every man according to his ways, according to the fruit of his doings." (Jer. 17:10 AMP)

COACH: The second block:

WORD: "If we say that we have no sin, we are only fooling ourselves, and refusing to accept the truth. But if we confess our sins to him, he can be depended on to forgive us and to cleanse us from every wrong. (And it is perfectly proper for God to do this for us because Christ died to wash away our sins)." (1 John 1:8–9 TLB)

COACH: Other blocks came through the journey of the apostle Paul, who was transformed (grew and changed) from the confession of being "chief of sinners," having "nothing good in (him)," deserving "only condemnation and death" to stating he was "more than a conqueror through (Christ, Jesus) who loved (him)," that he could "do all things through Christ who strengthens (him)," that "God's strength is made perfect in (his) weakness" and finally to say, "It is no longer I (self-centered ego) Paul who live, but Christ within me." One block builds upon the other. As your Coach, I know which building blocks from the Word to hand you at the right time. You need only remember which block (Word) is the cornerstone of the house of God's grace. It is none other than the Word from the cross—all this so you can be transformed by the renewing of your mind as you cast down the imaginations of the heart, deaden the deeds of the flesh and crucify the self. This means you can practice saying every day, "Today, I can stop having a form of godliness and denying the power thereof."

WORD: "For the message of the cross is foolishness to those who are perishing, but to us who are being saved it is the power of God." (1 Cor. 1:18 NIV)

Training Regimen #9

COURSE: The Sin unto Death

TRAINEE: What is it?

COACH: The "wall" Scriptures that fell on you.

TRAINEE: I broke through that wall, but I can't dodge the fact that my sin was "willful and deliberate."

COACH: So was King David's.

TRAINEE: The apostle Paul wrote that his sin was in ignorance.

COACH: So there are degrees of sin? Does the Word say that?

TRAINEE: I have not decided to go my own way or to reject Jesus, and my heart feels the thump effect of that triangle as it is rolled over—the edges of my conscience not worn off; however, I'm deeply afraid of offending God by my hypocrisy and deceitful heart.

COACH: Beautiful! You recall that "working out your salvation with fear and trembling" is amplified to read:

WORD: "(Self-distrust, that is, with serious caution, tenderness of conscience, watchfulness against temptation; timidly shrinking from whatever might offend God and discredit the name of Christ)." (Phil. 2:12 AMP)

TRAINEE: Can I in truth believe that, like King David, I am "a man after God's own heart"?

COACH: From now own, watch carefully for the clever deceptions of the enemy. He can even quote

Scripture in his effort to torment and deceive. The word *devil* comes from your word *traduce*, meaning "to expose, shame or blame by means of falsehood and misrepresentation" (*Merriam Webster's Collegiate Dictionary*, Tenth Edition). As your coach, I will never torment you with the Word. I convict of sin and of the Father's forgiveness (John 16:8–11).

TRAINEE: What about others who sin as I have, even our presidents?

COACH: The Father can raise up wounded healers for them. You, now, are one. Pray, as a nation, two Words for your president: Philippians 2:13 and 2 Corinthians 7:10. I can coach and help him "to will and to do (the Father's) good pleasure" and to have "godly sorrow over his sin."

TRAINEE: That would certainly rescue us, as a nation, from the "soap-opera" mentality.

COACH: Israel, as a nation, fared better as David developed godly sorrow. God will not bless people who try to serve him while they, at the same time, hold onto a bosom lust. The real crime here is unbelief. Your adultery was not only idolatry; it was also not believing his Word. He saw your struggle with it; therefore, he was patient with you in it. You can still come boldly to him (see

382

Eph. 3:12, Heb. 4:16) despite the long history of your struggle.

WORD: "It is of the Lord's mercies that we are not consumed, because his compassions fail not." (Lam. 3:22 KJV)

Training Regimen #10

COURSE: My Untrustworthy Heart

WORD: "The heart is deceitful above all things, and it is exceedingly perverse and corrupt and severely, mortally sick! Who can know it (perceive, understand, be acquainted with his own heart and mind)?" (Jer. 17:9 AMP)

COACH: *Heart* is the Old Testament's word for the seat of your emotional system sitting in the right brain. God made that portion of the brain for a reason. Feelings are his creation and, therefore, are good. Speaking of Jesus, the writer of Hebrews says that he was "anointed with gladness beyond his comrades" (Heb. 1:9). Yet he also was described by Isaiah as "a man of sorrows, and acquainted with grief" (Is. 53:3).

However, Jesus was never enslaved to his own emotional reactions. How he felt was never the issue; personal insult never provoked him, unless it affected the Father. He *saw* things from the Father's perspective. Recall the scene on Palm Sunday, where almost two million people prepared for the Passover celebration. As the Pharisees tried to stop the people from singing praises to Jesus, Jesus told the Pharisees that if the people kept quiet, the very stones would cry out (see Luke 19:28–44). That, by the way, makes perfect sense. Jesus, being the "Word made flesh" who created the rocks, would certainly have gotten a response from the rocks if the people did not give it. They would have demonstrated for a fact that they, too, have life or exist because of him. These were the Father's feelings as he watched his Son enter Jerusalem. Yet, a little while later, Jesus' mood shifted dramatically. He approached Jerusalem and wept over it (see Luke 19:41–44). These verses show that he was feeling what the Father felt as he saw their future, the destruction of Jerusalem in AD 70.

Later, his mood changed again. Angered by the activity at the temple, he began driving out the merchants and overturning their tables. Your archaeologists have discovered that those tables were very heavy; it took a lot of adrenaline to turn them over. Psalm 69:9 and John 2:17 tell you that zeal for his Father's house consumed

Jesus. The opposite of love is not anger or even hatred; it is indifference. Jesus strongly felt what the Father felt then and there.

WORD: "For even Christ did not please himself but, as it is written: 'The insults of those who insult you have fallen on me'" (Rom. 15:3 NIV).

COACH: If you don't choose to adopt God's feelings, you settle for your own.

TRAINEE: On one hand, I am not to "let the sun go down on (my) anger"; on the other hand, I am to "be angry but sin not" (see Eph. 4:26). It's like the saying, "Going to pieces is sometimes what keeps you from falling apart."

COACH: The balance comes in choosing to see or perceive people, circumstances, and so on from God's view.

TRAINEE: How is this done?

COACH: Part of what it means for you to "deny yourself and take up your cross" falls under the prayer that says, "Dear Father, I give my emotions to you and ask that you give me yours." Is this not what the apostle Paul learned?

WORD: "Put them all away: anger, wrath, malice, slander, and foul talk.... Put on compassion, kindness, lowliness, meekness, and patience, forbearing one another ... and forgiving one another." (Col. 3:8, 12, 13)

COACH: You are not a robot, programmed by feelings into action. Not only can you act your way into a new way of thinking; you can think your way into a new way of acting. Notice the word *put* in the above text. It is a decision. Just as you choose which pair of shoes to put on for different occasions, you can also choose which emotions to wear.

WORD: "Reckon ... yourselves to be dead ... unto sin." (Rom. 6:11 KJV)

TRAINEE: Yet again, what enables this choice?

COACH: It takes an act of faith to make such decisions about feelings. That faith moves into action when you lock it into the Word. God's Word gives you what his feelings are concerning anything you face or see or experience. When you stand on his feelings through a faith-decision, he is pleased. (See Heb. 11:6.)

The benefits of such a transformation through the renewal of the mind (see Rom. 12:2) are as follows:

A. While you may see differently than most of the world (for example, Jeremiah was called "the weeping prophet"), you will have an extraordinary objectivity in your outlook. When you look at the news and see the insane actions of a hardened criminal and ask, "How do you feel about this, Father?" you will find yourself moving away from the vindictive, reactionary, self-righteous response to a desire to see this criminal in the position of the penitent thief hanging on the cross next to Jesus, causing you to pray for salvation in the midst of punishment.

B. You'll be free to enter God's emotions rather than remain bound to your own. The reason Jesus could voice a cry of victory—"It is finished"—from the cross is because he saw what the Father saw. Great or small, whatever the concern, it pays to see it from God's perspective.

TRAINEE: I recall the story of Corrie Ten Boom.

COACH: The Beatitudes (Matt. 5:1–12), for example, tell you that you are "blessed" (happy) when poor in spirit, mournful, persecuted, and so on. These verses, when added to the following—"This is the day that the Lord hath made; we *will* rejoice and be glad in it" (Ps. 118:24 KJV), "for the joy of the Lord is your strength" (Neh. 8:10b KJV)—establish a biblical platform for feelings to also become faith-decisions.

As your Coach, heed my lead to see that the one Beatitude—"Blessed are the poor in spirit, for theirs is the kingdom of heaven"—with the Greek text reading, "How blest are those who know their need of God; the kingdom of Heaven is theirs"—is completely true. Matthew 5:3 (NEB) states that you are to choose to be happy when you come to know how much you need God.

TRAINEE: I am to develop the attitude of gratitude. One might say it is a "to-be-or-not-to-be attitude."

WORD: "All Scripture is given by inspiration of God, and is profitable for doctrine, for reproof, for correction, for instruction in righteousness, that the man of God may be complete, thoroughly equipped for every good work." (2 Tim. 3: 16-17 NKJV)

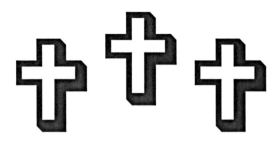

Beyond the research centered on the **"God-Particle,"** another recent scientific discovery shows that "the **"Laminin molecule**—*which holds the cells and tissue of our bodies together, and, without which our bodies would literally fall apart*—has the form of a *cross* [Dec. 2012 Midnight Call p. 22]." Has God placed into the very fabric of creation a picture of what it would take to bring our hearts back to His heart? The following Word, however, gives the most comprehensive survey to show that all of history is really His-story!

For by Him all things were created that are in heaven and that are on earth, visible and invisible, whether thrones or dominions or principalities or powers. All things were created through Him and for Him. 17 And He is before all things, and in Him all things consist. Colossians 1: 16-17 NKJV

He has made the earth by His power, He has established the world by His wisdom, and has stretched out the heavens at His discretion. 13 When He utters His voice, there is a multitude of waters in the heavens: "And He causes the vapors to ascend from the ends of the earth. He makes lightning for the rain, He brings the wind out of His treasuries." Jeremiah 10: 12-13 NKJV

Arthur Coffey has served as a parish pastor for fifteen years, an Army chaplain for twenty-three years, and a Veterans Affairs Medical Center chaplain for twelve years. He was mobilized for Operation Desert Shield, Operation Desert Storm, Operation Joint Endeavor, and the Humanitarian Aid tour to Guatemala.

Coffey is the recipient of the Witherspoon Award for "most creative use of Scripture," presented by the National Bible Association and the Armed Forces Chief of Chaplains.

He is also the recipient of a Veterans Affairs National Chaplain of the Month award for "outstanding service in the promotion of the Bible in ministry, healing and research."

In addition, Coffey presented his Alzheimer's research, centered on Scripture, at the Mayo Clinic, where it was voted the most outstanding of those presented and declared to be "pioneer research" because no other known research had ever used Scripture as the independent variable.

Coffey earned a doctorate in "wholistic" health care, awarded by Lutheran Theological Seminary. The exam committee proclaimed his research to be the best they had seen in the field.

CPSIA information can be obtained at www.ICGtesting.com
Printed in the USA
LVOW080253150213

320077LV00003B/15/P